A Special Issue of
Cognition and Emotion

Culture and Emotion

Edited by
Antony S.R. Manstead
University of Amsterdam, The Netherlands

Agneta H. Fischer
University of Amsterdam, The Netherlands

Published in 2002 by Psychology Press Ltd
27 Church Road, Hove, East Sussex, BN3 2FA

Simultaneously published in the USA and Canada
by Taylor & Francis Inc.
29 West 35th Street, New York, NY 10001, USA

www.psypress.co.uk

Psychology Press is a member of the Taylor & Francis Group

British Library Cataloguing in Publication Data
A catalogue record for this book is available from the British Library

ISBN 1-84169-924-1
ISSN 0269-9931

Index by Christine Boylan
Typeset by in the UK by DP Photosetting, Aylesbury, Bucks
Printed in the UK by Hobbs The Printers Ltd, Totton, Southampton
Bound in the UK by TJ International, Padstow, Cornwall

Contents

*This book is also a special issue of the journal Cognition and Emotion
which forms issue 1 of Volume 16 (2002).

COGNITION AND EMOTION, 2002, *16* (1), 1–9

Beyond the universality-specificity dichotomy

Antony S.R. Manstead and Agneta H. Fischer

University of Amsterdam, The Netherlands

For the past three decades theorising and research on the relationship between culture and emotion has tended to concentrate on the seemingly straightforward issue of whether or not emotions are universal. Within psychology this debate was reinvigorated in the 1960s by the pioneering research of Ekman and Izard, who were the first to conduct systematic cross-cultural studies on facial expressions in order to test Darwin's idea about the universality of emotion expressions. Ekman's original motivation in conducting this research was to try to settle the issue of whether emotion expressions are universal or culturally specific by collecting reliable empirical evidence, rather than relying on theoretical arguments, or the intuitions and judgements made by one anthropologist on the basis of his or her fieldwork. "I would just get the facts. I was excited that I might be able to settle a 100-year-old dispute, about such a fundamental issue" (p. 371), he writes in the afterword to the third edition of Darwin's (1872/1998) *The expression of the emotions in man and animals*. In this afterword, he provides a personal account of the dispute in which he remembers that he started the research with other assumptions, but that the evidence led him to conclude that there was no other way to interpret the data: "Our evidence, and that of others, shows only that when people are experiencing strong emotions, are not making any attempt to mask their expressions, the expression will be the same regardless of age, race, culture, sex and education. That is a powerful finding" (p. 391). This conclusion, however, was not universally shared by other researchers, and

Correspondence should be addressed to Dr Agneta H. Fischer, Social Psychology Program, University of Amsterdam, Roetersstraat 15, 1018 WB Amsterdam, The Netherlands.
E-mail: sp_Fischer@macmail.psy.uva.nl

We would like to thank Jerry Parrott for his invitation to edit this Special Issue and for his willingness to take on the role of Action Editor for a paper on which we were co-authors. If he had known at the time of asking us that his invitation was going to involve him in so much extra work after several years of being Chief Editor of this journal, he might have thought twice about issuing the invitation. We would also like to thank the authors whose papers are published here for their patience in waiting for editorial decisions and for their willingness to make revisions. Finally, a vote of thanks is due to those colleagues who were kind enough to provide reviews of papers submitted to this Special Issue.

© 2002 Psychology Press Ltd

http://www.tandf.co.uk/journals/pp/02699931.html   DOI:10.1080/0269993014000103

thus proved to be less self-evident and powerful than Ekman believed it to be. Both his theoretical arguments and his research methods have generated a lot of criticism concerning the validity and generalisability of his conclusions (e.g., Russell, 1994).

Although the work of Ekman and his colleagues has dominated the field for a long time, there was other research on culture and emotion. The fact that there was a dispute to be settled also implies that there were other perspectives on the issue. Early anthropologists, such as Mead, Bateson, or Birdwhistell, claimed that emotion expressions were far from universal, but they had little by way of specific evidence concerning how different emotions were in other cultures. From the 1970s onwards there was a steady stream of publications by cultural anthropologists and ethnographers, providing more compelling evidence in favour of the argument that the emotional lives of peoples from other cultures is different from that in the West. Some well-known case studies exemplify this line of work. In her book *Never in Anger*, Briggs (1970) reported that the Inuit neither experience nor display any anger because they consider angry thoughts and acts to be dangerous. Another frequently cited example is that of the Ilongot, who—according to Rosaldo's (1980) observations—consider *liget* to be the central emotion. *Liget* may be best described as a combination of energy, passion, or anger, but it is associated with a variety of sensations, such as enthusiasm, agitation, passivity, violence, separation, social withdrawal, and confusion. The Ilongot believe that they can only overcome heavy feelings of *liget* by means of head-hunting, a ritual in which a young man goes out to kill another person—preferably, but not necessarily, someone outside his own group. Still another example of cultural variation in emotion can be found in Levy's work on the Tahitians, who appear to lack words and scripts for sadness (Levy, 1973). When they are confronted with loss the Tahitians refer to their condition using nonspecific terms, such as "feeling troubled", or "not feeling a sense of inner push", or "feeling tired". This implies, according to Levy, that their feelings can be interpreted as something other than emotion, for example as illness, or as the harmful effects of a spirit.

These examples illustrate the general message emerging from this work, namely that emotions are shaped in important ways by culture, a position clearly at odds with the view that emotions are universal. The examples also show that one important source of cultural variation can be found in the cultural meaning attached to emotion concepts and emotion knowledge. For psychologists and cultural anthropologists the implications of cultural meanings for emotions differ, however. Psychologists, especially those favouring a universalist stance, do not consider cultural meaning systems to be essential for the emotion system. Cultural meanings may affect interpretations and ideologies concerning emotions, but they do not influence the way in which emotional reactions unfold. Cultural anthropologists, on the other hand, have developed a theoretical perspective in which they emphasise the primary importance of cultural meaning systems in both the experience and the expression of emotions. In contrast with the dominant psychological view, emotions are not seen as material things, as part of a physiological system, but rather as phenomena that occur in interactions between people, and are therefore constituted in social relationships. Given the presumption that emotions are interpreted, experienced, and expressed differently depending on the social and cultural context in which they occur, they clearly cannot be universal.

The debate became polarised and neither side could be convinced by the data or theoretical arguments offered by their opponents. One factor impeding progress was that the debate tended to focus on the either/or mutual exclusivity of the universalist and culturally relativist views of emotion. Another limitation was the incommensurability of findings generated by standardised and essentially quantitative research methods, on the one hand, and idiosyncratic and essentially qualitative research methods, on the other.

Not everyone was stuck in this trench war, however. Several commentators acknowledged that the fact that people living in radically different cultures largely agree in how to label a limited set of facial expressions need not imply that other facial expressions are also universally labelled, or that other facets of emotion, such as appraisals, behavioural responses, and regulation attempts are similar regardless of culture. Even the proposition that there exists a set of "basic" emotions that are universal with respect to appraisal and expression was challenged. In the absence of theoretical consensus several researchers were led to collect cross-cultural data on emotion attributes other than facial expression, in an effort to advance the debate.

Brandt and Boucher, for example, conducted a series of studies (e.g., Boucher & Brandt, 1981; Brandt & Boucher, 1985) in which they compared the responses of Americans with those of Malaysians, Koreans, and Samoans. They first asked the participants to describe events that elicit certain emotions. Subsequently, a separate group of respondents from each of these cultures was asked to identify which emotions resulted from the described events. The results showed that there was a high rate of agreement among the different groups, but the extent of this agreement varied as a function of type of emotion and cultural group. A huge cross-cultural study was initiated by Scherer and Wallbott, who collected questionnaire data in 37 countries from all over the world. Respondents were asked to report on antecedents, appraisals, physiological changes, verbal and nonverbal expression, and control attempts with regard to the seven so-called basic emotions (joy, anger, fear, sadness, disgust, contempt, and surprise). These data enabled the researchers to test hypotheses concerning the relative importance of universal and social and cultural factors, by examining the sizes of the statistical effects associated with different emotions, on the one hand, and different countries, on the other. They concluded that there was evidence both of emotion-specific patterns across cultures, supporting the case for universality, and of the cultural-specificity of emotions (Scherer & Wallbott,

1994). Thus, the findings did not support the extreme positions of either the universalists or the cultural relativists. A similar conclusion was reached by Mesquita and Frijda (1992), who reviewed the anthropological and psychological evidence on emotions across cultures and found that there are both cultural similarities and dissimilarities in emotions. They were led to conclude that the question is not so much *whether or not* there is cultural variation, but rather *to what extent*, and *at what level of analysis*, such cultural variation exists.

During the past decade the empirical evidence concerning cultural variation in emotion has expanded further (e.g., Cohen & Nisbett, 1994, 1997; Cohen, Nisbett, Bowdle, & Schwarz, 1996; Kitayama & Markus, 1994; Lutz & Abu-Lughod, 1990; Markus & Kitayama, 1991; Matsumoto, 1996; Russell, 1991, 1994; Watson-Gegeo & White, 1990). The findings of this research are generally consistent with the view that an extreme position in this controversy is untenable. In particular it has been shown that whether or not one finds evidence of cultural similarities or differences very much depends on the methodological approach one adopts: Which emotion and which specific component is being studied, and in reaction to which event and under which social circumstances? Perhaps unsurprisingly, it also makes a difference whether one uses forced-choice formats or open questions, emotion labels or component descriptions, questionnaires or observational techniques. Thus, the fact that sometimes few or no cultural differences are found does not necessarily plea for a universalist position; it may rather be due to the way in which emotions have been assessed in the research concerned. Equally, evidence of the presence of cultural differences in emotional response may arise from the fact that the comparisons being made are in some sense inappropriate, either because the emotions are not equivalent or because the participants differ in some respect that is not exclusively "cultural". There is every reason for being ultra-cautious in drawing conclusions on the basis of cross-cultural research on emotion.

The papers selected for inclusion in this Special Issue bear witness in their different ways to a new awareness of the need to approach the issue of the relation between culture and emotion in a way that goes beyond the universalism-relativism debate. One issue that is attracting increased research attention is the role of *emotion language* in emotion research. Although cultural anthropologists have quite often studied emotion language, this has in the past tended to be a topic that was overlooked by psychologists. Now, there is growing consensus among psychologists that emotion language is an important issue in cross-cultural research. Three papers included here address the issue of language. The paper by Semin, Görts, Nandram, and Semin-Goossens is concerned with the extent to which the linguistic representation of emotions and emotion events is influenced by the extent to which the culture in question values interpersonal relationships and interdependence, rather than personal autonomy and independence. It is argued that in interdependence-oriented cultures emotion terms serve as what the authors call "relationship-markers", and are represented by more concrete terms, whereas in independence-oriented cultures emotion terms serve as "self-markers", and are represented by more abstract terms. The authors report two studies in which they find support for these predictions. As well as being consistent with previous findings on cultural variation in attributional tendencies, these results suggest that emotions and the events that give rise to them are more closely intertwined with interpersonal relations in interdependent cultures than they are in independent cultures.

The paper by Kitayama and Ishii draws on similar theoretical concepts by making use of Hall's (1976) distinction between "low context" and "high context" cultures. Low context cultures are ones in which the verbal content of utterances is relatively more important in conveying information to others, whereas high context cultures are ones in which contextual and nonverbal cues are relatively more important in communication. Using (American) English and Japanese as examples of low context and high context languages, respectively, the authors predict that native speakers of English will be relatively more attuned to the evaluation of word meaning when processing an emotionally spoken evaluative word, whereas native speakers of Japanese will be relatively more attuned to vocal emotion when processing such a word. They use a modified Stroop task to test these predictions and find that the interference effect of competing word evaluation is stronger for Americans than for Japanese participants, whereas the interference effect of competing vocal emotion judgements is stronger for Japanese than for Americans. These findings suggest that there are cultural differences in the relative emphasis accorded to one or other channel of emotional utterances.

Fontaine, Poortinga, Setiadi, and Markam's paper addresses the what the authors call "cognitive structure" of emotion terms, by which they mean the cognitive representation of similarities and differences between emotion terms. They compare the cognitive structure of such terms in Indonesia and the Netherlands. They began by selecting 120 emotion terms on the basis of local ratings of protoypicality as exemplars of emotion. Analyses of ratings of these terms revealed similar structures in the two cultures. Fifty of these terms were deemed to be translation-equivalent, and 42 of these 50 terms were found to be cognitively equivalent. These 42 terms therefore meet the authors' criteria for exhibiting good fit with a common cognitive structure of emotion terms. However, closer analysis of the location of the terms "shame" and "guilt" showed that they were closer to "fear" and further away from "anger" in Indonesia than in the Netherlands. These findings show that evidence of cross-cultural consistencies and cross-cultural differences can be found within the same dataset.

An influential way of thinking about cultural differences in emotion was introduced by Markus and Kitayama (1991), who analysed the consequences of different types of self-concepts for the occurrence, experience, and expression of emotion. They argued that individualistic cultures tend to promote independent selves, whereas collectivistic cultures tend to promote interdependent selves. Furthermore, these differences in self-concept influence the degree to which certain emotions are felt and expressed. Independent selves are more likely to experience and express "socially disengaged" emotions, such as pride or anger, which tend to set the individual apart from others, whereas interdependent selves are more likely to experience and express "socially engaged" emotions, such as shame or contentment, because these emotions strengthen social bonds. These theoretical proposals provided additional impetus to the tendency for cross-cultural comparisons regarding emotion to draw on the well-established distinction between individualistic and collectivistic cultures, a distinction that began with Hofstede's (1980) pioneering research on work-related values. This Special Issue contains three papers that testify to the continuing influence of Hofstede's ideas.

Becht and Vingerhoets report on the results of a large-scale cross cultural study of crying, with a focus on the extent to which respondents reported mood change following crying. By mood change the authors mean a change of mood in a positive direction. The authors expected mood change to be positively associated with individualism-collectivism and negatively associated with masculinity-femininity, two of the dimensions that emerged from Hofstede's research. In the event, only the predicted association with masculinity-femininity proved to be significant, reflecting a tendency for crying to be more likely to result in positive mood change in feminine countries, that is, countries in which there is relatively little emphasis placed on gender role differences, where cooperation is valued, and where there is a concern for the less fortunate members of society. Also predictive of mood change, independently of other predictors, was gross domestic product per capita, which suggests that the material circumstances of a society have an impact on its citizens' emotional lives in ways that are difficult to capture using psychological variables.

The paper by Basabe, Paez, Valencia, Gonzalez, Rimé, and Diener also uses the Hofstede dimensions to analyse country differences in emotional variables by conducting secondary analyses of existing large-scale datasets, adding cultural variables such as the Hofstede dimensions and measures of socioeconomic development and climate as potential predictors. The key indices of emotion used in this research are subjective well-being and "affect balance" (positive minus negative affect). Both subjective well-being and affect balance were positively associated with individualism, controlling for all the other predictors. Aside from the substantive findings of this study, an interesting methodological point raised by the authors is the extent to which individual self-reports of, say, affect balance can be averaged to yield an index of the emotional climate of the culture in question. By demonstrating that societal indices of affect balance relate in similar ways to cultural variables as do individual-level measures, the authors make a good empirical case for treating the averaged scores of representative samples of a country's citizens as an index of the emotional climate of that country.

Markus and Kitayama's (1991) argument that the effects of individualism and collectivism on emotion can be understood in terms of differences in the way the self is construed is not the only way to interpret such effects. A somewhat different (but nevertheless complementary) explanation is one that focuses on *cultural concerns*. Cultural concerns are goals, desires, or ideals that are consistent with and promoted by core values in a given culture. An example of such cultural concerns is honour. The effects of honour concerns on emotions has been the topic of a number of investigations (e.g., Cohen & Nisbett, 1994; Rodriguez Mosquera, Manstead, & Fischer, 2000). A typical finding is that people who by virtue of the culture in which they have grown up presumably have a heightened concern with honour react differently to events that threaten their honour than do their counterparts who are less concerned with honour. These differences in emotional reaction are due not only to differences in the way that the instigating event is appraised, but also to different appraisals of one's coping resources and one's social environment. For men in particular, a strong concern for honour carries with it the implication that the only appropriate way to respond to an insult is by getting angry and being aggressive.

The paper by Mesquita and Karasawa is an example of how cultural differences in self-construal, measured at the individual level, give rise to differences in concerns that in turn help to account for differences in emotion. They compare "selfways" (the characteristic ways in which individuals participate in their culture) in America and Japan, and argue that the types of concern associated with emotions vary as a function of differences in these selfways. Their respondents completed questionnaires assessing emotions and concerns four times a day during the period of one week. Surprisingly, Japanese respondents living in Japan were more likely than American respondents to report that they experienced no emotions at all. Consistent with the authors' expectations, Americans rated the emotional events in their lives in more positive terms than did the Japanese. Also consistent with predictions was the finding that the degree to which independent and interdependent concerns predicted pleasantness varied as a function of culture. Among Japanese respondents, interdependent concerns were more predictive of pleasantness than were independent concerns; among American respondents, independent and interdependent concerns were equally predictive of pleasantness. These findings are consistent with the argument that differences in concerns give rise differences in the quality of emotional lives.

Rodriguez Mosquera, Manstead, and Fischer's paper also focuses on cultural concerns. The concerns in question are honour concerns and the central question addressed in the study is whether differences in concern for honour can account for cultural differences in the way that Spanish and Dutch participants respond to insults. It is found that Spanish participants are more likely than Dutch participants to react emotionally to offences that threaten family honour, and that degree of concern for family honour mediated this effect of nationality on emotional reactions to threats to family honour. Thus, the more the self is psychologically concerned with family honour, the more intense is one's emotional reaction in the face of offences that threaten family honour. Here, is further evidence, then, that cultural differences in the types of concern that people regard as being at stake can account for the quality of their emotional response to given events.

The fact that there is variation in concerns within cultures as well as between them is a salutary reminder of a fact that is often recognised but seldom researched by those interested in cultural variation in emotion, namely, that cultures are not monolithic. Societies are stratified to a greater or lesser extent in terms of wealth, social status, region, and gender, and each subgrouping within a society can be regarded as having its own subculture. Furthermore, in the second half of the 20th century most Western societies became "multicultural," as a result of economic and/or political migration. The tendency on the part of researchers to compare nationals of one country with nationals of another country thus runs the risk of overlooking important subcultural variation in emotion within a given society. The USA has a longer history of being a multicultural society than most Western countries, and the final paper included in this Special Issue, by Vrana and Rollock, investigates the extent to which ethnicity (among other factors) influences emotional responses to imagined emotional scenarios on the part of white Americans and Afro-Americans. Compared to whites, black participants are found to be more facially expressive of positive emotion and less facially expressive of negative emotion. Blacks (especially males) react more strongly to emotional imagery in terms of elevated blood pressure. Finally, imagined interactions with blacks give rise both to more positive and to more negative facial expressions on the part of all participants, regardless of ethnicity. The authors interpret these findings as showing that blacks, by comparison with whites, are more autonomically reactive to emotional situations, and are themselves more likely to be responded to emotionally, findings that have implications for health and for interpersonal encounters.

In conclusion, as will be noticed in the course of reading this Special Issue, the methods, approaches, and topics of the present contributions are as variable as the emotions in various cultures can be. There is clearly no one way of doing the job, and there is no single theoretical approach that dominates the field. We regard this is an advantage and believe that methodological eclecticism is likely to be beneficial to the development of research on emotions. We believe that the contributions to this Special Issue provide insight and contribute to knowledge, and we hope that they will also inspire further research that attempts to unravel the complex links between emotions and culture.

Manuscript received 6 January 2001

REFERENCES

Boucher, J. D., & Brandt, M. E. (1981). Judgement of emotion: American and Malay antecedents. *Journal of Cross-cultural Psychology, 12,* 272–283.

Brandt, M. E., & Boucher, J. D. (1985). Judgements of emotions from the antecedent situations in three cultures. In I. R. Lagunes & Y. H. Poortinga (Eds.), *From a different perspective: Studies of behavior across cultures* (pp. 348–362). Lisse, the Netherlands: Swets & Zeitlinger.

Briggs, J. L. (1970). *Never in anger: Portrait of an Eskimo family.* Cambridge, MA: Harvard University Press.

Cohen, D., & Nisbett, R. E. (1994). Self-protection and the culture of honor: Explaining southern violence. *Personality and Social Psychology Bulletin, 20,* 551–567.

Cohen, D., & Nisbett, R. E. (1997). Field experiments examining the culture of honor: The role of institutions in perpetuating norms about violence. *Personality and Social Psychology Bulletin, 23,* 1188–1199.

Cohen, D., Nisbett, R. E., Bowdle, B. F., & Schwarz, N. (1996). Insult, aggression and the southern culture of honor: An "experimental ethnography". *Journal of Personality and Social Psychology, 70,* 945–960.

Darwin, C. (1998). *The expression of the emotions in man and animals.* New York: Oxford University Press. (Original work published 1872).

Hall, E. T. (1976). *Beyond culture.* New York: Anchor.

Hofstede, G. (1980). *Culture's consequences: International differences in work-related values.* Beverley Hills, CA: Sage.

Kitayama, S., & Markus, H. (Eds.) (1994). *Emotion and culture: Empirical studies of mutual influence.* Washington, DC: APA.

Levy, R. I. (1973). *Tahitians: Mind and experience in the Society Islands.* Chicago, IL: Chicago University Press.

Lutz, C., & Abu-Lughod, L. (Eds.) (1990). *Language and the politics of emotion.* New York: Cambridge University Press.

Markus, H. R., & Kitayama, (1991). Culture and the self: implications for cognition, emotion and motivation. *Psychological Review, 98,* 224–253.

Matsumoto, D. (1996). *Unmasking Japan: Myths and realities about the emotions of the Japanese.* Stanford, CA: Stanford University Press.

Mesquita, B., & Frijda, N. H. (1992). Cultural variations in emotions: A review. *Psychological Bulletin, 112,* 179–204.

Nisbett, R. E., & Cohen, D. (1996). *Culture of honor: The psychology of violence in the South.* Boulder, CO: Westview.

Rodriguez Mosquera, P. M., Manstead, A. S. R., & Fischer, A. H. (2000). The role of honor-related values in the elicitation, experience and communication of pride, shame and anger: Spain and the Netherlands compared. *Personality and Social Psychology Bulletin, 26,* 833–844.

Rosaldo, M. Z. (1980). *Knowledge and passion: Ilongot notions of self and social life.* Cambridge, UK: Cambridge University Press.

Russell, J. A. (1994). Is there universal recognition of emotion from facial expressions? A review of cross-cultural studies. *Psychological Bulletin, 115,* 102–141.

Russell, J. A. (1991). Culture and the categorization of emotions. *Psychological Bulletin, 110,* 426–450.

Scherer, K. R., & Wallbott, H. G. (1994). Evidence for universality and cultural variation of differential emotion response patterning. *Journal of Personality and Social Psychology, 66,* 310–328.

Watson-Gegeo, K. A., & White, G. M. (Eds.) (1990). *Disentangling: Conflict discourse in Pacific societies.* Stanford, CA: Stanford University Press.

COGNITION AND EMOTION, 2002, *16* (1), 11–28

Cultural perspectives on the linguistic representation of emotion and emotion events

Gün R. Semin, Carien A. Görts, Sharda Nandram, and Astrid Semin-Goossens

Free University Amsterdam, The Netherlands

It is argued that the linguistic representation of emotions and events giving rise to them is influenced by the cultural regulation of the relationship between a person and others. Such cultural variations are expected to be reflected in how emotions and emotion events are represented in language. The two studies provide support for the hypothesis that in a culture where relationships and interdependence are valued emotion terms function as relationship-markers and emotion events are represented by the use of concrete linguistic terms when compared with cultures that emphasise the value of the individual. Moreover, we also found support for the argument that emotion terms function predominantly as self-markers in cultures that value individuality and that they are represented by more abstract terms (adjectives, nouns). The implications of these findings are discussed.

The two studies reported here examine cultural variations in the linguistic representation of emotions, and events that give rise to emotions by investigating how people talk about them. We focus on talk and in particular on specific linguistic features of words used in emotion-talk, because our linguistic habits are shaped by recurrent cultural patterns of representing, acting, feeling, interpreting, and experiencing social events. Differences in cultural practices are therefore likely to give rise to variations in recurrent features of talk. For instance, variations in how the person is culturally construed is likely to imply different constructions of emotions, since emotional events predominantly characterise the qualities of the types of relationships between a person and his/

Correspondence should be addressed to Gün R. Semin, Social Psychology Department, Free University Amsterdam, van der Boechorststr. 1, 1081 BT Amsterdam, The Netherlands: email: GR.Semin@psy.vu.nl

The research reported here was supported by a Netherlands Organisation for Scientific Research-Pionier Grant No.PGS 56-381 to the first author. The authors would like to thank Wolanda Werkman, Sandra Zwier, and Zita Meijer and three anonymous reviewers for their helpful and constructive comments on an earlier version of this paper. In particular, we would like to thank Agneta Fischer and Tony Manstead for their excellent editorial guidance, detailed comments, and professionalism.

http://www.tandf.co.uk/journals/pp/02699931.html   DOI:10.1080/02699930143000112

her social world (Markus & Kitayama, 1991, 1994). Accordingly, the cultural formation of the person can be regarded to play an important role in shaping the interpretation of emotions and the events giving rise to them across cultures (cf. Hofstede, 1980; Markus & Kitayama, 1991; Mauss, 1938/1985; Sampson, 1985; Semin & Rubini, 1990; Shweder & Bourne, 1982; Triandis, 1988, 1989, 1994a,b; 1995, inter alia). As Kitayama, Markus, and Matsumoto (1995) argue emotions play a central role in "managing relationships with other persons, defining the self, maintaining the self's worth or dignity and organising appropriate action in many social situations" (p. 442). One would therefore expect an individual-centred management of social events (cognitively and emotionally) to be a prominent feature in cultures that value individualism. In contrast, if a socio-centred management of events is a central cultural practice, then emotional events will be construed primarily interpersonally. As a consequence, one would expect emotion terms to be more prominent or accessible as *relationship-markers* in cultures where thoughts, feelings, and actions in conformity and harmony with in-group members are valued and where group-goals prevail over individual-goals. In contrast, in cultures where individual preferences and goals frequently prevail over group goals, and thoughts, feelings, and actions independently of others are emphasised emotions are more likely to be individual or *self-markers*.

One possible way of discovering whether emotions are used as *relationship-markers* versus *self-markers* is by means of the relative prominence of different grammatical categories (e.g., verbs, adjectives, and nouns) that are spontaneously mentioned. In the research we report here, the *linguistic category model* (LCM; Semin & Fiedler, 1988, 1991) provided a framework to examine the relative prominence of different emotion terms and the linguistic characteristics of emotion event descriptions. This is a model of interpersonal language that furnishes the means to investigate—among other things—the type of linguistic devices that are used to represent particular events. In this model, a distinction is made between four different categories of interpersonal terms. *Descriptive-action-verbs* are the most concrete terms and are used to convey a description of a single, observable event and preserve perceptual features of the event (e.g., "A punches B"). Similarly, the second category *(interpretive-action-verbs)* describes specific observable events. However, these verbs are more abstract in that they refer to a general class of behaviours and do not preserve the perceptual features of an action (e.g., "A hurts B"). The next category *(state-verbs)* typically describes an unobservable emotional state and not a specific event (e.g., "A hates B"). Finally, *adjectives* (e.g., "A is aggressive") constitute the last and most abstract category. These generalise across specific events and objects and describe only the subject. They show a low contextual dependence and a high conceptual interdependence in their use. In other words, the use of adjectives is governed by abstract, semantic relations rather than by the contingencies of contextual factors. The opposite is true for action verbs (e.g.,

Semin & Fiedler, 1988; Semin & Greenslade, 1985). The most concrete terms retain a reference to the contextual and situated features of an event.

We applied this model to examine different facets of emotion terms and emotion events in the two comparative studies reported below. The general hypothesis behind these studies was the following. In cultures where group-goals and thus the value of relationships prevail over individual ones concrete language use (e.g., predominantly interpersonal verbs) will be more accessible than abstract language (e.g., adjectives, nouns), because concrete language marks relationships and preserves situational information. However, in cultures where individual goals and preferences are more prominent, we expected abstract language to be more accessible. In the first study, we focused on (a) the relative prominence of different linguistic categories in the spontaneous listing of emotion terms. This language-based analysis was complemented by examining (b) whether the causes of emotion events are perceived to be predominantly individual or interpersonal; and (c) the degree to which significant others are perceived to shape emotion events. The second study investigated cultural variations in the degree to which free descriptions of emotion events are seen as person-centred. This was determined by using the LCM to investigate the relative abstractness or concreteness of the events as a function of culture.

STUDY 1

The first issue that we examined was driven by the following considerations. If distinctive linguistic expressions of emotion function as either relationship or individual, self-markers, then there should be systematic differences in their accessibility as a function of cultural background. What does this mean within the general framework of the LCM? One can make a general distinction between interpersonal verbs and adjectives and nouns (Semin & Fiedler, 1991). Sentences with interpersonal verbs always require a subject and an object. Interpersonal verbs are transitive and always represent an event in terms of the relationship between two people. Interpersonal adjectives do not. They are decontextualised qualifiers of persons. In the context of the first study, we were particularly interested in the relative prominence of verbs of state (e.g., to love, to surprise, to envy) versus adjectives (e.g., love, surprised, envious) as a function of the cultural background of people.

An objection that one may raise against classifying nouns or adjectival emotion terms as decontextualised self-markers is that their referents always implies a relationship and cannot be conceived of otherwise. To be in love, envious, or surprised always involves some other for this individual state to be present in the first place. Obviously, this is correct of any emotion-term—emotions are regulatory states in relation to "something" or "somebody". However, there is always a choice to express a relation by either incorporating the object of emotion as an integral part of a linguistic representation (e.g., "I envy Agneta'') or decontextualising the state from the object, as is apparent in cases such as ''I am envious'', or ''I am ashamed'', ''I am angry''. In these latter cases, the choice of an adjective in sentence construction is a preferential expression of the individual's state rather than the explicit expression of a relationship in which the state arises. If people are asked to spontaneously generate as many emotion-terms as they could think of, then the relative proportion of relationship-markers (state verbs) and self-markers should vary as a function of the cultural prevalence of whether emotion events are managed in an individual or socio-centred manner. Our first hypothesis was therefore the following.

1. For participants from a cultural background where the value of relationships and group-goals is prominent, linguistic categories marking relationships (state verbs) should be more accessible than those marking the self (adjectives, or nouns). The reverse pattern was predicted for participants who emphasise the value of the individual.

The study had two further facets. The first one was designed to investigate the type of emotion events (i.e., significant emotion events or significant life events) that are freely generated. In particular, we were interested to examine whether the type of events that participants generate would typically be more interpersonal or individual events as a function of the cultural background of our participants. The type of difference that we were interested in would be between ''being delighted or happy to meet an old friend after many years'' (interpersonal event) versus ''being delighted or happy to pass a difficult exam'', or ''winning in a lottery'' (individual-centred event). We hypothesised that:

2. Members of a culture for whom relationships are more significant are more likely to generate interpersonal emotion events than members of a culture that emphasise the value of the individual. In the latter case, we expected relatively more mention of individual emotion events.

Finally, this study included an investigation of the influence that significant others have upon the shaping of critical, emotion-inducing life events (e.g., marriage, beginning a new job). A critical life event has a strong emotional impact and can make deep inroads on a person's life. The shaping of such an event is culturally informative because it provides another construct to demonstrate differences in the representation of how emotions are constituted. For members of a cultural community that emphasises the importance of relationships, significant others were expected to be influential in the shaping of critical life events—something that was not predicted in the case of communities that value individualism. Our final hypothesis was:

3. In cultural communities that emphasise relationships significant others (i.e., parents, relatives, and friends) would be perceived as more influential in shaping critical life events, than in individual-centred cultures.

Method

Overview.   Hindustani-Surinamese and Dutch participants were given four tasks. The first consisted of an emotion-term generation task, in which they had to list as many emotion terms that came to their mind. Then, half of the subjects were given the task of generating examples of five critical life events, whereas the other half were asked to generate five critical emotions that one can experience. The first group then had to generate the emotions that are likely to occur in such critical life events. In contrast, those who listed the critical emotional experiences had to list the types of situations that were likely to give rise to them. Finally, they all had to judge the relative contribution that significant others (family, friends, etc.) made to shape the events that they had listed. The critical between-subjects variable was culture (Hindustani-Surinamese vs. Dutch). Each task had different within-subjects variables that are elaborated upon in the method and results sections.

Participants.   A total of 84 participants (35 females and 49 males) took part in this study on a paid voluntary basis. Forty-six of the participants (20 males and 26 females) were Dutch (M_{Age} = 22.77 years; SD = 3.26) and 38 (21 males and 17 females) were Hindustani-Surinamese (M_{Age} = 22.84 years; SD = 2.62). The Dutch sample consisted only of native Dutch speakers. They were all students at the Free University. The Hindustani-Surinamese participants were selected on the basis of their chief conversational language in their social life, which was Hindustani. All these participants could read *and* write Hindustani; they were all bilinguals (they could also speak Dutch). Except for six, all the Surinamese participants were born in Surinam and had been in the Netherlands for an average of 12.14 years. All Hindustani-Surinamese were students at the Free University, except for two who were already in employment. One Hindustani-Surinamese participant did not specify his occupation. The fact that our Hindustani-Surinamese participants were all resident in Amsterdam means that despite a strong sense of cultural identity with strong group and family ties, they were nevertheless exposed to a Western individualistic culture. It should be noted that this inevitable bias created by their exposure could be regarded as working against rather than in favour of the hypotheses under consideration.

Additionally, we administered a 17-item independence-interdependence scale with three subdimensions to measure the cultural orientation of the two samples (Semin, Semin-Goossens, & Taris, 1996). This scale showed that the two samples differed from each other in the expected direction. The three subscales were: (1) *Traditional interdependence.* This scale measures an element of continuity in a stable social and physical environment. This sub-scale comprises of items that identify a social coexistence form that remains stable and is also geographically fixed. (2) *Independence-dependence*. This subscale is characterised by items that have to do with how problem solving and decision making are tackled, namely individually or in consultation with others. (3) *Family interdependence*. This scale focuses on reliance upon family and friends in general, that is with regard to problems, happiness, and the role of respect in socialisation. A multivariate ANOVA using these three scales as dependent variables with culture and sex as between-subjects factors yielded a significant multivariate main effect for Culture, $F(3, 76) = 26.87$; $p < .001$. The univariate analyses showed that the Hindustani-Surinamese and the Dutch differed significantly on two of the three subdimensions. The main difference is manifested in the traditional interdependence measure, $F(1, 78) = 52.34$; $p < .01$, where the Hindustani-Surinamese scored significantly higher ($M = 3.27$) than did the Dutch ($M = 1.92$). No significant interactions with sex were found. The significant difference on the second subdimension (independence-dependence), $F(1, 78) = 4.75$; $p < .05$, showed that the Dutch scored higher ($M = 3.81$) with regard to consulting others or relying on second opinions on important decisions and problems than did the Hindustani-Surinamese ($M = 2.29$).[1]

Procedure. Participants were given a booklet. The first page had a very brief instruction (in the respective languages of the participants) in which they were simply asked: "Please list as many emotion words that come to your mind—if the space below is not sufficient then you can use the back of this page". All participants received this spontaneous emotion generation task first, because we did not want their responses to this task to be influenced by possible demands that may have been generated by the other tasks (e.g., whether significant others may shape an emotion event). Moreover, we assumed that a free emotion-term generation task would be unlikely to prime their subsequent answers in any systematic way since the remaining tasks asked for explicit judgements or event descriptions.

After completing this task participants were randomly allocated into one of two conditions. Half of the participants received the following instruction (*critical event condition*): "We are interested in specific events that can influence a person's life in a critical manner. To contrast, there are a number of events that happen in daily life, which have no particular long-term consequences for a person's life. In the following, we would like you to list 5 critical life events that can make deep inroads on a person's life." Twenty-three Dutch and 18 Surinamese participants were in this condition. After the participants completed the critical event task, they were asked to list the emotion(s) that somebody would experience during each of these events.

---

[1] Scales and scale construction data can be obtained from the first author.

The remaining half of the participants received identical introductory instructions except that in their case the word "event" was substituted by "emotional experience" (*critical emotional experience condition*). Twenty-three Dutch and 20 Hindustani-Surinamese participants were in this condition. After having written down the critical emotional experiences, they were asked to list the types of events that they thought would lead to these emotional experiences. Thus, for each of the five emotions they listed the types of events that would give rise to the emotion.

All participants were then asked to turn back at the very first list of emotions they had generated. They were asked to take the first, the fourth and the last emotion from this list (thus randomising the type of emotion examined and its salience) and write down the events that they thought would give rise to these emotions.

Finally, participants were asked to rate the five critical life events that they had generated on six scales. The instruction was as follows: "Please indicate how likely or unlikely it is that each of the five critical life events that you have listed is influenced by each of the following persons". They were then given detailed instructions of the meanings of the 7-point scale, the ends of which were anchored with "highly improbable" (1) and "highly probable" (7). For each event they had to rate the degree to which: (a) they themselves; (b) their parents; (c) their relatives—other than parents; (d) their friends; (e) others; and, (f) uncontrollable factors were likely to influence the event.

Results

The emotion-generation task. We start with the analysis of the general features of the responses participants gave to the first task of listing as many emotion terms as came to their minds. Thereafter we turn to the analyses examining the specific hypothesis regarding the differences in which emotions are coded grammatically in language.

In a first analysis, we calculated the total number of emotions that each participant listed. Dutch participants mentioned a significantly higher number of emotions ($M = 10.24$; $SD = 2.94$) than did the Hindustani-Surinamese ($M = 5.89$; $SD = 2.56$), $F(1, 80) = 43.82$; $p < .001$.

The main hypothesis was examined by analysing the relative proportion of grammatical categories utilised in the listing of emotions.[2] Each emotion word that was mentioned was categorised either as a verb of state (to hate). an

---

[2] The grammatical category analysis is much more self-evident in Dutch and Hindustani-Surinamese than in English. In English, a participant could list "love, hate, surprise" and could be referring to either a verb or a noun rendering the analysis of grammatical category somewhat difficult. Both the Dutch or Hindustani-Surinamese language do not pose this difficulty because the three grammatical categories have manifestly distinct forms which are very clearly distinguishable (e.g., in Hindustani: love $\approx$ *pyar*; to love $\approx$ *pyar karna*; lovely $\approx$ *pyari*, etc. In Dutch: surprise $\approx$ *verrassing*; to surprise $\approx$ *verrassen*; surprising $\approx$ *verrassend*).

TABLE 1
Relative proportion of grammatical categories mentioned in the emotion generation
task as a function of culture

	State verbs	Adjectives	Nouns
Hindustani-Surinamese	0.30 (SD=0.14)	0.18 (SD=0.22)	0.52 (SD=0.28)
Dutch	0.14 (SD=0.24)	0.26 (SD=0.31)	0.60 (SD=0.37)

adjective (hateful), or a noun (hate). A MANOVA was conducted using culture (Dutch vs. Hindustani-Surinamese), and sex (Female vs. Male) as the two between subjects variables and grammatical categories as repeated measures (verbs vs. nouns). We did not use all three dependent variables (i.e., verbs, nouns and adjectives) as the three levels of grammatical category are tied and the proportions add up to 1.00. This MANOVA yielded the expected multivariate main effect for culture, $F(3, 77) = 3.33$; $p < .05$. The univariate tests revealed that there was a significant difference between the cultures for the proportion verbs used, $F(1, 74) = 8.43$; $p < .005$, and a tendency for the proportion of nouns used, $F(1, 74) = 2.93$; $p < .10$. As can be seen in Table 1, the Hindustani-Surinamese mentioned more state verbs than did the Dutch and tended to use somewhat fewer state referent nouns than did the Dutch. The respective proportions of adjectives for the Hindustani-Surinamese and the Dutch was not significant, $F(1, 74) < 1.00$).

Use of grammatical emotion categories in events.   Next, we analysed the emotions that participants had generated for the critical life events or critical emotion experience tasks in terms of the grammatical categories. This MANOVA had three between-subjects variables, namely, culture, sex, and version (event task first vs. emotion task first). The dependent variables in this case were the proportion of the verbs, adjectives, and nouns that were mentioned. All three were entered into the analysis because 5% of the answers by the Dutch and 3% of the answers by the Surinamese could not be coded thereby removing the interdependence between the three variables. The multivariate main effect for culture was significant, $F(3, 77) = 4.50$; $p < .006$). The univariate analyses provided support for the general hypothesis. The Hindustani-Surinamese sample mentioned more verbs ($M = 0.30$; SD = .33) than did the Dutch ($M = 0.10$; SD = 0.25), $F(1, 75) = 11.08$; $p < .001$, but a significantly lower proportion of nouns ($M = 0.59$; SD = 0.33) than did the Dutch ($M = 0.82$; SD = 0.30), $F(1, 75) = 11.33$; $p < .001$. The univariate culture effect using proportion of adjectives as the dependent variable was not significant. These results mirror those obtained in the first task and suggest that the first finding is a stable one.

The second hypothesis was that Hindustani-Surinamese participants would generate relatively more interpersonal events as giving rise to emotional experiences than did the Dutch. For these analyses we had two separate measures. The first one came from the five critical life events that participants had listed. The second set consisted of the events that they generated as giving rise to the first, fourth, and final emotions on the very first emotion-term generation task. The respective events mentioned by each participant were coded by two independent coders as either an interpersonal event (e.g., meeting an old friend, being helped by a colleague, etc.) or a noninterpersonal event (e.g., passing an exam, winning in a lottery, etc.) The overall intercoder reliability[3] was high $(r = .87)$.

The first analysis used the number of interpersonal events (out of a total of five for each participant) mentioned by the participants as the dependent variable in an ANOVA with culture (Hindustani-Surinamese vs. Dutch) and sex (female vs. male) as the two between-subjects variables. We obtained only a significant main effect due to culture, $F(1, 36) = 5.70$; $p < .03$. Consistent with our expectations, the Hindustani-Surinamese participants mentioned significantly more interpersonal events $(M = 3.59$; $SD = 1.50)$ than did the Dutch $(M = 2.65$; $SD = 0.89)$. An analysis of the relative proportion of interpersonal events resulted in the same outcome. This two-way ANOVA also yielded only a significant main effect for culture, $F(1, 74) = 7.89$, $p < .006$, supporting the prediction that the Hindustani-Surinamese participants mentioned relatively more interpersonal events $(M = 0.61$; $SD = 0.23)$ than did the Dutch participants $(M = 0.51$; $SD = 0.19)$.

The contribution of significant others to critical life events.   For Hindustani-Surinamese participants, we expected significant others (e.g., parents, friends, and family) to have a stronger influence on the shaping of critical life events than for the Dutch. With respect to the latter group, we expected the "self" to be regarded as more influential than significant others. To this end we performed a multivariate analysis of variance, with culture and sex as the two between-subjects variables and the likelihood ratings for the influence of self, parents, family, friends, others, and uncontrollable factors on the shaping of the event as dependent measures. This analysis yielded only a significant multivariate main effect for culture, $F(5, 76) = 5.82$; $p < .001$, supporting the prediction. The univariate analyses yielded significant main effects for the influence exerted by self, $F(1, 80) = 4.02$; $p < .05$; parents, $F(1, 80) = 17.96$; $p < .001$, family, $F(1, 80) = 24.37$; $p < .001$, and friends, $F(1, 80) = 11.70$; $p < .001$. As can be seen

---

[3] One of the coders was fluent in Hindustani and Dutch, the second only in Dutch. The first translated all the events listed by the Hindustani-Surinamese subjects into Dutch. She then coded the both the Dutch events and the Hindustani Surinamese events in their respective languages. The second coder did the same except that in this case all events were in Dutch.

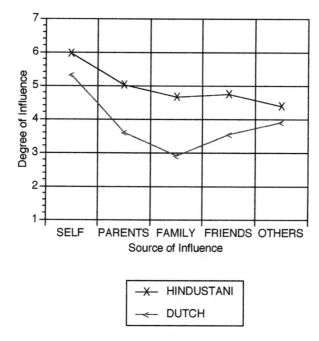

Figure 1. The relative contribution of parents, family, and friends to critical life events.

in Figure 1, all these main effects are in the expected direction, showing that for the Hindustani-Surinamese sample, Self, Parents, Family, and Friends exert a stronger influence on the shaping of major life events than it did for the Dutch.

Discussion

The results of this study display a convergent pattern in the three general features of emotion events that were examined here. First, we found as predicted that the proportion of state verbs accessed by the Hindustani-Surinamese participants is twice as much as the proportion mentioned by the Dutch. These results suggest that the active emotion vocabularies of the two communities display a systematic difference in terms of the feature under investigation, namely, the grammatical category by which emotions are marked. Moreover, we found that the same pattern is consistent and holds irrespective of whether participants are asked to list five significant emotions or list emotions associated with critical life events. The Hindustani-Surinamese sample produces a higher proportion of emotion-terms that mark interpersonal relationships (i.e., verbs) when compared with the Dutch sample where emotions are more likely to be marked in terms of abstracted or decontextualised states (namely nouns). These findings provide support for the notion that the linguistic construction of emotional events may vary systematically between cultures. This evidence is not in terms of the particular content of the emotions in question, their intensity or semantic signification, but rather the differential accessibility of specific grammatical categories in the two samples.

We know that interpersonal verbs constitute a more concrete grammatical category than adjectives and nouns (cf. Semin & Fiedler, 1988, 1991). Whereas interpersonal verbs (or verbs of state, such as *to like, to surprise*) can only be used with a sentence subject and object and refer to a particular event or concrete relationship between a subject and an object, adjectives and nouns abstract from the immediacy of events. They refer to qualities or qualitative states of the person that are detached from a specific constellation. One implication of this finding is that, for the Hindustani-Surinamese, emotions are more concrete events that are anchored more directly in the here and now. In contrast, for the Dutch, emotions are marked more prominently as intrapersonal states. They are abstracted from the here-and-now and thus decontextualised to the level of the experiencing person. That is, for them emotions are marked more abstractly overall than for the Hindustani-Surinamese. Whereas for the Hindustani-Surinamese emotions are more strongly indicative of *interpersonal* rather than solitary experiences, for the Dutch emotional experience is marked by the predominant use of individual-centred and decontextualised terms. The systematic differences in grammatical category can also be seen as providing *indirect* evidence for the same conclusion. Although emotional experience is more an *inter*-psychological event for the Hindustani-Surinamese, it constitutes an *intra*-psychological one for the Dutch.

Whereas the analysis addressed linguistic features of spontaneously elicited emotion terms, the next analysis addressed the characteristics of events that give rise to emotions. Again, we deployed different methods to elicit the reports of events that are associated with emotions. Irrespective of whether participants were asked to note significant life events, or to simply write down those events that gave rise to three of the emotions which they listed, we found a pattern that converged with the emotion data. Hindustani-Surinamese participants listed proportionately more interpersonal events than did the Dutch participants— irrespective of the method that was used to elicit these events. These results provide evidence for the hypothesis that for the Hindustani-Surinamese participants' emotional events are predominantly interpersonal ones, whereas for the Dutch participants they constitute individual-centred events and experiences.

The final source of evidence provided by the results concerns the role different people play in shaping critical life events. The Hindustani-Surinamese perceived that the shape of significant life events is strongly influenced by significant others, namely, family, friends, and parents. This finding is consistent with the fact that they also construed emotions in interpersonal terms, and regard emotion events to be interpersonal. In contrast, for the Dutch the pattern is reversed, as expected. We found that if one compares the relative influence of self to the influence that their parents, family, friends, or others may have then the self was perceived to influence significant life events significantly more relative to all these other target groups. In this type of cultural context, parents, family, and friends turn out not to be very significant in the shaping of important events. In turn, this is consistent with the findings that for them emotions are predominantly individual experiences as are the events that give rise to them.

STUDY 2

In a second study we addressed the linguistic structure of emotion events in a different way. The focus of the first study was on the differential accessibility of grammatical categories as a function of participants' cultural background. In the second study we examined whether the overall pattern of predicate use (e.g., verbs and adjectives) in the representation of an emotion event varies as a function of cultural background. There is earlier work on cultural differences in attributional tendencies (e.g., Miller, 1984; Morris & Peng, 1994; Semin & Zwier, 1997; Shweder & Miller, 1985). This research suggests, for instance, that Indian participants use a more concrete situationalist attributional style than, for instance, their more individualistic American counterparts (e.g., Miller, 1984). The general finding across diverse studies is that individual-centred cultures preferentially deploy internal attributes of persons in representing social events, whereas relationship centered cultures resort to focal or situational features. To our knowledge, this pattern of outcomes has as yet not been examined in the context of emotion events. Moreover, the linguistic category model provides a systematic tool for the examination of the relative abstractness of event representations as a function of cultural differences. As we mentioned earlier, the LCM permits an examination of the degree to which a representation of an event is abstract or concrete, as measured by the types of predicates used in an event description (see Semin & Fiedler, 1989, and the Method section below). The following hypothesis was tested in this study. The language used to represent emotion events should be more abstract in cultures where individual preferences and goals prevail over group goals. In contrast, in cultures where relationships are valued emotion events should be represented by the use of more concrete language. Abstract and concrete were operationalised in terms of the linguistic category model.

Method

Participants.   A total of 165 students participated in the study on a paid voluntary basis. They consisted of 83 Dutch students from the Free University Amsterdam (41 men and 42 women, with a mean age of 21.8 years) and 82 participants from two universities in Turkey, one in Istanbul and the other in Mersin. The Turkish sample consisted of 40 men and 42 women, with a mean age of 22.4 years.

Procedure.   Participants filled out a questionnaire which consisted of two parts: An event-description task and an emotion-description task. They received one of two different versions of the questionnaire. These versions differed as to whether participants were asked to report about himself or herself or about a close friend of the same-sex.[4] In the first version, they were asked to describe a positive and a negative event which they themselves had experienced and which had had a significant impact on them. They were given 10 lines to describe each event. After they had completed the first event-description, they were asked to name the emotions that they had experienced during this event. They had 8 lines for this. They were then asked to describe the second event and subsequently the particular emotions experienced in this event. The order in which they described the positive and negative event was randomised. The second version of the questionnaire asked participants to think about a close friend of the same sex. Their task was identical to the self-referent task, except that it was now for a close friend. The procedure was similar to the first version of the questionnaire.

Participants completed the questionnaires in their native language. The Dutch version was translated into Turkish and then back-translated by an independent translator (Brislin, 1970) in order to ascertain for equivalence in meaning between the two questionnaires.

Design.   The event- and emotion-description tasks both consisted of a 2 (culture: Dutch vs. Turkish) $\times$ 2 (target: self vs. friend) $\times$ 2 (event valence: positive vs. negative) design with the last variable as a within-subjects variable. The effects for the target variable will not be discussed as this variable did not show any systematic effect whatsoever.

Coding of open-ended answers. The Dutch data were coded by one of the authors and the Turkish data by a Turkish Dutch bilingual who had received extensive instructions about the coding proceeding. Before coding the Turkish data, the bilingual coded 10% of all Dutch data (inter-rater reliability, $r = .85$). Differences between both coders on the Dutch data were resolved by discussion before the bilingual started coding the Turkish data.

Dependent variables.   In the case of the emotions we first calculated the number of discrete emotion terms that were listed (e.g., "disappointment", "frustration", and "I hated him" were coded as three distinct emotion terms). Then the overall *abstraction of the emotions* was coded. This involved coding each emotion reference as either adjectives or nouns (e.g., "happy" or "sadness"), state verbs (e.g., "to hate"), interpretative action verbs (e.g., "to fall silent"), and descriptive action verbs (e.g., "to cry") (see Semin & Fiedler, 1988, 1991 for details of the linguistic category model). These categories reflect

---

[4] The self-other condition was introduced to control for the potential contribution of perspective upon emotion events. As it turned out this variable did not yield any systematic effects.

an increase in abstraction from descriptive action verbs to adjectives or nouns. Weights were applied to these categories in such a way that a higher score reflects a higher level of abstraction (see Semin & Fiedler, 1989). This was accomplished by a simple monotonic weighting scheme using 1, 2, 3, and 4, to weigh descriptive action verbs (DAV), interpretative action verbs (IAV), state verbs (SV), and adjectives or nouns (ADJ/NOUN) respectively (Semin & Fiedler, 1989). The abstraction level of the emotion terms was calculated by the following formula:

$$\frac{(nDAV \times 1) + (nIAV \times 2) + (nSV \times 3) + (nADJ/NOUN \times 4)}{(nDAV + nIAV + nSV + nADJ/NOUN}$$

The abstraction level ranges from 1 (very concrete, only DAVs) to 4 (very abstract, only ADJ/NOUNs).

The linguistic *abstraction of the events* giving rise to emotions was scored in the same way as the emotion descriptions.

Results

Abstraction level of events and emotions.   To test the prediction that Dutch event-descriptions are more abstract than the Turkish ones, a 2 (culture: Dutch vs. Turkish) × 2 (event valence: positive vs. negative) ANOVA was conducted. The second variable was a within-subjects variable and the level of abstraction of the event-descriptions constituted the dependent variable. As expected, the level of abstraction of the Dutch event-descriptions ($M = 1.76$: SD $= 0.44$) was higher than the level of abstraction of the Turkish event-descriptions ($M = 1.59$, SD $= 0.44$), $F(1, 154) = 5.59$, $p < .05$. The same analysis with the abstraction score of emotion terms allowed us to test the hypothesis that the Dutch used more abstract emotion terms than did the Turks. As expected, the Dutch described emotions more abstractly ($M = 3.96$, SD $= 0.14$) than did the Turks ($M = 3.68$, SD $= 0.49$), $F(1, 148) = 25.18$, $p < .001$.

Discussion

The results of this study provide additional support for the hypothesis that the language used to represent emotions and emotion events is more abstract in descriptions provided by members of a culture who emphasise the individual than members of cultures who value interdependence. The latter were found to use a more concrete language for the same tasks. These findings are convergent with earlier work on cultural differences in attributional tendencies (e.g., Miller, 1984; Morris & Peng, 1994; Shweder & Miller, 1985). It would appear to be the case that there are general cognitive differences between members of collectivistic and individualistic communities in the manner in which they represent and process information about their social world. Whereas collectivists display a stronger reliance on more concrete and immediate event-based representations and processing of information, individualists appear to rely more on an abstracted, decontextualised coding and representation of events and persons. This general tendency is also reflected in the emotion vocabularies or the manner in which emotion is coded by the respective cultures.

GENERAL DISCUSSION AND CONCLUSIONS

The general pattern emerging from these two studies suggests that emotions and emotion events are more interpersonally configured within an interdependent cultural context than they are within an independent one. The first two converging sources of evidence come from the linguistic coding of emotions. We found that concrete emotion categories implying situated relationships are more accessible (Study 1) and that emotion events are more concretely described (Study 2) in interdependent cultural contexts relative to independent cultural contexts. The latter are more likely to access abstract emotion terms. Moreover, they are more inclined to describe emotion events abstractly.

The finding of concrete versus abstract descriptions of emotion events (Study 2) is in line with the research suggesting that contextualizing predicates are more prominently used in attributional explanations in cultures where interdependence is more prominent (e.g., Miller, 1984; Miller & Bersoff, 1992; Morris & Peng, 1994, inter alia). Moreover, this is also in line with the notion that the self itself is contextualised in such cultural contexts (e.g., Cousins, 1989; Markus & Kitayama, 1991). The argument developed here dovetails quite well with an observation that White (1994) makes. He notes that "It is difficult for A'ara speakers to even talk about emotions as abstract or discrete states of mind independent of these context linkages" (pp. 226–227). Furthermore, he notes that most vernacular terms used by the A'ara to denote emotions are verbs.

These findings are complemented by the second set of findings about the types of events that give rise to emotional experiences. In the first study, we found—again with two convergent methods—that for participants from an interdependent cultural background, such events are more likely to involve interpersonal situations than for participants from independent cultural contexts. The second study yielded convergent evidence. Representations of events were more concrete for the Turks and more abstract for the Dutch sample. Finally, the first study shows that significant others are seen as exerting a stronger influence on how such events are shaped in the case of interdependent participants.

The current research strategy of relying on self-generated emotions or emotion events rather than specifying a specific set of emotions presents some advantages over some other approaches in the comparative study of emotions. First of all, it avoids potential problems of focusing on a particular emotion rather than others. Frijda and Mesquita (1994) have for instance criticised "the extent to which cross-cultural emotion psychology is plagued by a preoccupation with emotion labels" (p. 82). Moreover, research in this field has often been concerned with whether the specific events that give rise to particular emotions lead to comparable conclusions across cultures. This type of focus makes generalisation very difficult. Obviously, we are not suggesting that self-generation methods provide a panacea, but they present a possible avenue to examine general features of emotions that vary across cultures.

One of the more speculative implications of the current research has to do with the implications of the nature of relationships and how they are maintained. If it is the case that the formation of identities is predicated on relationships in an interdependent culture then it is inevitable that there is a relative permanence of relationships. That is, once relationships are formed they are more likely to be stable over time and the changes in this sphere are likely to be less variable than in an independent cultural context. In an independent culture, one would expect interpersonal relations to be more likely to have ''mobility''. In short, one would expect that interpersonal relationships do not have the same permanence as they do in interdependent cultures. Therefore, it is possible that interpersonal relationships are more strongly bounded by emotions in communities where interdependence is valued and they are more permanent whereas emotions in independent communities are more likely to be typified by the permeability of relationships. One way of speaking about experiences or events that are detached from distinctive events or situations is by resorting to abstraction. This is one possible sociocultural factor that may be regarded as contributing to the emergence, use of, and access to a more abstract vocabulary (e.g., nouns and adjectives).

Finally, the current work may have some implications for emotional communication. If the manner in which emotion is marked (relationship vs. self) differs systematically, as do the situations that give rise to it, then it is likely that there are subtle differences in the way interdependent and independent cultures engage in talking about emotions. This, in our view, is one of the interesting challenges for future research in this field. The findings in this study suggest that the communicative implications of emotion-talk are different to the extent that in an independent context talking about emotions is more likely to be an invitation to talk and analyse the self. In contrast, emotion-talk in an interdependent context is much more likely to be talk about a social event within which the self and others are interfaced. Moreover, this may also imply that emotion-talk has stronger action implications in interdependent cultures—namely, to undertake or do things jointly in contrast to an independent context where emotion talk may simply remain ''analytic talk''. Examining the general cultural features of the configuration of emotion-talk and its social implications, rather than of particular emotions, in our view, may open new vistas for comparative research in this field, as well as throw light on our own culture's conceptions of emotions.

Manuscript received 31 October 1999
Revised manuscript 30 October 2000

REFERENCES

Brislin, R. W. (1970). Back-translation for cross-cultural research. *Journal of Cross-Cultural Psychology*, *1*, 185–216.

Cousins, S. (1989). Culture and selfhood in Japan and the US. *Journal of Personality and Social Psychology*, *56*, 124–131.

Frijda, N. H., & Mesquita, B. (1994). The social roles and functions of emotions. In S. Kitayama & H. Markus (Eds.), *Culture and emotion: Empirical studies of mutual influence* (pp.51–88). Washington, DC: APA.

Hofstede, G. (1980). *Culture's consequences*. Beverly Hills, CA: Sage.

Kitayama, S., Markus, H. R., & Matsumoto, H. (1995). *Culture, self, and emotion: A cultural perspective on 'self-conscious' emotions*. In J. P. Tangney & K. W. Fischer (Eds.), *Self-conscious emotions: The psychology of shame, guilt, embarrassment and pride* (pp. 439–465). New York: Guilford Press.

Markus, H. R., & Kitayama, S. (1991). Culture and the self: Implications for cognition, emotion, and motivation. *Psychological Review*, *98*, 224–253.

Markus, H. R., & Kitayama, S. (1994). The social construction of self and emotion: Implications for social behavior. In S. Kitayama & H. Markus (Eds.), *Culture and emotion: Empirical studies of mutual influence* (pp. 89–130). Washington, DC: APA.

Mauss, M. (1985). A category of the human mind: the notion of person; the notion of self. (W. D. Halls, Trans.). In M. Carrithers, S. Collins, & S. Lukes (Eds.), *The category of the person* (pp. 1–25). Cambridge, UK: Cambridge University Press. (Original work published 1938).

Miller, J. G. (1984). Culture and the development of everyday social explanation. *Journal of Personality and Social Psychology*, *46*, 961–978.

Miller, J. G., & Bersoff, D. M. (1992). Culture and moral judgment: how are conflicts between justice and interpersonal responsibilities resolved? *Journal of Personality and Social Psychology*, *62*, 541–554.

Morris, M. W., & Peng, K. (1994). Culture and cause: American and Chinese attributions for social and physical events. *Journal of Personality and Social Psychology*, *67*, 949–971.

Sampson, E. E. (1985). The decentralization of identity: Toward a revised concept of personal and social order. *American Psychologist*, *40*, 1203–1211.

Semin, G. R. & Rubini, M. (1990). Unfolding the concept of person by verbal abuse. *European Journal of Social Psychology*, *20*, 463–474.

Semin, G. R., & Fiedler, K. (1988). The cognitive functions of linguistic categories in describing persons: Social cognition and language. *Journal of Personality and Social Psychology*, *54*, 558–568.

Semin, G. R., & Fiedler, K. (1989). Relocating attributional phenomena within a language-cognition interface: The case of actors' and observers' perspectives. *European Journal of Social Psychology*, *19*, 491–508.

Semin, G. R., & Fiedler, K. (1991). The linguistic category model: Its bases, applications, and range. In W. Stroebe & M. Hewstone (Eds.), *European Review of Social Psychology* (Vol. 2, pp. 1–30) Chicester, UK: Wiley.

Semin, G. R., & Greenslade, L. (1985). Differential contributions of linguistic factors to memory based ratings: Systematizing the systematic distortion hypothesis. *Journal of Personality and Social Psychology*, *49*, 1713–1723.

Semin, G. R., Semin-Goossens, A., & Taris, T. (1996). *INDCOL—an instrument to measure facets of individualism-collectivism*. Vrije Universiteit, Unpublished manuscript.

Semin, G. R., & Zwier, S. (1997). Social cognition. In J. W. Berry, M. H. Segall, & Ç. Kagitçibasi (Eds.), *Handbook of cross-cultural psychology: Vol. 3. Social behavior and applications* (2nd ed., pp. 51–75). Boston, MA: Allyn & Bacon.

Shweder, R. A., & Bourne, E. J. (1982). Does the concept of the person vary cross-culturally? In A. J. Marsella & G. M. White (Eds.), *Cultural conceptions of mental health and therapy* (pp. 97–137). Dordrecht: Riedel.

Shweder, R. A., & Miller, J. (1985). The social construction of the person: How is it possible? In K. J. Gergen & K. E. Davies (Eds.), *The social construction of the person* (pp. 27–49). New York: Springer.

Triandis, H. C. (1988). Collectivism v. individualism: A reconceptualisation of a basic concept in cross-cultural social psychology. In G. K. Verma & C. Bagley (Eds.), *Cross-cultural studies of personality, attitudes and cognition* (pp. 60–95). London: Macmillan.

Triandis, H. C. (1989). Cross-cultural studies of individualism and collectivism. In *Nebraska symposium on motivation* (pp. 41–133). Lincoln, NE: University of Nebraska Press.

Triandis, H. C. (1994a). *Culture and social behavior*. New York: McGraw-Hill.

Triandis, H. C. (1994b). Major cultural syndromes and emotion. In S. Kitayama & H. Markus (Eds.), *Culture and Emotion: Empirical studies of mutual influence* (pp. 285–305). Washington, DC: APA.

Triandis, H. C. (1995). *Individualism and collectivism*. Boulder, CO: Westview.

White, G. M. (1994). Affecting culture: Emotion and morality in everyday life. In S. Kitayama & H. Markus (Eds.), *Culture and emotion: Empirical studies of mutual influence* (pp. 219–239). Washington, DC: APA.

COGNITION AND EMOTION, 2002, *16* (1), 29–59

Word and voice: Spontaneous attention to emotional utterances in two languages

Shinobu Kitayama and Keiko Ishii

Kyoto University, Japan

Adopting a modified Stroop task, the authors tested the hypothesis that processing systems brought to bear on comprehension of emotional speech are attuned primarily to word evaluation in a low-context culture and language (i.e., in English), but they are attuned primarily to vocal emotion in a high-context culture and language (i.e., in Japanese). Native Japanese (Studies 1 and 2) and English speakers (Study 3) made a judgement of either vocal emotion or word evaluation of an emotionally spoken evaluative word. Word evaluations and vocal emotions were comparable in extremity in the two languages. In support of the hypothesis, an interference effect by competing word evaluation in the vocal emotion judgement was significantly stronger in English than in Japanese. In contrast, an interference effect by competing vocal emotion in the word evaluation judgement was stronger in Japanese than in English. Implications for the cultural grounding of communication, emotion, and cognition are discussed.

In every culture and language, emotionally nuanced utterances play a central role in the making of many figurative meanings. For example, consider an utterance, "Good!" When this line (carrying a positive word evaluation) is spoken in a harsh tone of voice (carrying a negative vocal emotion), the listener is likely to infer that the speaker does not really mean it and, in fact, that he/she wishes to convey something else (Sperber & Wilson, 1986). Systematic research by Scherer and colleagues has amassed considerable evidence that vocal emotion is accurately recognised on at least relatively gross dimensions of pleasantness and arousal (e.g., Banse & Scherer, 1996; Scherer, 1986). Further, a growing number of studies, conducted mostly with English speakers, have begun

Correspondence should be addressed to Shinobu Kitayama, Faculty of Integrated Human Studies, Kyoto University, Sakyo-ku, Kyoto 606-8501 Japan. E-mail: kitayama@hi.h.kyoto-u.ac.jp

This research was supported by National Institute of Mental Health Grant 1R01 MH50117-01 and Ministry of Education Grants B-20252398 and C-10180001. We thank Mayumi Karasawa for running Study 2, Cynthia M. Ferguson for running Study 3, Taro Hirai for data analysis, and Ann Marie and Peter Jusczyk for technical advice and support. We also thank members of the Kyoto University cultural psychology lab, who commented on an earlier draft of the paper.

http://www.tandf.co.uk/journals/pp/02699931.html   DOI:10.1080/0269993943000121

to suggest some different ways in which both verbal content (*what* is said) and vocal tone (*how* it is said) are implicated in speech processing (Kitayama, 1996; Kitayama & Howard, 1994) and social perception (see DePaulo & Friedman, 1998, for a review).

Although the general, pan-cultural significance of both verbal content and vocal tone in the comprehension of emotional speech is beyond doubt, cultural or linguistic dimensions will also have to be taken into account in a more comprehensive analysis of the issue. The current work explores whether the specific mechanisms underlying emotional information processing may be moderated by cultural or linguistic factors. To the extent that such cultural or linguistic moderation exists, an enquiry into the cultural variation in emotional information processing will provide a significant insight into the interface between culture and emotion.

One important clue for a cultural variation in emotional information processing comes from some observations of communicative practices and conventions of different cultures and languages.[1] It has been suggested that the *relative* emphasis given to verbal content *vis-à-vis* vocal tone may differ considerably across cultures and languages. Specifically, scholars in anthropology, linguistics, and cross-cultural psychology, have suggested that a global difference exists in this particular aspect of communicative practices and conventions between individualist languages and cultures and collectivist ones (Gudykunst *et al.* 1996; Hall, 1976; Kashima & Kashima, 1998; Semin & Rubini, 1990). Hall (1976) proposed that in some Western cultures and languages (e.g., North America/English) a greater proportion of information is conveyed by verbal content. Correspondingly, contextual cues including nonverbal ones such as vocal tone are likely to serve a relatively minor role. Hall referred to these cultures and languages as *low-context*. Low-context communicative practices appear to be grounded in a cultural assumption that the thoughts of each individual are unknowable in principle unless they are explicitly expressed in words. By contrast, in some East Asian cultures and languages (e.g., Japan/Japanese), the proportion of information conveyed by verbal content is relatively lower and, correspondingly, contextual and nonverbal cues are likely to play a relatively greater role. These languages are therefore called *high-context*. High-context communicative practices appear to be grounded in a contrasting cultural assumption that the thoughts of each individual are knowable in principle once enough context is specified for an utterance.

---

[1] Such practices and conventions are simultaneously *both* cultural in that they embody shared meaning systems *and* linguistic in that they rely on symbolic means of communication. Thus, the current work does not seek to differentiate relative effects of cultural *vis-à-vis* linguistic factors. We will return to this issue in the Discussion section.

Existing evidence is consistent with Hall's analysis. For example, Ambady, Koo, Lee, and Rosenthal (1996) found that choice of politeness strategies in social communication (cf. Brown & Levinson, 1987) is influenced more by the content of communication in the United States, but is influenced more by relational concerns (i.e., contextual information) in Korea. Focusing on Japanese communicative practices, several observers have noted that utterances in daily communications in Japan are often ambiguous when taken out of context (Barnlund, 1989; Borden, 1991; Ikegami, 1991). For example, "*i-i*" literally means "good". When this utterance is used in a specific social context, however, it can mean praise ("It is good"), mild distancing of the self from the other ("It is good that you don't do it", meaning "you don't have to do it"), or even outright rejection ("It is good that we are finished", meaning "go away!"). The intended meaning of a communication is so dependent on the immediate social and relational context that it can diverge considerably from its literal verbal meaning. In a more systematic, cross-linguistic study, Kashima and Kashima (1998) have noted that in the languages of individualist cultures (e.g., English, German) it is often obligatory to include relevant pronouns in constructing grammatically permissible sentences. These structural features of the languages lend themselves to verbally explicit, low-context forms of communication. In contrast, the languages of collectivist cultures (e.g., Japanese, Chinese, Korean, and Spanish) tend to leave the use of pronouns largely optional, which is conducive to verbally ambiguous, high-context forms of communication. Further, recent research on cultural variations in cognition has also demonstrated that people in Eastern cultures are more sensitive to contextual information in a variety of inference tasks than are those in Western cultures (Kitayama, 2000; Nisbett, Peng, Choi, & Norenzayan, 2001).

In the current paper, we examine whether and to what extent the high- versus low-context patterns of communicative practices and conventions may be reflected in the nature of processing systems that are brought to bear on the comprehension of emotional utterances. By emotional utterances we mean emotionally spoken words that have emotional verbal meaning. In particular, we focused on one low-context language (i.e., English) and one high-context language (i.e., Japanese). Our analysis draws on an emerging body of research in cultural psychology. This literature suggests that psychological systems acquire cross-culturally divergent operating characteristics (or "biases") depending on the practices and public meanings prevalent in a given cultural community (Fiske, Kitayama, Markus, & Nisbett, 1998; Markus, Kitayama, & Heiman, 1996). A number of studies have been conducted in the recent years, making this perspective quite promising in diverse domains, including self-perception and evaluation (e.g., Heine, Lehman, Markus, & Kitayama, 1999; Kitayama, Markus, Matsumoto, & Norasakkunkit, 1997), social cognition (Morris & Peng, 1994), reasoning (Nisbett et al., 2001), emotion (Kitayama, Markus, & Kurokawa, 2000; Mesquita & Frijda, 1992), motivation (Iyengar & Lepper, 1999), and mental health (Kitayama & Markus, 2000; Suh, Diener, Oishi, & Triandis, 1998). Extrapolating from this literature, it would seem reasonable to expect that processing systems implicated in the comprehension of emotional utterances are closely interdependent with communicative practices and conventions of a given culture and language and, thus, cross-culturally or linguistically variable to some significant extent .

Specifically, in low-context cultures and languages, both speakers and listeners are likely to engage in a communicative endeavour with the implicit rule of thumb that what is said in word is what is meant. The speakers craft their messages and, in turn, the listeners comprehend them with this rule of thumb in mind. Thus, for example, when someone says "Yes", the listener ought to construe, first, the utterance to mean an affirmation of some kind. Only after this initial assignment of meaning may an adjustment be made on the basis of other contextual cues including the attendant vocal tone (see Gilbert & Malone, 1995, for a similar analysis). Once socialised in such a linguistic and cultural system, individuals will have developed a well-practised attentional bias that favours verbal content. In contrast, in high-context cultures and languages, both speakers and listeners are likely to engage in a communicative endeavour with the implicit cultural rule of thumb that what is said makes best sense only in a particular context. The speakers craft and the listeners, in their turn, comprehend messages with this rule of thumb in mind. Thus, for example, when someone says "Yes" in a relatively reluctant tone of voice, the tone of the voice should figure more prominently, along with other available contextual cues, for the listener to infer the "real" meaning of the utterance. Once socialised in such a linguistic or cultural system, individuals will have developed a well-practised attentional bias that favours vocal tone.

If the culturally divergent attentional biases predicted above are overlearned through recurrent engagement in one or the other mode of daily communications, they should be quite immune to intentional control to nullify them. This possibility can be tested with a Stroop-type interference task (MacLeod, 1991; Stroop, 1935). This task is suitable for examining the degree to which one or another channel of emotional information captures attention even when the listener has to ignore it. Two specific predictions can be advanced. First, suppose individuals are asked to ignore the verbal content of an emotional utterance and, instead, are asked to make a judgement about its vocal tone. Under these conditions, native speakers of English (a low-context language) should find it relatively difficult to ignore the verbal meaning. This attentional bias should result in an interference effect; that is, performance of the focal judgement (in both accuracy and speed) should be better if the attendant word meaning was congruous than if it was incongruous. In contrast, native speakers of Japanese (a high-context language) should find it relatively easy to ignore the verbal meaning, leading to a lesser degree of interference. Second, consider the reverse task, in which individuals have to ignore the vocal tone of the utterance and, instead, to make a judgement of its verbal content. Under these conditions, native Japanese speakers should find it relatively difficult to ignore the vocal tone. Again, this attentional bias should cause an interference effect; that is, performance of the word meaning judgement is better if the attendant vocal tone is congruous than if it is incongruous. In contrast, the native English speakers should find it relatively easy to ignore the vocal tone, hence resulting in a lesser degree of interference.

The three studies reported below were conducted with the foregoing cross-cultural predictions in mind. Studies 1 and 2 were done in Japanese with native Japanese speakers and, separately, Study 3 was conducted in English on native English speakers (Americans). Because there were no previous studies on cultural differences in the processing of emotional utterances in general, let alone any studies pertaining directly to our predictions, our effort was exploratory in virtually every step of the research endeavour. Inevitably, some limitations ensued, which will be discussed below. However, the three studies, when taken as a whole, offer a unique opportunity to perform a valid test of our predictions. In what follows, we will first report the three studies separately and then draw a comparison between the Japanese results and the American results.

In all studies, we orthogonally manipulated both word evaluation and vocal emotion. Importantly, word evaluations and vocal emotions were comparable in the two languages. Respondents were asked to make either: (1) a judgement of word evaluation as pleasant or unpleasant while ignoring the attendant vocal emotion, or (2) a judgement of vocal emotion as pleasant or unpleasant while ignoring the attendant word evaluation. The focus was to determine whether and to what extent performance in a judgement on one of the stimulus dimensions would be interfered with by competing information on the other, judgement-irrelevant dimension. Such an interference effect would occur to the extent that respondents fail to ignore the judgement-irrelevant channel of information. An interference effect by competing word evaluation in the vocal tone judgement should be prominent primarily for native English speakers, whereas an interference effect due to competing vocal emotion in the word meaning judgement should be prominent primarily for native Japanese speakers.

STUDIES 1 AND 2

The purpose of Studies 1 and 2 was to collect pertinent data from native Japanese speakers. Because we anticipated a major interference effect in word evaluation judgement for Japanese, we decided to determine first if we could in fact find such an effect. Thus, Study 1 examined word evaluation judgement. Vocal emotion judgement was added to the experimental design in Study 2.

Method

Respondents and Procedure.   A total of 50 undergraduates (23 males and 27 females) at a Japanese national university participated in Study 1 and another group of 60 female undergraduates at a Japanese women's college participated in Study 2. The participation partially fulfilled course requirements. All were native speakers of Japanese. Each respondent was seated in front of a personal computer and wore a pair of headphones. The respondents were informed that the study was concerned with the perception of spoken words. They were told that they were to hear many words that varied in both their emotional meaning and the emotional tone of the voice with which they were spoken. In the word evaluation judgement condition (run in both Studies 1 and 2), respondents were instructed to make a judgement of the meaning of each word as pleasant or unpleasant while ignoring the attendant tone of voice. In the vocal tone judgement condition (included only in Study 2), respondents were instructed to make a judgement of vocal tone as pleasant or unpleasant while ignoring the attendant word evaluation.

Study 1 consisted of 208 trials, preceded by 10 practice trials. The order of the 208 experimental trials was randomised for each respondent. Out of the 208 utterances, 144 constituted critical stimuli used in testing our prediction (see the Materials section), while the rest were included as fillers. Study 2 used only the critical stimuli and thus consisted of 144 trials, preceded by 10 practice trials. Utterances used on these 10 trials were quite ambiguous on the judgement-irrelevant dimension, but they had very clear emotional valence on the focal dimension.

The respondents were asked to place the first finger of their left hand on the "d" key of the computer keyboard, the first finger of their right hand on the "k" key, and both thumbs on the space bar. The keys were appropriately labelled. On each trial "x" appeared at the centre of the screen. When the respondents pressed the space bar, a word was presented 500 ms later. They were to make a judgement of either the meaning of the word or the tone of the voice and report their judgement by pressing the "d" key if the word meaning/vocal tone was pleasant and the "k" key if it was unpleasant. They were asked to respond as quickly as possible without sacrificing accuracy in judgement. Response time was measured in ms from the onset of each utterance. One second after the response, the next trial began with a presentation of "x".

Materials.   We used 26 evaluatively positive words and 26 evaluatively negative words. All words were quite unequivocal in meanings and associated evaluations. In the absence of any word frequency norms in Japanese, it was impossible to control for word frequency, but every attempt was made to sample words that were quite familiar and presumably fairly high in frequency of occurrence in everyday life. In order to ensure that the word meaning was manipulated as intended, we asked a group of 13 undergraduates to rate the pleasantness of the meaning of each word on a 5-point rating scale (1 = "very unpleasant", 5 = "very pleasant"). The positive words were rated as being quite pleasant and the negative words as quite unpleasant (see below).

Subsequently, these words were used to construct spoken stimuli. Specifically, 26 native speakers of Japanese, half of whom were males, were asked to read a different subset of several words, both positive and negative, in one of two emotional tones, *either* a smooth and round tone, which is commonly recognised to be pleasant, *or* a harsh and constricted tone, which is commonly recognised to be unpleasant (Kitayama, 1996; Scherer, 1986). In this way, each of the 52 words was spoken in two tones by one male and one female speaker so that there resulted a set of 208 (52 × 2 × 2) utterances.

These utterances were tape recorded in a random order and submitted to a pre-test. First, to confirm that the intonation was perceived as pleasant or unpleasant, independent of word meaning, these utterances were low pass filtered at 400 Hz so that semantic content was virtually indiscernible. The 13 undergraduates who provided the pleasantness ratings for word meaning also judged the emotional tone of the voice as pleasant or unpleasant on a 5-point rating scale (1 = "very unpleasant", 5 = "very pleasant"). Out of the 104 utterances intended to be positive in vocal tone, 51 had mean pleasantness ratings that were higher than the midpoint of the scale (= 3). Out of the 104 utterances intended as negative, 93 had means that were lower than the midpoint. These 144 utterances were adopted as critical experimental stimuli. They are listed in Appendix A. The pleasantness ratings for these (content-filtered) utterances were submitted to a 2 × 2 Multivariate Analysis of Variance (MANOVA), which revealed only a significant main effect for vocal emotion, $F(1, 140) = 213.84$, $p < .0001$. The pertinent means are summarised in the "Japanese set" rows of the lower half of Table 1. Neither word evaluation nor the interaction between word evaluation and vocal emotion approached statistical significance, $Fs < 1$. Hence, vocal emotion was successfully manipulated independent of word evaluation.[2]

Second, to confirm that word evaluation was independent of the variation in vocal emotion, the mean pleasantness ratings of the 144 utterances were analysed within a MANOVA. Only the main effect for word evaluation proved significant, $F(1, 140) = 823.06$, $p < .0001$ (see the upper half of Table 1). Note that the effect on vocal emotion was less extreme than that on emotional word meaning. Further, apart from a relatively small number of "outliers", there was little overlap in the two distributions. Hence, if observed, an interference caused

---

[2] To ensure that the perceived pleasantness of intonation for the content-filtered utterances paralleled closely that for the original, unfiltered utterances, another group of 35 undergraduates were given the same rating task on the original utterances. The mean pleasantness ratings for the original utterances closely paralleled those for the content-filtered utterances.

TABLE 1

Mean ratings of vocal emotions for the content-filtered utterances and mean ratings of word evaluations for the words in the Japanese set (used in Studies 1 and 2) and the American set (used in Study 3)

Vocal emotion	Word evaluation								
	Positive			Neutral			Negative		
	n	*M*	(SD)	*n*	*M*	(SD)	*n*	*M*	(SD)
Pleasantness ratings for word meanings									
Positive									
Japanese set	30	4.07	(0.56)	–	–	–	21	1.74	(0.28)
American set	17	4.20	(0.25)	13	2.95	(0.21)	10	1.73	(0.27)
Neutral									
Japanese set	–	–	–	–	–	–	–	–	–
American set	13	4.22	(0.20)	14	3.00	(0.14)	20	1.84	(0.25)
Negative									
Japanese set	47	4.06	(0.60)	–	–	–	46	1.68	(0.31)
American set	9	4.15	(0.92)	15	2.95	(0.16)	18	1.78	(0.23)
Pleasantness ratings for vocal emotions									
Positive									
Japanese set	30	3.34	(0.25)	–	–	–	21	3.30	(0.26)
American set	17	3.84	(0.28)	13	3.69	(0.12)	10	3.65	(0.11)
Neutral									
Japanese set	–	–	–	–	–	–	–	–	–
American set	13	3.09	(0.21)	14	3.14	(0.18)	20	3.13	(0.15)
Negative									
Japanese set	47	2.42	(0.35)	–	–	–	46	2.34	(0.47)
American set	9	2.21	(0.29)	15	2.27	(0.15)	18	2.20	(0.19)

by competing vocal emotion in a judgement of word evaluation would suggest a bias of the processing system that favours vocal information—a bias that is strong enough to overcome the more potent effect of word evaluation.

In addition, two more aspects of utterances that might influence performance in the judgements of word evaluation and vocal tone were examined (see Table 1). First, the 35 undergraduates who rated the pleasantness of intonation for the original utterances were also asked to judge how clear the pronunciation was or alternatively how easy it was to understand the word (1 = "very unclear/very difficult", 5 = "very clear/very easy"). The order of these two tasks was counterbalanced. A 2 × 2 MANOVA performed on the mean clarity ratings computed for each utterance showed a significant main effect of vocal emotion, $F(1, 140) = 28.91, p < .0001$, with those spoken in negative intonations judged to be less clear and more difficult to comprehend than those spoken in positive intonations. Second, the length of each utterance was measured. The main effect of vocal emotion and the interaction between word evaluation and vocal emotion were far from significant, $Fs < 1$. Nevertheless, positive words ($M = 980$) were somewhat longer than negative words ($M = 910$) although the difference did not reach statistical significance, $F(1, 140) = 2.20$, $p > .10$. The effects of these two aspects of the utterances were therefore statistically controlled in the analyses to follow.[3]

Results and discussion

Both accuracy and response time were analysed. To control for the effects of clarity and length of utterances on response time, the following steps were taken. With the entire dataset in each judgement condition, response time was regressed on both utterance clarity and utterance length. For each data point we obtained a predicted response time—a value predicted as a linear function of both clarity and length of utterances. Deviations from the predicted values (i.e., residuals) were added to the overall mean response time to obtain adjusted response times. In Study 2, this procedure was taken separately for the two judgement conditions. The adjusted response times were subsequently analysed in two ways. First, relevant means were computed separately for each respondent over utterances in each of the four pertinent conditions (i.e., word evaluation × vocal emotion). They were submitted to a MANOVA with respondents as a random variable. Significant Fs (denoted as F_1s) indicate the generalisability of the effects over respondents. Second, relevant means were computed separately for each utterance over respondents. They were then submitted to a MANOVA with utterances as a random variable. Significant Fs (denoted as F_2s) indicate the generalisability of the effects over utterances.

An analogous analysis was performed on accuracy. Because the dependent variable was dichotomous (1 = "correct" or 0 = "incorrect"), a logistic regression was performed on the entire set of data in each judgement condition. For each data point we obtained a predicted probability of correct response as a function of clarity and length. Deviations from the predicted values were subsequently computed for each of the data points. These deviation scores were added to the overall accuracy to yield adjusted accuracies, which were combined in two different ways for MANOVAs. First, relevant means were computed separately for each respondent over utterances in each condition, and they were submitted to a MANOVA with respondents as a random variable. Second, relevant means were computed separately for each utterance over respondents,

---

[3] We also performed analysis without the statistical control described here. The results were no different.

and they were submitted to a MANOVA with utterances as a random variable. Note that these means can be interpreted as probabilities of correct responses. Hence, before the MANOVAs the means were first arc-sine transformed. To facilitate readability, however, all means reported below are original probabilities. In all analyses reported below, unless otherwise noted, only those effects that proved significant in both the subject-wise analysis and the utterance-wise analysis will be reported.

Study 1: Word evaluation judgement

Accuracy.   A 2 × 2 × 2 MANOVA (vocal emotion × word evaluation × gender of respondents) was performed on the accuracy measure. A Stroop-type interference would be revealed by a reliable interaction between vocal emotion and word evaluation. The analysis showed this interaction to be highly significant, $F_1(1, 48) = 9.55$, $p < .005$ and $F_2(1, 140) = 6.38$, $p < .02$. The means are shown in Table 2. As predicted, the judgement of positive words tended to be less accurate if the attendant vocal intonation was negative than if it was positive and, conversely, the judgement of negative words tended to be less accurate in the latter condition than in the former. No gender effects approached statistical significance.

TABLE 2
Mean accuracy and response time as a function of vocal intonation and word meaning in the word evaluation judgement condition of Study 1 (conducted in Japan with native speakers of Japanese)

Vocal emotion		Word evaluation	
		Positive	*Negative*
Positive			
Accuracy	*M*	0.97	0.95
	(SD)[a]	(0.03)	(0.10)
RT (ms)	*M*	974	992
	(SD)	(174)	(165)
Negative			
Accuracy	*M*	0.96	0.97
	(SD)	(0.09)	(0.14)
RT(ms)	*M*	1004	972
	(SD)	(176)	(166)

[a] Standard deviations are based on the subject-wise analysis and thus signify the dispersion of pertinent means over the respondents.

Response time.   In the MANOVA performed on the response time measure, the critical interaction between vocal emotion and word evaluation also proved significant, $F_1(1, 48) = 34.40$, $p < .0001$ and $F_2(1, 140) = 3.85$, $p = .05$. The means are shown in Table 2. As predicted, the judgement of positive words tended to be slower if the attendant vocal intonation was negative than if it was positive and, conversely, the judgement of negative words tended to be slower in the latter than in the former. No gender effects were found.

Discussion of Study 1.   Study 1 showed an interference effect due to vocal emotion in word evaluation judgement for native Japanese speakers. Because this happened despite the fact that variation in vocal emotion was less extreme than that in word evaluation, the effect may be taken to suggest a close attentional attunement on the part of native Japanese speakers to vocal tone. Nevertheless, because this is the first demonstration of this sort, it calls for a replication. Moreover, Study 1 did not examine a reversed judgement task in which individuals have to make a judgement of vocal emotion as pleasant or unpleasant while ignoring the attendant word evaluation. Hence, Study 2 examined vocal emotion judgement as well as word evaluation judgement.

Study 2: Judgements of both word evaluation and vocal tone

Accuracy.   A $2 \times 2 \times 2$ MANOVA (judgement type × vocal emotion × word evaluation) was performed on the accuracy measure. In general, word evaluation judgement was far more accurate than vocal emotion judgement ($Ms = 0.95$ vs. 0.77), $F_1(1, 58) = 5.74$, $p < .02$ and $F_2(1, 140) = 5.50$, $p < .02$, thereby confirming the pre-test result (see Table 1) that word evaluation was much more unequivocal than vocal emotion. Further, the MANOVA revealed the predicted interaction between vocal emotion and word evaluation, $F_1(1, 58) = 18.17$, $p < .0001$ and $F_2(1, 140) = 14.94$, $p < .0005$. Pertinent means are given in Table 3. In both judgements, accuracy was higher when the two channels of information were congruous than when they were incongruous and, further, this interactive pattern was equally strong in the two judgement conditions.

Response time.   A MANOVA performed on the response time for correct responses revealed a significant main effect for judgement, $F_1(1, 58) = 20.24$, $p < .0001$ and $F_2(1, 140) = 855.05$, $p < .0001$, again showing that vocal emotion judgement was much more difficult, and thus more time-consuming than word evaluation judgement. Further, the predicted interaction between word evaluation and vocal emotion proved significant, $F_1(1, 58) = 18.30$, $p < .0001$ and $F_2(1, 140) = 10.46$, $p < .0005$. The pertinent means are given in Table 3. In both judgements, response time was shorter when the two channels of emotional

TABLE 3
Mean accuracy and response time as a function of vocal emotion and
word evaluation in the two judgement conditions of Study 2 (conducted in
Japan with native speakers of Japanese)

| | | Word evaluation | | | |
| | | Word meaning judgement | | Vocal tone judgement | |
Vocal emotion		Positive	Negative	Positive	Negative
Positive					
Accuracy	M	0.97	0.94	0.78	0.67
	(SD)[a]	(0.05)	(0.07)	(0.16)	(0.21)
RT(ms)	M	992	1020	1280	1356
	(SD)	(198)	(239)	(331)	(323)
Negative					
Accuracy	M	0.95	0.96	0.77	0.82
	(SD)	(0.06)	(0.06)	(0.16)	(0.12)
RT (ms)	M	1034	1000	1346	1278
	(SD)	(189)	(222)	(323)	(314)

[a] Standard deviations are based on the subject-wise analysis and thus signify the dispersion of pertinent means over the respondents.

information were congruous than when they were incongruous. Finally, the second order interaction including judgement type turned out to be significant only in the utterance-wise analysis, $F_1(1, 58) = 2.16$, n.s. and $F_2(1, 140) = 7.17$, $p < .01$, reflecting the fact that the vocal emotion × word evaluation intonation interaction was somewhat stronger in the vocal emotion judgment than in the word evaluation judgement.

Discussion of Study 2. Studies 1 and 2 show that vocal emotions are activated at least as quickly or as strongly as word evaluations among native Japanese speakers. In view of the fact that the vocal emotions were much less extreme and thus more ambiguous than were the word evaluations, the pattern would seem to be consistent with the hypothesised attentional bias in high-context cultures—the one favouring vocal emotion. If this interpretation is right, a very different attentional bias should appear under comparable conditions in a low-context culture/language (in North America/English). For native English speakers, word evaluation should have a distinct attentional advantage over vocal emotion. Thus, there should be a considerable interference by competing word evaluation in the vocal emotion judgement, but little or no such effect by competing vocal emotion information in the word evaluation judgement. This prediction was tested in Study 3.

STUDY 3

Method

Respondents and procedure. A total of 38 undergraduates (14 males and 24 females) at a North American state university participated in the study to partially fulfil their course requirements. All were native speakers of English. Each respondent was seated in an individual booth, and wore a pair of headphones. The respondents were told that the study was concerned with the perception of spoken words. They were told that they were to hear many words which varied in both their emotional meaning and the emotional tone of the voice with which they were spoken. Approximately half the respondents (18) were instructed to make a judgement of the meaning of each word as pleasant or unpleasant while ignoring the attendant tone of the voice, and the remaining respondents were instructed to make a judgement of the vocal intonation as pleasant or unpleasant while ignoring the attendant word meaning.

The study was composed of 178 trials in the word evaluation judgement condition and 162 trials in the vocal emotion judgement condition, respectively (see below). In both cases, the experimental trials were preceded by 10 practice trials. On these practice trials, utterances were clear on the focal dimension, but quite ambiguous on the judgement-irrelevant dimension. The order of the experimental trials were randomized for each respondent. Respondents were asked to place the first finger of their left hand on a key placed on the left-hand side of a response box placed in front of them, the first finger of their right hand on another key on its right-hand side. On each trial, a word was presented 500 ms after a brief beep sound. Respondents were asked to make one of the two judgements and report their judgement by pressing the left key if the judgement was "pleasant" and right key if it was "unpleasant". The keys were appropriately labelled. Respondents were asked to respond as quickly as possible without sacrificing accuracy of judgement. Response time was measured in ms from the onset of each utterance. One second after the response, the next trial began with a beep sound.

Materials. A total of 63 words of relatively short length (4 through 6 letters long) were prepared. According to the normative ratings provided by Kitayama (1991), these words were either positive, neutral, or negative in word evaluation (see Table 1). Next, a female college student was trained to read these words in each one of three vocal tones, that is, a smooth and round tone (emotionally positive), a monotonic and business-like tone (emotionally neutral), *or* a harsh and constricted tone (emotionally negative), yielding 189 utterances (63 words $\times$ 3 different vocal tones). In order to select experimental stimuli, these utterances were low pass filtered at 400 Hz so that semantic content was virtually indiscernible. The vocal tone of each filtered utterance was rated by 23 respondents (10 males and 13 females) on a 5-point rating scale (1 = "very unpleasant", 5 = "very pleasant"). Utterances with the mean ratings of 3.5 or greater were employed in the positive vocal tone condition, those with mean ratings below 2.5 were used in the negative vocal tone condition, and those with the ratings between 2.6 and 3.4 were used in the neutral vocal tone condition. In this way, 131 of the 189 utterances were selected (see Appendix B).

The mean pleasantness ratings of vocal tone and word meaning for the utterances employed in each of the nine conditions (3 × 3) are summarised in the "American set" row of Table 1. The meaning ratings are based on our earlier research (Kitayama, 1991), in which a group of 33 respondents from the same population judged the pleasantness of each word on the same rating scale. Inspection of Table 1 reveals that the manipulation of vocal emotion was independent of the word evaluation manipulation. In a 3 × 3 MANOVA per-formed on the vocal emotion ratings, vocal emotion accounted for approxi-mately 90% of the total variance, and the interaction between vocal emotion and word evaluation was statistically negligible, accounting only for 1% of this variance. Likewise, the word evaluations did not vary across the three vocal emotion conditions. Both word evaluations and vocal emotions were largely comparable between the Japanese set and the American set (but see below for a more detailed discussion of this issue). Finally, the utterances with neutral tones (680 ms) were somewhat longer than those with either positive (640 ms) or negative tones (630 ms). In subsequent analyses, this variable was statistically controlled.

In the current research we examined judgement of pleasantness and, there-fore, only those utterances that were either positive or negative on the judgement-relevant dimension were included in the design. Thus, in the word evaluation judgement condition, only those words that had either positive or negative evaluations were used, resulting in a set of 89 utterances. These utterances were repeated twice to yield a total of 178 trials. Likewise, in the vocal emotion judgement condition, only those utterances that had either posi-tive or negative vocal emotions were used, resulting in a set of 81 utterances. These utterances were repeated twice to yield a total of 162 trials.

Results and discussion

Following the procedure of Studies 1 and 2, we first controlled for potential effects of word length on both accuracy and response time.[4] Because the neutral emotion/evaluation condition was included only on the dimension that was irrelevant to the focal judgement, the design was not factorial. We therefore

---

[4] In this work, no clarity ratings were obtained and, thus, no attempt was made to control for this aspect of utterances. Note, however, the results of Studies 1 and 2 were no different regardless of whether this control was used.

report results separately for the two judgement conditions, followed by an analysis with judgement type as an additional experimental variable. In the latter analysis, the neutral conditions were excluded. All pertinent means are reported in Table 4.

Word evaluation judgement

Accuracy. Judgement accuracies were submitted to a $2 \times 2 \times 2 \times 2$ MANOVA (word evaluation × vocal emotion × repetition × gender of respondent). A Stroop interference effect would be reflected in a significant vocal emotion × word evaluation interaction. This critical interaction was statistically negligible, $Fs < 1$. As predicted, the level of accuracy was high whether the attendant vocal emotion was congruous, incongruous, or neutral (all $Ms = 0.95$).

TABLE 4
Mean accuracy and response time as a function of vocal emotion and word evaluation in the two judgement conditions of Study 3 (conducted in the US with native speakers of English)

	Word evaluation					
	Positive		Neutral		Negative	
Vocal emotion	M	(SD)[a]	M	(SD)	M	(SD)
Word evaluation judgement						
Accuracy						
First half						
Positive	0.96	(0.06)	–	–	0.90	(0.11)
Neutral	0.96	(0.05)	–	–	0.91	(0.07)
Negative	0.95	(0.09)	–	–	0.94	(0.05)
Second half						
Positive	0.98	(0.04)	–	–	0.96	(0.06)
Neutral	0.97	(0.05)	–	–	0.96	(0.04)
Negative	0.95	(0.06)	–	–	0.93	(0.06)
Response time						
First half						
Positive	1030	(234)	–	–	1082	(272)
Neutral	1057	(237)	–	–	1187	(348)
Negative	1015	(182)	–	–	1113	(269)
Second half						
Positive	1041	(306)	–	–	1081	(337)
Neutral	1010	(258)	–	–	1102	(308)
Negative	1059	(330)	–	–	1065	(304)

(Continued)

TABLE 4
(Continued)

	Word evaluation					
	Positive		Neutral		Negative	
Vocal emotion	M	(SD)[a]	M	(SD)	M	(SD)
Vocal emotion judgement						
Accuracy						
First half						
Positive	0.92	(0.08)	(0.79)	(0.17)	0.78	(0.19)
Neutral	–	–	–	–	–	–
Negative	0.78	(0.24)	(0.89)	(0.15)	0.96	(0.13)
Second half						
Positive	0.93	(0.09)	(0.88)	(0.11	0.90	(0.16)
Neutral	–	–	–	–	–	–
Negative	0.87	(0.18)	(0.92)	(0.10)	0.96	(0.09)
Response time						
First half						
Positive	943	(231)	(962)	(215)	1162	(339)
Neutral	–	–	–	–	–	–
Negative	979	(210)	(937)	(200)	912	(220)
Second half						
Positive	875	(181)	(955)	(215)	989	(213)
Neutral	–	–	–	–	–	–
Negative	892	(182)	(884)	(184)	856	(184)

[a] Standard deviations are based on the subject-wise analysis and, thus, signify the dispersion of pertinent means over the respondents.

Response time. In a MANOVA performed on the response time, the critical interaction between vocal emotion and word evaluation was again marginal, $F_1(1, 36) = 2.45$, $p > .10$ and $F_2 < 1$. As predicted, mean response time was no different whether the attendant vocal emotion was congruous, incongruous, or neutral ($Ms = 1062$ vs. 1060 vs. 1090).

Vocal emotion judgement

Accuracy. The pertinent means in the vocal emotion judgement showed a very different pattern from the one for the word evaluation judgment. The vocal emotion × word evaluation interaction proved highly significant, $F(2, 36) = 5.64$, $p < .01$ and $F(2, 75) = 14.68$, $p < .0001$. As predicted, there was a cross-over pattern that showed a Stroop-type interference. Accuracy was much lower if the attendant word evaluation was incongruous ($M = 0.83$) than if it was congruous ($M = 0.94$), with the neutral word evaluation condition falling in between ($M = 0.87$). No other effects attained statistical significance. Among others, the same pattern appeared in both halves of the presentations, but the effect was somewhat weaker, although still evident and statistically significant, in the second half.

Response time.   Inspection of the relevant data in Table 4 reveals a strong interference effect. As in the accuracy analysis, the vocal emotion × word evaluation interaction was highly significant, $F_1(2, 36) = 17.24$, $p < .0001$ and $F_2(2, 75) = 9.08$, $p < .0005$. As predicted, it took less time to make the vocal emotion judgement if the attendant word evaluation was congruous ($M = 857$) than if it was incongruous ($M = 1006$), with the neutral word evaluation conditions falling in between ($M = 935$). This same pattern appeared in both halves of the presentations, but the effect was somewhat weaker, although still evident and statistically significant, in the second half.

Combined analysis

After excluding the data from the utterances with neutral word evaluation (in the vocal emotion judgement condition) and those from the utterances with neutral vocal emotion (in the word evaluation judgement condition), we performed a MANOVA with an additional variable of judgement type included in the design. As can be expected from the foregoing patterns of data, the vocal emotion × word evaluation × judgement type interaction was significant for both accuracy and response time, $F_1(1, 34) = 10.16$, $p < .005$ and $F_2(1, 49) = 6.59$, $p < .02$, and $F_1(1, 34) = 19.17$, $p < .0001$, and $F_2(1, 49) = 9.56$, $p < .005$, respectively. An interference of competing information in the irrelevant channel was observed in the vocal emotion judgement, but not in the word evaluation judgement.

COMPARISON BETWEEN JAPANESE AND AMERICAN RESULTS

In this section, a comparison is drawn between the Japanese data from Studies 1 and 2 and the American data from Study 3. Because the two sets of studies were conducted separately, care must be taken to eliminate any alternative interpretations that may result from the procedural differences between them.

As summarised in Table 1, both vocal emotions and word evaluations were reasonably comparable between the Japanese set and the American set. To begin with, the word pleasantness ratings for both positive and negative words were quite similar between the two stimulus sets. Although they were somewhat more polarised in the American set than in the Japanese set, in no case did the difference prove to be significant. Further, vocal emotions were far more ambiguous than were word evaluations. Although this was the case for both sets, it was somewhat more pronounced in the Japanese set than in the American set. Specifically, positive vocal emotions were less positive than positive word evaluations; but this difference was greater in the Japanese set (0.74; $Ms = 3.32$ vs. 4.06) than in the American set (0.43; $M = 3.75$ vs. 4.18). Likewise, negative vocal emotions were less negative than negative word evaluations; but this difference was again somewhat greater in the Japanese set (0.67; $M = 2.38$ vs. 1.71) than in the American set (0.45; $M = 2.20$ vs. 1.75). In short, the relative ambiguity of vocal emotion *vis-à-vis* word evaluation was somewhat greater in the Japanese set than in the American set. Everything else being equal, then, an interference by competing word evaluation in the vocal emotion judgement should be more likely in Japanese (where vocal emotions were less clear) than in English (where they were clearer). Likewise, an interference by competing vocal emotion in the word evaluation judgement should be more likely in English than in Japanese. Note, however, that both these "default predictions" are opposite in direction to our theoretical predictions. Thus, the inadvertent difference between the two sets of stimuli worked against our hypothesis, thereby posing no threat on the validity of our comparison.

Another concern comes from the fact that the number of utterances was different across the conditions of the two sets of studies, varying from a minimum of 9 to a maximum of 47 (see Table 1). To guard against any potential effects of the number of trials devoted to each condition, we limited the analyses in the present section to the first nine utterances that entered the experimental trials from each of the four crucial conditions defined by word evaluation (positive vs. negative) and vocal emotion (positive vs. negative). We also excluded from the analysis the stimuli with ambiguous vocal emotions used in Study 1 and those with neutral vocal emotions or word evaluations used in Study 3. There resulted nine sets of four utterances, 36 in total, that varied with respect to the order by which they appeared in the experiment. In a supplementary analysis described later, we treated the order of appearance as an additional variable. To the extent that any cultural difference occurs from the very beginning of the study, the varying number of trials between the two sets is an unlikely source of alternative explanations.

Finally, one alternative interpretation for the absence of any interference effect by vocal emotion in the American/word meaning judgement condition might be that there was only one speaker for the American speech stimuli and, therefore, the American respondents were habituated to the vocal features of this single speaker. This interpretation would be less plausible, however, if the absence of the interference effect in this condition was observed from the very beginning of the study.

Results and discussion

Accuracy. For each respondent, mean accuracies were computed over the nine utterances in each of the four experimental conditions defined by word evaluation and vocal emotion. These means, presented in Table 5, were submitted

TABLE 5
Mean accuracy and response time as a function of vocal emotion and word evaluation in the two judgement conditions for native Japanese and English speakers (based on the first 9 utterances that appeared in each condition, see text for detail)

| | | Word evaluation | | | |
| | | Word meaning judgement | | Vocal tone judgement | |
Vocal emotion		Positive	Negative	Positive	Negative
Japanese speakers					
Positive					
Accuracy	*M*	0.98	0.95	0.78	0.65
	(SD)	(0.05)	(0.11)	(0.20)	(0.24)
RT	*M*	1009	1032	1346	1443
	(SD)	(186)	(228)	(327)	(336)
Negative					
Accuracy	*M*	0.93	0.97	0.81	0.82
	(SD)	(0.09)	(0.13)	(0.19)	(0.17)
RT	*M*	1149	1065	1443	1398
	(SD)	(221)	(258)	(336)	(388)
English speakers					
Positive					
Accuracy	*M*	0.98	0.90	0.89	0.77
	(SD)	(0.06)	(0.12)	(0.10)	(0.19)
RT	*M*	1032	1124	1196	1394
	(SD)	(226)	(308)	(215)	(287)
Negative					
Accuracy	*M*	0.94	0.92	0.78	0.98
	(SD)	(0.10)	(0.08)	(0.25)	(0.12)
RT	*M*	1028	1171	1234	1152
	(SD)	(180)	(318)	(229)	(235)

to a MANOVA with two between-subjects variables (country and judgement type) and two within-subjects variables (word evaluation and vocal emotion).

Before testing our main predictions, it is important to reiterate that vocal emotions were far more ambiguous than were word evaluations and, furthermore, this was more pronounced in the Japanese set than in the American set. As may be anticipated, accuracy was significantly lower for vocal emotion judgement than for word meaning judgement, $F(1, 143) = 65.09$, $p < .0001$. Furthermore, this was more pronounced for Japanese (Ms = 0.77 vs. .96) than for Americans (Ms = 0.86 vs. .94). The interaction between judgement type and country was significant, $F(1, 143) = 12.37$, $p < .001$.

More importantly, there was a highly significant word evaluation × vocal emotion interaction, $F(1, 143) = 45.39$, $p < .0001$. As expected, this interaction was qualified by judgement type and country. Specifically, both word evaluation × vocal emotion × judgement type and word evaluation × vocal emotion × country × judgement type interactions were significant, $Fs(1, 143) = 8.14$, and 6.20, $ps < .005$, $< .02$, respectively. To facilitate the comparison, we computed an index of interference effect by subtracting the mean accuracy for the incongruous utterances (where vocal emotion and word evaluation had a different valence) from the mean accuracy for the congruous utterances (where the two had the same valence). This interference index takes a positive value if there exists a Stroop-type interference (i.e., greater accuracy for the congruous utterances than for the incongruous utterances), the value of zero if there is no such effect, and a negative value if there exists an effect that is opposite in direction to the Stroop-type interference. As can be seen in Figure 1, in the United States there was a remarkably strong interference for the vocal emotion

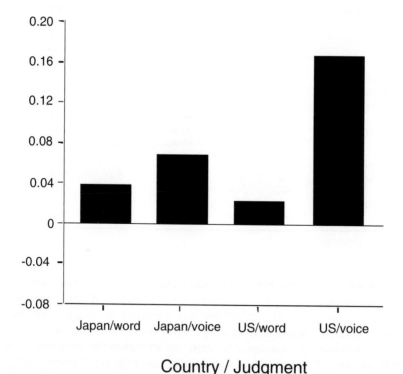

Figure 1. The Stroop-type interference effect in judgement accuracy (= mean accuracy for the congruous utterances; mean accuracy for the incongruous utterances). The interference effect is strongest in the US vocal emotion judgement condition, moderate in both judgement conditions in Japan, and nonexistent in the US word evaluation judgement condition.

judgement, $t(143) = 6.11, p < .001$. But such an effect virtually vanished for the word evaluation judgement, $t = 1.23$, n.s. By contrast, in Japan the interference was significant in both judgements, $ts(143) = 2.79$ and $3.81, ps < .01$, for the vocal emotion judgement and the word evaluation judgement, respectively. As predicted, the interference in the vocal emotion judgement was significantly greater in the United States than in Japan, $t(143) = 2.96, p < .01$. Finally, the interference in the word evaluation judgment was statistically significant in Japan but not in the United States, but this difference was negligible, $t < 1$.

Response time

For each respondent, mean response times were computed over the nine utterances in each of the four experimental conditions defined by word evaluation and vocal emotion. These means were submitted to a MANOVA with two between-subjects variables (country and judgement-type) and two within-subject variables (word evaluation and vocal emotion). As in the accuracy analysis, performance was much worse for vocal tone judgement than for word meaning judgement ($Ms = 1334$ vs. 1068), $F(1, 143) = 27.93, p < .0001$. Further, this was somewhat more pronounced for Japanese ($Ms = 1394$ vs. 1064) than for Americans ($Ms = 1233$ vs. 1089), $F(1, 143) = 3.63, p = .06$. This pattern corresponds to the fact that vocal emotions were more ambiguous than word evaluations and, moreover, that this difference was somewhat more pronounced for Japanese than for English. Importantly, as would be predicted, the word evaluation × vocal emotion interaction proved significant, $F(1, 143) = 15.07$, $p < .0002$. Furthermore, this interaction was qualified by judgement type and country. Thus, the word evaluation × vocal emotion × judgement type interaction and the word evaluation × vocal emotion × country × judgement type interaction were both significant, $Fs(1, 143) = 8.68$ and 10.54, $ps < .01$, respectively.

Again, to facilitate the comparison, an interference index was computed by subtracting the mean response time for the congruous utterances from the mean response time for the incongruous utterances. This index takes a positive value if there is a Stroop-type interference effect (i.e., a shorter response time for the congruous utterances than for the incongruous utterances). The results are summarised in Figure 2. In the United States, a strong interference effect was found in the vocal emotion judgement, $t(143) = 4.29, p < .01$; but no such effect was obtained in the word evaluation judgement, $t < 1$. In fact, the interference was significantly greater in the vocal emotion judgement than in the word evaluation judgement , $t(143) = 3.52, p < .01$. In Japan, however, the pattern was reversed. Thus, while a significant Stroop-type interference was observed in the word evaluation judgement, $t(143) = 3.80, p < .01$, this effect attained only marginal statistical significance in the vocal emotion judgement, $t(143) = 1.68$, $p < .10$. Most importantly, in support of our main prediction, in the vocal

(msec)

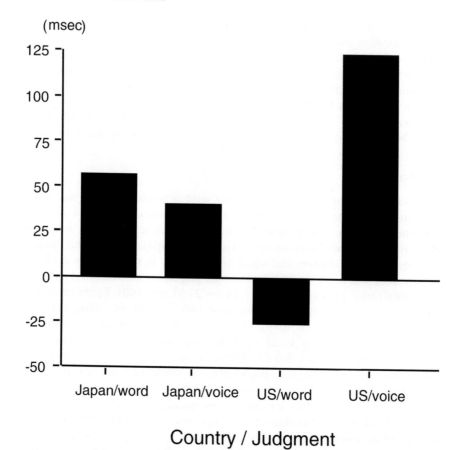

Country / Judgment

Figure 2. The Stroop-type interference effect in response time (= mean response time for the incongruous utterances; mean response time for the congruous utterances). The interference effect is strongest in the US vocal emotion judgement condition, moderate in both judgement conditions in Japan, and nonexistent in the US word evaluation judgement condition.

emotion judgement the interference was significantly greater in the United States than in Japan, $t(143) = 2.26$, $p < .05$, but in the word meaning judgement it was significantly greater in Japan than in the United States, $t(143) = 2.34$, $p < .05$.

Order effect

Did the same pattern hold from the beginning of the study? To address this issue, for each order of appearance, we computed the interference index (i.e., the difference between the average value for congruous utterances and the average value for incongruous utterances). The interference index is plotted separately for accuracy and response time in Figures 3 and 4, respectively. There was a considerable variation over the course of the study. However, the overall results reported in Figures 1 and 2 are best approximated for the utterances that appeared for the first time in each condition. In both accuracy and response time, there was a strong interference in the American word evaluation judgement condition; but there was none—in fact, a negligible tendency in the opposite direction, in the American vocal emotion judgement condition. Between these two extremes fell the two judgement conditions of Japan. Notably, no interference was evident for the word evaluation judgement in the United States from the very beginning. Hence, the fact that a single speaker was used to produce American stimuli does not account for the absence of interference in the word evaluation judgement. Further, the presence of the essentially identical pattern from the beginning of the study eliminates the differing numbers of trials across the studies as a potential source for alternative account. Finally, this fine-grained analysis revealed a considerable practice effect. Most conspicuously, the failure of Americans to ignore competing word evaluation in the vocal emotion judgement quickly dissipated, although it never fully disappeared, over the course of the study.

GENERAL DISCUSSION

The three studies reported here—the first of their kind in the literature—demonstrate a cultural difference in spontaneous allocation of attention either to vocal emotion or to word evaluation in comprehension of emotional speech. Japanese respondents showed a moderate interference effect in both the word evaluation judgement and the vocal emotion judgement. In contrast, American respondents showed a strong interference effect in the vocal emotion judgement, but no such interference was found in the word evaluation judgement. Overall, an interference effect by competing word evaluation in the vocal emotion judgement was stronger for Americans than for Japanese; but an interference effect by competing vocal emotion in the word evaluation judgement was stronger for Japanese than for Americans. The Japanese studies and the American study were largely comparable and, further, one confound between the two sets of stimuli (the greater ambiguity of vocal emotions in the Japanese set than in the American set) worked against our hypothesis. Hence, the present data can be taken to support the hypothesis that Americans are attentionally more attuned to word evaluation than are Japanese; but Japanese are more attuned to vocal emotion than are Americans.

In the stimuli used in the current work, vocal emotion was considerably less extreme than was word evaluation. Accordingly, it would be prudent to limit our conclusions to a cultural difference in the *relative* emphasis on one or the other channel of emotional speech. Nevertheless, some additional insights can be

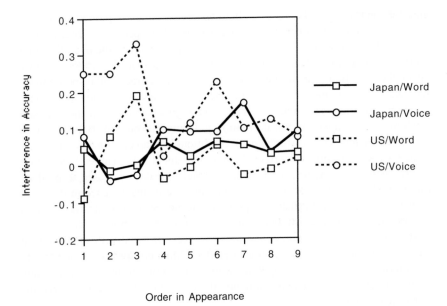

Figure 3. The interference index in accuracy over the course of the study. The overall pattern observed in Figure 1 is best captured for the utterances that appeared first in each condition.

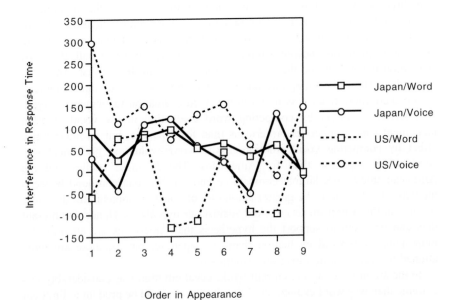

Figure 4. The interference index in response time over the course of the study. The overall pattern observed in Figure 2 is best captured for the utterances that appeared first in each condition.

gained by interpreting the present findings in the light of this feature of the stimuli. First, Japanese respondents failed to ignore vocal emotion in a judgement of word evaluation despite the fact that the former was much more ambiguous and less extreme than the latter. Although indirect, this pattern is consistent with the suggestion that the processing systems of the native Japanese speakers are biased in favour of vocal emotion over word evaluation. Second, the massive interference by word evaluation in the vocal emotion judgement observed for the Americans was likely mediated by both the greater extremity of word evaluation and a processing bias that favours word evaluation over vocal emotion. Third, the absence of any interference by vocal emotion in the word evaluation judgement for Americans may be due in part to the fact that the manipulated vocal emotions were relatively weak. With a sufficiently strong manipulation of vocal emotion, Americans would fail to ignore it (Sanchez-Burks, 1999, study 3), but even in this case the interference should be less for Americans than for Japanese.

The present work has a number of limitations that should be addressed in future research. Most obviously, it would be ideal to run the Japanese part and the American part with an identical procedure and design. More subtly, yet equally importantly, a more sophisticated set of steps should be taken to develop spoken stimuli. First, to go beyond the analysis of a cross-cultural difference in the relative emphasis on one or the other channel of emotional speech and to perform a more stringent test of the absolute attentional bias that might exist in the respective cultures and languages, it is imperative to equate the polarity of both word evaluation and vocal emotion in the two languages. Second, to ensure the generality of the findings, it is important to use multiple speakers of both sexes to create stimuli. Third, it would be better if it were possible to exert a much finer control over vocal features other than vocal emotion between the two languages. This would be possible if, for example, Japanese-English bilinguals were used to produce both Japanese and English stimulus materials.

Although needing to be followed up with studies with an improved design and procedure, the present evidence is quite consistent with a broader, cultural psychological analysis of the interdependencies between cultural practices and meanings and psychological processes and structures (Bruner, 1990; Fiske et al., 1998; Shweder & Sullivan, 1993). Specifically, Markus and Kitayama (1991; Kitayama et al., 1997; Markus et al., 1996) have proposed that a variety of daily practices available in a given cultural context reflect certain assumptions about the self, such as independence and interdependence, that are taken for granted therein. Thus, low-context communication practices available in North America may be rooted in the assumption of selves as mutually independent and autonomous and, thus, "informationally insulated". In contrast, high-context communicative practices commonly available in Japan, which require the speaker to be implicit and indirect, may be rooted in the assumption of selves as interdependent and, thus "informationally connected". In general agreement with this line of analysis, several theorists have pointed out close connections between the cultural conception of person and language use (Kashima & Kashima, 1998; Semin & Rubini, 1990). Importantly, this global characterisation of the two models of the self is consistent with the simultaneous presence of considerable within-culture variations. Thus, for example, even though the North American culture may be quite low-context in general, this cultural characteristic may be more pronounced in some types of situations (e.g., business transaction) and for some subgroups (e.g., those with a Protestant heritage; Sanchez-Burks, 1999).

Another important dimension of culture concerns traditionally held forms of subsistence and economy, and associated levels of social mobility and population density (Berry, 1976; Nisbett & Cohen, 1996; Triandis, 1994). It could be argued that relatively high levels of social mobility and relatively low levels of population density, associated with economies of hunting, gathering, and herding (the last of which in turn may be relatively more common in the historical development of many European civilisations), should render any substantial sharing of tacit knowledge quite difficult and infeasible. Accordingly, they might have encouraged a low-context mode of communication. In contrast, relatively low levels of social mobility and relatively high levels of population density, associated with agricultural economies (which in turn may be relatively more common in the historical development of many Asian civilisations), should make it easier and in fact quite realistic to achieve a long-term sharing of considerable tacit knowledge. Accordingly, they might have encouraged a high-context mode of communication.

Our theoretical analysis, which focuses on high- versus low-context communicative practices, is reminiscent of the Whorfian hypothesis of linguistic relativity. This hypothesis proposes that ways of thinking and perceiving depend significantly on characteristics of the specific language used. So far, research on this hypothesis has been concerned mostly with structural features of language (e.g., availability of words, expressions, or grammatical forms; Hardin & Banaji, 1993; Hunt & Agnoli, 1991; Lucy, 1992). Evidence here is by no means very supportive of the hypothesis. In contrast, we have suggested, along with some others (e.g., Krauss & Chiu, 1998), that it is use of language and associated practices of communication that play a central role in forming biases in the psychological structures implicated in the processing of verbal and nonverbal information. Because in any communicative practice, linguistic and non-linguistic or cultural aspects are tightly connected and even inseparably meshed with each other, it is hardly possible to isolate the "language *per se*" from the entire cultural pattern of practices. Hence, we suspect that it is rather futile to debate, as in past work on linguistic relativity, whether "language *per se*" can *cause* differences in psychological structures and processes (e.g., Au, 1983; Bloom, 1981). It seems more fruitful for researchers to explore specific processing biases that can be traced back to certain known parameters of practices of different cultural groups. Nevertheless, future work may examine people speaking native or non-native languages in their own or foreign cultural contexts. In this way, it will be possible to obtain some clues regarding the relative contribution of "cultural" versus "linguistic" factors to the present findings.

Aside from the issues revolving around culture, communication, and cognition, much more research should be devoted in the future to the processing of emotional utterances. By studying the process of meaning making as a matter of comprehending written texts, as is typically the case in the contemporary cognitive literature, information that is vital to the human act of meaning making may be ignored or overlooked, and thus resulting data and theories will be partial at best and, worse, can be misleading to the degree that what is true about visual information processing does not directly translate into what happens in auditory processing. Accordingly, a systematic exploration of the processing of emotional utterances, especially the intricate and dynamic interplay between vocal information and verbal information throughout the course of information processing, is long overdue (Kitayama, 1996). To us, this presents a challenging direction for future research on communication, cognition, and emotion. And the current work provided initial evidence that psychological systems brought to bear on this processing are variable to a significant extent across cultures and, hence, while clearly grounded in a common human heritage, they also reflect substantial cultural interventions.

Manuscript received 15 September 1999
Revised manuscript received 27 October 2000

REFERENCES

Ambady, N., Koo, J., Lee, F., & Rosenthal, R. (1996). More than words: Linguistic and nonlinguistic politeness in two cultures. *Journal of Personality and Social Psychology, 70,* 996–1011.

Au, T.K. (1983). Chinese and English counterfacturals: The Sapir-Whorf hypothesis revisited. *Cognition, 15,* 162–163.

Banse, R., & Scherer, K.R. (1996). Acoustic profiles in vocal emotion expression. *Journal of Personality and Social Psychology, 70,* 614–636.

Barnlund, D.C. (1989). *Communicative styles of Japanese and Americans: Images and realities.* Belmont, CA: Wadsworth.

Berry, J.W. (1976). *Human ecology and cognitive style: Comparative studies in cultural and psychological adaptation.* New York: Sage/Halsted.

Bloom, A. (1981). *The linguistic shaping of thought.* Hillsdale, NJ: Erlbaum.

Borden, G.A. (1991). *Cultural orientation: An approach to understanding intercultural communication.* Englewood Cliffs, NJ: Prentice-Hall.

Brown, P., & Levinson, S. (1987). *Politeness: Some universals in language usage.* Cambridge, UK: Cambridge University Press.

Bruner, J. (1990). *Acts of meaning.* Cambridge, MA: Harvard University Press.

DePaulo, B.M., & Friedman, H.S. (1998). Nonverbal communication. In D.T. Gilbert, S.T. Fiske, & G. Lindzey (Eds.), *Handbook of social psychology* (Vol. 2, pp. 3–40). New York: McGraw Hill.

Fiske, A.P., Kitayama, S., Markus, H.R., & Nisbett, R.E. (1998). The cultural matrix if social psychology. In D. T. Gilbert, S. T. Fiske, & G. Lindzey (Eds.), *Handbook of social psychology* (Vol. 2, pp. 915–981). New York: McGraw Hill.

Gilbert, D.T., & Malone, P.S. (1995). The correspondence bias. *Psychological Bulletin, 117,* 21–38.

Gudykunst, W.B., Matsumoto, Y., Ting-Toomey, S., Nishida, T., Kim, K., & Heyman, S. (1996). The influence of cultural individualism-collectivism, self-construals, and individual values on communication styles across cultures. *Human Communication Research, 22*, 510–543.

Hall, E.T. (1976). *Beyond culture.* New York: Doubleday.

Hardin, C.H., & Banaji, M.R. (1993). The influence of language on thought. *Social Cognition, 11*, 277–308.

Heine, S.J., Lehman, D.R., Markus, H.R., & Kitayama, S. (1999). Is there a universal need for positive self-regard? *Psychological Review, 106*, 766–794.

Hunt, E., & Agnoli, F. (1991). The Whorfian hypothesis: A cognitive psychology perspective. *Psychological Review, 98*, 377–389.

Ikegami, Y. (1991). "DO-language" and "BECOME language": Two contrasting types of linguistic representation. In Y. Ikegami (Ed.), *The empire of signs: Semiotic essays on Japanese culture* (pp. 285–326). Philadelphia: John Benjamins.

Iyengar, S.S., & Lepper, M.R. (1999). Rethinking the value of choice: A cultural perspective on intrinsic motivation. *Journal of Personality and Social Psychology, 76*, 349–366.

Kashima, E.S., & Kashima, Y. (1998). Culture and language: the case of cultural dimensions and personal pronoun use. *Journal of Cross-Cultural Psychology, 29*, 461–486.

Kitayama, S. (1991). Impairment of perception by positive and negative affect. *Cognition and Emotion, 5*, 255–274.

Kitayama, S. (1996). Remembrance of emotional speech: Improvement and impairment of incidental verbal memory by emotional voice. *Journal of Experimental Social Psychology, 32*, 289–308.

Kitayama, S. (2000). Cultural variations in cognition: Implications for aging research. In P.C. Stern & L.L. Cartensen (Eds.), *The aging mind: Opportunities in cognitive research* (pp. 218–237). Washington, DC: National Academy Press.

Kitayama, S., & Howard, S. (1994). Affective regulation of perception and comprehension. In P.M. Niedenthal & S. Kitayama (Eds.), *The heart's eye: Emotional influences in perception and attention* (pp. 41–65). New York: Academic Press.

Kitayama, S., & Markus, H.R. (2000). The pursuit of happiness and the realization of sympathy: Cultural patterns of self, social relations, and well-being. In E. Diener & Suh, E. (Eds.), *Subjective well-being across cultures* (pp. 113–161). Cambridge, MA: MIT Press.

Kitayama, S., Markus, H.R., & Kurokawa, M. (2000). Culture, emotion, and well-being: Good feelings in Japan and the United States. *Cognition and Emotion, 14*, 94–123.

Kitayama, S., Markus, H.R., Matsumoto, H., & Norasakkunkit. (1997). Individual and collective processes in the construction of the self: Self-enhancement in the United States and self-criticism in Japan. *Journal of Personality and Social Psychology, 72*, 1245–1267.

Krauss, R., & Chiu, C. (1998). Language and social behavior. In D. Gilbert., S. Fiske., & G. Lindzey (Eds.), *Handbook of social psychology* (Vol. 2, pp. 41–88). New York: McGraw Hill.

Lucy, J.A. (1992). *Language diversity and thought: A reformulation of the linguistic relativity hypothesis.* Cambridge, UK: Cambridge University Press.

MacLeod, C.M. (1991). Half century of research on the Stroop effect: An integrative review. *Psychological Bulletin, 109*, 163–203.

Markus, H.R., & Kitayama, S. (1991). Culture and the self: Implications for cognition, emotion, and motivation. *Psychological Review, 93*, 224–253.

Markus, H.R., Kitayama, S., & Heiman, R.J. (1996). Culture and "basic" psychological principles. In E.T. Higgins & A.W. Kruglanski (Eds.), *Social psychology: Handbook of basic principles.* (pp. 857–913) New York: Guilford Press.

Mesquita, B., & Frijda, N.H. (1992). Cultural variations in emotions: A review. *Psychological Bulletin, 112*, 179–204.

Morris, M., Peng, K. (1994). Culture and cause: American and Chinese attributions for social and physical events. *Journal of Personality and Social Psychology, 67*, 949–971.

Nisbett, R.E., Peng, K., Choi, I., & Norenzayan, A. (2001). Culture and systems of thought: Holistic vs. analytic cognition. *Psychological Review, 108*, 291–310.

Nisbett, R.E., & Cohen, D. (1996). *Culture of honor: The psychology of violence in the South.* Boulder, CO: Westview.

Sanchez-Burks, J. (1999). *Ascetic Protestantism and cultural schema for relational sensitivity in the workplace.* Unpublished doctoral dissertation, University of Michigan.

Scherer, K.R. (1986). Vocal affect expression: A review and a model for future research. *Psychological Bulletin, 99,* 143–165.

Semin, G.R., & Rubini, M. (1990). Unfolding the concept of person by verbal abuse. *European Journal of Social Psychology, 20,* 463–474.

Shweder, R.A., & Sullivan, M. (1993). Cultural psychology: Who needs it? *Annual Review of Psychology, 44,* 497–523.

Sperber, D., & Wilson, A. (1986). *Relevance: Communication and cognition.* Cambridge, MA: Harvard University Press.

Stroop, J.R. (1935). Studies of interference in serial verbal reaction. *Journal of Experimental Psychology, 18,* 643–662.

Suh, E., Diener, E., Oishi, S., & Triandis, H.C. (1998). The shifting basis of life satisfaction judgments across cultures: Emotions versus norms. *Journal of Personality and Social Psychology, 74,* 482–493.

Triandis, H.C. (1994). *Culture and social behavior.* New York: McGraw Hill.

APPENDIX A

Words used in the Japanese studies (Studies 1 and 2)

Word meaning	
Positive	*Negative*
Positive voice tone	
AKURUI (BRIGHT)	BAKA (FOOL)
ANSHIN (SAFETY)*	BINBOU (POVERTY)
ATATAKAI (WARM)	FUAN (ANXIETY)*
AZAYAKA (VIVID)	HETA (CLUMSY)
EGAO (SMILE)	ITAI (PAINFUL)
IKOI (RELAXATION)*	JIGOKU (HELL)
JIYUU (FREEDOM)	KENKA (QUARREL)
JUNSUI (PURITY)	KITANAI (DIRTY)
KAPPATSU (ACTIVE)*	KUSAI (STINKING)
KAWAII (CUTE)	MAZUI (UNSAVORY)
KIREI (BEAUTIFUL)*	MIJIME (MISERABLE)*
KUTSOROGI (RELAXATION)	MUNASHII (FRUITLESS)
NAGOYAKA (GENTLE)	NIKUI (HATRED)*
SAWAYAKA (REFRESHING)*	OBAKE (GHOST)
SHINSETSU (KINDNESS)	OSOROSHII (TERRIBLE)*
SUBARASHII (WONDERFUL)*	TSUMARANAI (BORING)
SUKI (LIKING)	ZASETSU (SETBACK)
URESHII (JOYFUL)	
IRESHII (JOYFUL)	
UTSUKUSHII (BEAUTIFUL)	
WARAI (LAUGHTER)*	
YASASHII (GENTLE)*	
YASURAGI (CALMNESS)	

(Continued)

APPENDIX A

(Continued)

Word meaning	
Positive	*Negative*
Negative voice tone	
AI (LOVE)	BAKA (FOOL)*
AKARUI (CHEERFUL)*	BINBOU (POVERTY)*
ANSHIN (SAFETY)	FUAN (ANXIETY)*
ATATAKAI (WARM)	FUKOU (UNHAPPINESS)*
AZAYAKA (VIVID)	HETA (CLUMSY)*
EGAO (SMILE)	ITAI (PAINFUL)*
IKOI (RELAXATION)*	JIGOKU (HELL)*
JIYUU (FREEDOM)*	KEGA (INJURY)*
JUNSUI (PURITY)*	KENKA (QUARREL)*
KAPPATSU (ACTIVE)*	KITANAI (DIRTY)*
KAWAII (CUTE)*	KOJIKI (BEGGAR)*
KIMOCHIII (PLEASANT)*	KOWAI (FEARFUL)
KIREI (BEAUTIFUL)	KURAI (DARK)
KUTSUROGI (RELAXATION)*	KURUSHII (AFFLICTING)*
MIRYOKU (CHARM)*	KUSAI (STINKING)*
NAGOYAKA (GENTLE)	MAZUI (UNSAVORY)*
OYATSU (AFTERNOON TEA)*	MIJIME (MISERABLE)
SAWAYAKA (REFRESHING)*	MUNASHII (FRUITLESS)*
SHINSETEU (KINDNESS)*	NIKUI (HATRED)*
SUBARASHII (WONDERFUL)	OBAKE (GHOST)
SUKI (LIKING)*	OSOROSHII (TERRIBLE)*
URESHII (JOYFUL)*	TSUKARE (FATIGUE)*
UTSUKUSHII (BEAUTIFUL)*	TSUMARANAI (BORING)
WARAI (LAUGHTER)*	TSURAI (TOUGH)*
YASASHII (GENTLE)*	WAGAMAMA (SELF-INDULGENT)
YASURAGI (CALMNESS)*	ZASETSU (SETBACK)*

Note: Words marked by askerisks (*) were used twice, spoken in both a male voice and a female voice.

APPENDIX B

Words used in the American study (Study 3)

	Word meaning				
Positive		Neutral		Negative	
Positive voice tone					
COMEDY	EAGER	TREND	HABIT	TERROR	CANCER
TALENT	PRIZE	CUSTOM	ROUTE	HUNG	HATRED
MATURE	CHARM	TRACK	SWITCH	FAULT	DEVIL
SMILE	LUCKY	STONE	SHEET	INJURY	PANIC
TRUST	FUNNY	TRACE	MARGIN	UGLY	SHAME
PROUD	AWARD	DETECT	PANEL		
GLORY	ENJOY	EXTRA			
HUMOR	CASH				
WISDOM					
Neutral voice tone					
TALENT	ENJOY	BORDER	EXTRA	CANCER	FAULT
MATURE	GLORY	MARGIN	CHAIR	INJURY	GUILT
HUMOR	PRIZE	LOCATE	TRACE	DAMAGE	WASTE
SMILE	PROUD	STAMP	STONE	HARED	STORM
FUNNY	JOKE	LABEL	SHEET	VICTIM	FOOL
AWARD	CASH	ROUTE	FENCE	TERROR	PALE
TRUST		SPARE	PAUSE	PANIC	SNAKE
				ERROR	CRIME
				ANGRY	HUNG
				FALSE	UGLY
				BLAME	WORSE
Negative voice tone					
WISDOM	ENJOY	BORDER	HABIT	CANCER	BLAME
TALENT	GLORY	MARGIN	TREND	INJURY	FAULT
MATURE	PROUD	LOCATE	CHAIR	DAMAGE	GUILT
CHARM	EAGER	STAMP	TRACE	HATRED	WASTE
AWARD	JOKE	LABEL	PANEL	VICTIM	STORM
		SPARE	FENCE	TERROR	FOOL
		SWITCH	PAUSE	DEVIL	CRIME
		CUSTOM		ANGRY	UGLY
				FALSE	WORSE

COGNITION AND EMOTION, 2002, *16* (1), 61–86

Cognitive structure of emotion terms in Indonesia and The Netherlands

Johnny R.J. Fontaine

University of Leuven, Belgium

Ype H. Poortinga

Tilburg University, The Netherlands and University of Leuven, Belgium

Bernadette Setiadi and Suprapti S. Markam

Universitas Indonesia, Jakarta, Indonesia

We investigated the cognitive structure of emotions in Indonesia and The Netherlands in a series of three studies. Sets of 120 emotion terms were selected based on local ratings of prototypicality for "emotion". With similarity sortings a three-dimensional (evaluation, arousal, dominance) and a four-cluster (positive emotion, sadness, fear, anger) structure was found in each group. Of 50 pairs of translation-equivalent terms, 42 pairs were also found to be cognitively equivalent. With these equivalent terms a good fit of a common cognitive emotion structure was demonstrated in both countries. In a fourth and final study, the location of two social emotions, "shame" and "guilt", in the common structure was found to be closer to "fear" and somewhat further away from "anger" in Indonesia than in the Netherlands.

The four studies reported in this article form the initial phase of a larger culture-comparative project to examine the emotions of guilt and shame (see also Breugelmans et al., 2000). The present studies were conducted in Indonesia and The Netherlands, two societies that are considered to vary considerably in respect of these two emotions (Geertz, 1961; Triandis, 1988). First, we needed to have an overview of the emotion domain in samples of Indonesian and Dutch respondents and to explore whether cross-culturally consistent points of reference could be empirically identified. This part of our research relies on the cognitive representation of emotions by means of emotion terms (Shaver, Wu, &

Correspondence should be addressed to Johnny Fontaine, Department of Psychology, University of Leuven, Tiensestraat 102, 3000 Leuven, Belgium; e-mail: Johnny.Fontaine@psy.kuleuven.ac.be

We would like to thank Nico Frijda and Batja Mesquita for their contribution, especially during the earlier stages of the project on which this article is based.

http://www.tandf.co.uk/journals/pp/02699931.html   DOI:10.1080/02699933014000130

Schwartz, 1992), which we will refer to as the "cognitive structure of emotions". We present this preliminary phase in some detail, because it seems relevant for cross-cultural emotion research, in terms of both methodology and results. It is a necessary step to enable in the fourth and final study an examination of the location of guilt and shame in the emotion domain, as well as possible cultural similarities and differences in this location.

The cognitive structure of emotions

Within a cultural group, the cognitive structure of emotions can be conceptualised as the cognitive representation of differences and similarities between emotion terms (Shaver, Schwartz, Kirson, & O'Connor, 1987). Because any language only contains a limited vocabulary, it is feasible to gain an overview of their interrelationships. Moreover, as emotion processes or aspects thereof deemed relevant within a culture are likely to be coded into emotion terms (Levy, 1984), they offer access to culture-specific representations of the emotion domain. Furthermore, it has been found that the cognitive representation of emotion terms resembles characteristics of emotion processes. For example, the number of appraisals and the number of action tendencies shared by pairs of emotions closely relate to the cognitive similarity between corresponding emotion terms (Frijda, 1987). In addition, there is evidence for a close relationship between the correlational structure of current affect based on questionnaire research and perceived similarities between emotion terms (Reisenzein & Schimmack, 1999). In short, an analysis of the cognitive structure of emotions offers a way of gaining knowledge about emotions.

Cross-cultural differences in cognitive representations. To understand cross-cultural variations in cognitive representation of emotions one has to distinguish three aspects, namely: emotion terms (linguistic); representation of facets of emotion processes and states in terms of cognitive similarities and differences between emotion terms (representational); and emotion processes and states themselves (internal).

The correspondence, or absence of correspondence, between an emotion term used by one group and a term used by another group can be studied by means of translation procedures. Based on these procedures one can conclude whether or not a pair of terms shows translation equivalence; usually such conclusions depend on whether or not bilingual experts agree about the translation of emotion terms (Brislin, 1980, 1986). However, such evidence is not conclusive, since neither the absence nor the presence of a pair of translation-equivalent emotion terms can provide decisive information about the equivalence or nonequivalence of the associated psychological events (Russell, 1991).

There is neither theoretical nor empirical evidence that the entire domain of emotions (i.e., all relevant aspects of all commonly distinguished emotions) is reflected to a similar extent in the cognitive structure of emotions. This difficulty is particularly evident when a componential theory of emotions is adopted (Frijda, 1986; Lazarus, 1991; Scherer, 1984). For example, one aspect that seems to be only marginally represented in the cognitive structure of emotions is emotion regulation. Respondents appear to make clear distinctions between an emotional state, a corresponding tendency to act in a certain way, and social norms about what can be expressed and how it has to be expressed (Ekman, 1973). For instance, Heider (1991) found that Minangkabau respondents reported aggressive behaviour quite explicitly when asked to describe the consequences of anger in general, whereas the actual expression of anger is not socially acceptable and appears to be seldom observed. This suggests that substantial differences in emotion expression (Rimé, Mesquita, Philippot, & Boca, 1991) can be compatible with cross-cultural invariance in cognitions about emotions.

With respect to emotion processes and states as such, it has been frequently reported that cultural context can shape these. An emotion term is then seen as designating a state or process that is intrinsically related to an aspect of cultural context found only in the specific society in which the term is used (Lutz, 1988; Lutz & White, 1986). An example is the emotion of "*liget*" among the Ilongots, as described by Rosaldo (1980). This is an emotion that is related to the practice of headhunting. Although this emotion can apparently be described for a Western reader—which implies that the meaning is communicable—its occurrence may be specific to the cultural context of the Ilongots. As mentioned above, strong relationships have been observed between basic characteristics of emotion processes, like appraisals and action tendencies, and the cognitive structure of emotions. Therefore, cross-cultural differences with respect to these characteristics should be represented in the cognitive emotion structure.

If one considers a large set of emotion terms, and the cognitive representation of their interrelationships within each of two cultures, evidence of a lack of cross-cultural equivalence is open to various interpretations (Poortinga & Van de Vijver, 1987; Van de Vijver & Leung, 1997). However, this is much less true in the case of evidence of equivalence. Nonequivalence can be due to a language not having a term for certain emotions, or to terms having only partial overlap in meaning (linguistic differences). Another possibility is that there are pervasive differences between cultural groups with respect to which aspects are represented in the cognitive structure of emotions (representational differences). Still another explanation is that cultural context shapes emotion processes not only incidentally (reports usually are limited to a few emotions; Mesquita & Frijda, 1992), but extensively (internal differences).

By contrast, evidence of cross-cultural equivalence of cognitive emotion structures is less easy to dismiss. First, equivalence of structures cannot be established psychometrically unless there exists at least a sizeable subset of emotion terms that are translation-equivalent (linguistic similarities). Second, equivalence implies that there are similarities between cultural groups with respect to those aspects of emotion processes that are represented in the cognitive structure of emotions (representational similarities). Third, equivalence also implies that those characteristics of the emotion process that are represented must be cross-culturally similar (internal similarities). If anyone of these three conditions is not met, it is difficult to see how invariance of cognitive structure of emotions could emerge.

Dimensional and hierarchical organisation of the cognitive structure of emotions. Cross-culturally, the cognitive structure of emotions has been mainly studied at one of three hierarchically ordered levels. The highest and most inclusive level pertains to the dimensionality of the cognitive emotion structure of the entire emotion domain (insofar as it is represented in emotion terms) and the interpretation of these dimensions. A less inclusive level is that of emotion clusters. The question is whether distinguishable groups of emotion terms can be identified, and whether there is correspondence across cultural populations in this respect. The most concrete level is that of individual emotion terms. The focus of research is the position of the terms within a cognitive structure of emotions. Cross-cultural variation at the highest level also implies variation at lower levels; for example, if the dimensional structure is different across cultures, clusters of emotions cannot be interpreted as having identical meaning.

Structural analyses of emotion terms, like factor analysis and multi-dimensional scaling, typically result in two or three dimensions (Russell, 1983, 1991). The first dimension is always a pleasantness or valence dimension; emotion terms can be systematically ordered on a positive-negative dimension. Two other dimensions that often emerge are activation (active-passive) or arousal (high-low), and dominance (strong-weak). These two dimensions are not always found in a single study, but they do appear systematically when considering multiple studies. The reason for discrepancies between studies should probably be sought in the selection of emotion terms. If the emotion words pertain more to interpersonal relationships, dominance can be expected as the second dimension; otherwise arousal is likely to emerge as the second dimension (Russell, 1991). The three-dimensional structure in the emotion domain is reminiscent of the Evaluation-Potency-Activation (EPA) dimensions in the connotative or affective meaning of words identified by Osgood and replicated in many societies (Osgood, May, & Miron, 1975). As far as current knowledge goes, it seems likely that the three dimensions universally span the entire emotion domain.

In addition to this dimensional tradition, there are analyses of discrete entities in the cognitive structure of the emotion domain (Boucher, 1979; Brandt & Boucher, 1986; Shaver et al., 1987). Terms referring to the same emotion, including terms pertinent to specific classes of situations or levels of intensity, should cluster together. This view is often combined with a prototype approach to cognitive structure of emotions (e.g., Shaver et al., 1987). According to prototype theory there exists a level of categorisation with an optimal trade-off between inclusiveness and informativeness, which is referred to as the basic level (Rosch, 1978). In cross-cultural studies on the cognitive structure of emotions, two high order clusters, distinguishing positive versus negative emotions, tend to emerge. At a somewhat lower level of inclusiveness four basic emotion categories have been identified, corresponding to anger, fear, sadness, and positive emotion (Shaver et al., 1992). At the next level down, a number of smaller subclusters emerge that do not appear to be entirely stable across cultural groups (Shaver et al., 1992). Such lack of consistency may be due to the fact that idiosyncratic effects of individual stimuli and sampling fluctuations are likely to play a stronger role at lower levels, with the result that more stable clusters can be expected at higher levels of inclusiveness.

The lowest level in emotion structures is that of the separate emotion words. In lexical analyses, evidence for substantial translation equivalence has been reported, especially for those terms that refer to so-called basic emotions (Russell, 1991). At the same time, as noted above, the mere fact that two terms are translation-equivalent is insufficient evidence of their cognitive equivalence.

Existing evidence suggests cross-cultural equivalence at more abstract levels (Shaver et al., 1987, 1992; Russell, 1991). However, the record does not allow for a more precise conclusion, because research tends to suffer from one or two shortcomings. Some studies aim explicitly at comparing cognitive emotion structures, but work with a set of translated emotion terms across cultural groups (e.g., Russell, Lewicka, & Niit, 1989). With this kind of study there is a risk of imposing a "Western structure", as the selection of terms is Western. Other studies have been carried out in a single cultural group (e.g., Church, Katigbak, Reyes, & Jensen, 1998; Lutz, 1988). The culture-specific structural configuration is then interpreted as reflecting the same or different underlying dimensions as found elsewhere, without there being an explicit criterion for either interpretation. Thus, for the empirical identification of equivalence and inequivalence in the cognitive structure of emotions a combined culture-specific culture-comparative approach is needed. A culture-specific approach is needed in order to assure that the local reality is taken into account. A culture-comparative approach is needed to investigate empirically whether and to what extent equivalence is present.

Guilt and shame in the cognitive structure of emotions

The analysis of the location of a separate emotion term in a cognitive emotion structure is possible once such a structure has been identified. In the present project, guilt and shame were selected for further analysis. Both pertain to self-regulation in the social environment. In Western literature, guilt is characterised by the transgression of a moral norm for which the subject takes personal responsibility, leading to a focus on the wrongdoing and to self-punishment and reparative behaviour (Izard, 1977; Lindsay-Hartz, De Rivera, & Mascolo, 1995; Tangney, 1990). With shame, the mere transgression of a social norm is a sufficient trigger for the emotional reaction. In such situations, the disdain of others is experienced or feared and the subject wishes to disappear from the scene (Izard, 1977). In shame, the focus is on the self that is being experienced in a negative way (Tangney, 1990).

There has been a long-standing interest in guilt and shame in both psychological and anthropological literature (e.g., Benedict, 1946; Geertz, 1961; Piers & Singer, 1953; Tangney, 1990). Some authors even consider them to be basic emotions (Izard, 1977). There is an extensive record distinguishing between guilt cultures and shame cultures (Benedict, 1946; Creighton, 1990). This idea has also been incorporated into recent theorising on individualism and collectivism, guilt being more prevalent in individualistic cultures and shame in collectivistic cultures (Triandis, 1988; Triandis, Leung, Villareal, & Clack, 1985). This implies a relatively stronger orientation toward shame in Indonesia and toward guilt in The Netherlands. Moreover, anthropological research indicates that Indonesian society qualifies as a shame culture (Geertz, 1961; Keeler, 1983). An extensive study by Heider (1991) analysed the emotion structure of Minangkabau and Javanese Indonesians. In this study only a cluster of shame terms emerged, but there was no separate cluster for guilt terms. When further probing the meaning of the emotion terms by asking for antecedents and consequences, Heider found that the typical guilt antecedent of wrongdoing was reported with the emotion word *takut*, which can be translated as ''fear''.

The distinction between guilt and shame cultures appears to refer to differences in both the prevalence and the salience of these emotions. Differences in relative prevalence (with guilt being more prevalent in guilt cultures and shame in shame cultures) do not as such necessarily imply differences in the cognitive structure of emotions. Equivalent emotions may just happen more frequently in one cultural context than in another. However, it is also implied that the same type of situation (norm violations in a general sense) will tend to elicit shame in a shame culture and guilt in a guilt culture. Such a cross-cultural difference in salience should have an effect on the position of the emotion terms in a cognitive emotion structure. If (social) behaviour is primarily sanctioned by shame in Indonesia, we can expect shame to show closer relationships than guilt to other negative emotions, as compared with The Netherlands, whereas for guilt the reverse pattern should hold.

Outline of the four studies

Three of the studies reported here pertain to the cognitive mapping of emotion terms and the equivalence of the cognitive representations in Indonesian and Dutch samples. We start with a brief description of how independent collections of emotion terms were obtained via local respondents, minimising the possibility of cultural imposition. In the second study the cognitive structure of emotions in Indonesian and Dutch samples is studied using data from a free-sorting task in which respondents placed emotion terms in categories according to their similarity in meaning. We analyse the data of each sample separately and examine at face value cross-cultural differences and similarities in dimensional and clustering representations of structure.

In the third study, translation-equivalent pairs of terms are identified, based on a number of sources. The cognitive equivalence of these pairs is analysed, as translation equivalence does not necessarily imply cognitive equivalence. The resulting set of translation- and cognitively equivalent terms is then used to link the two datasets from Study 2 and to examine whether they fit into a single structure. This allows a more precise assessment of whether and to what extent there is invariance of cognitive structure of emotions across the two cultural groups.

The fourth and final study focuses on the position of guilt and shame within the cognitive structure of emotions, with a view to examining cross-cultural differences in location in relation to the distinction between guilt and shame cultures. This analysis combines data from the previous studies with ratings of the relationships of the two target emotions with other emotion terms.

STUDY 1: SELECTION OF EMOTION TERMS

In order to investigate the cognitive emotion structure within a cultural group, it is necessary to select emotion terms that represent (aspects of) emotions in the group concerned. For the selection of such terms, we relied on the prototype approach that has been used successfully in previous research (Fehr & Russell, 1984; Shaver et al., 1987). The selection of terms for each cultural group was based on ratings of the prototypicality of emotion terms in that group.

Method

Emotion lists. Lists of emotion terms were generated based on various sources of information. The main source in each cultural group was a free-listing task (see Fontaine, Poortinga, Setiadi, & Suprapti, 1996). Seventy-three Indonesian and 60 Dutch students were asked to write down as many emotion words as they could in a period of 10 minutes. Terms mentioned at least three times were accepted and this resulted in an initial list of 137 terms in Indonesia and of 78 terms in the Netherlands. In order to ensure a comprehensive coverage of the emotion domain, the Indonesian list was extended with terms from an existing Indonesian list of emotion terms[1] (Markam, unpublished report).

---

[1] It would have been interesting to have also relied on the emotion lists generated by Heider (1991). Unfortunately, we did not have these at our disposal at the time of data collection in Indonesia.

Furthermore, the Dutch list was extended with terms translated from the (American) emotion list reported by Shaver et al. (1987) and terms from the Indonesian list that were readily translatable into Dutch.[2] This resulted in a list of 153 words in Indonesian and a list of 136 terms in Dutch. The terms of these two lists were rated with respect to prototypicality.

Respondents. A total of 71 Indonesian (56 women and 15 men) and 89 Dutch (79 women and 10 men) psychology students participated on a voluntary basis.

Procedure. The terms in the Indonesian and Dutch lists were rated with respect to prototypicality for "emotion" (*perasaan*, in Indonesian; *emotie* in Dutch).[3] Respondents were asked to rate each word from the list on a 4-point scale. The scale points were 0 (certainly not an emotion), 1 (unlikely to be an emotion), 2 (likely to be an emotion), and 3 (certainly an emotion).

Results and discussion

In the approach we followed, terms are assumed to be organised around prototypes, each term resembling a given prototype to a greater or lesser extent. Therefore, the prototypicality rating task was expected to yield an ordering of terms rather than a dichotomy between emotion terms and nonemotion terms. Terms with high scores were regarded as clearly belonging to the emotion domain.[4] For instance, the five most prototypical terms in Indonesia were *bahagia* ("happy"), *cinta* ("love"), *benci* ("hate"), *senang* ("joy'), and *sedih* ("sad"); in the Netherlands, the five most prototypical terms were *blijheid* ("joy"), *boosheid* ("anger"), *bedroefdheid* ("sadness"), *woede* ("rage"), and *verdriet* ("sadness"). In Indonesia, the five terms with the lowest prototypicality rating were *sakit* ("ill"), *sadar* ("consciousness"), *terhambat* ("impeded"), *pusing* ("dizzy"), and *cape* ("tired"); in The Netherlands, the least prototypical terms were *verwaarlozing* ("neglect"), *eerlijkheid* ("honesty"), *belemmering* ("impediment"), *onafhankelijkheid* ("independence"), and *onhandigheid* ("clumsiness").

---

[2] The emotion research of Shaver et al. (1987) constituted landmark research on the cognitive structure of emotions and because English is related to Dutch (*The atlas of mankind*, 1982), we considered it as an interesting point of reference. It would have been interesting to extend the Indonesian emotion list with Dutch emotion terms, but practical limitations of the project did not allow this.

[3] Despite the translation equivalence of the two terms, *emotie* and *perasaan* themselves could convey different meanings. However, this is ruled out by the similarities in results, reported later in this article.

[4] A full table of prototypicality ratings can be obtained on request from the first author.

In both Indonesia and in The Netherlands, the 120 emotion terms with the highest average rating were selected for further study of the cognitive emotion structure. In Indonesia, all emotion terms with a prototypicality rating of 1.94 or higher were selected; in The Netherlands the cut-off point was 1.19.[5]

In anticipation of Study 4, it is worth noting that "shame" received higher prototypicality ratings than "guilt" in both samples. In terms of rank order, *malu* ("shame") and *bersalah* ("guilt") occupied the 12th and 37th positions, respectively, in Indonesia; whereas *schaamte* ("shame") and *schuld* ("guilt") were ranked 24th and 53rd, respectively, in The Netherlands.

STUDY 2: CATEGORIZATION OF EMOTION TERMS

The cognitive structure of emotions was investigated by means of similarity sortings of the emotion words. For reasons already discussed a prototype approach was followed. In method and procedure we largely followed Shaver et al. (1987).

Method

Respondents. A total of 109 Indonesian (81 women and 28 men) and 105 Dutch (59 women and 46 men) students participated. The Indonesian students cooperated on an unpaid basis; the Dutch students received a small amount of money (Dfl10).

Procedure. The 120 emotion terms were each printed on a small card. Each participant received the set of cards and was asked to sort the terms in categories of similar emotions. The instructions, which mentioned that there were no rules regarding the number of categories, were taken from Shaver et al. (1987). Respondents were told that they could work on the task for an hour.

Results

The perceived similarity between two emotion terms was computed as the number of respondents who placed these terms in the same category. The dissimilarity between two emotion terms, on which all further analyses were based, was equal to the number of respondents who did not place these terms in the same category.

Dimensional structure. This was analysed in each set of 120 terms by means of nonmetrical Classical Multidimensional Scaling (CMDS), a technique

---

[5] The ratings in The Netherlands tended to be lower. This suggests differences in the use of scale points (response styles) (Van Hemert, Van de Vijver, Poortinga, & Georgas, 2001; Van Herk, 2000).

that allows for the representation of emotion words as points in a space, with the distance between two points representing dissimilarity in sorting (Borg & Groenen, 1997; Davison, 1983; Kruskal & Wish, 1978). These analyses were carried out with PROC MDS in SAS.[6] As a measure of the fit of the configurations we relied on the RSQ (Young & Lewyckyj, 1979), which is the squared correlation between the (optimally transformed) dissimilarity data and the Euclidean distances computed under the model. This statistic can be taken as the percentage of variance in the data explained by a configuration.

In the Indonesian and Dutch samples, the a priori expected three-dimensional structure explained 90% and 88%, respectively, of the variance (see Table 1, first two rows of the left column). After an orthogonal Procrustes rotation (which preserves the distances between points), the three dimensions could in both cases be interpreted as pleasantness or evaluation (separating positive from negative emotion terms), dominance or potency (separating anger terms from fear and sadness terms), and arousal or activation (separating sadness from fear and anger terms) (see Figures 1 and 2). These results are consistent with the previous findings mentioned in the Introduction.

Hierarchical structure.   The hierarchical structure of the emotion domain was investigated by means of Average Linkage Hierarchical Cluster Analyses

TABLE 1
Overview of fit (R^2) of three-dimensional culture-specific and consensus MDS configurations

No. of terms in configuration	Culture-specific configuration	Consensus configuration
120 selected emotion terms		
Indonesia	.90	.87[a]
The Netherlands	.88	.87[a]
50 translation-equivalent terms		
Indonesia	.92	.85
The Netherlands	.90	.81
42 cognitive equivalent terms		
Indonesia	.92	.88
The Netherlands	.94	.90

[a] This consensus emotion space was computed via Multidimensional Scaling (MDS) with partial overlap. The 42 equivalent pairs of emotion terms were each assigned a single position in the emotion space. The remaining 78 Dutch and 78 Indonesian terms had a specific position in the consensus configuration.

---

[6] All analyses were carried out with the UNTIE-option.

(ALHCA) on the distances between the emotions in the three-dimensional configurations.[7] These analyses were performed with PROC CLUSTER in SAS. There are various criteria for the identification of the optimal number of clusters. We mainly relied on the pseudo F, which is based on the ratio of between- and within-cluster variance, but related statistics, that is, Cubic Clustering Criterion (CCC) and pseudo t^2 (*SAS/STAT user's guide*, 1994), were also taken into consideration. In addition, we used the RSQ that reflects the fit of the cluster solution and can be interpreted as the percentage of variance in the distances between emotions terms accounted for by the cluster solution.

ALHCA of the Indonesian emotion terms showed first a distinction between positive and negative emotion terms (see Figure 1). The RSQ for this two-cluster solution was .47. All three criteria, CCC, pseudo F and pseudo t^2, pointed to four clusters as the optimal number. These clusters could be interpreted as positive emotion, sadness, fear, and anger. This solution, which corresponds most closely to a basic level categorisation, accounted for 74% of the variance. At a lower order level of categorisation, both the CCC and the pseudo F pointed to 19 clusters, accounting for 94% of the variance. A tree structure of the 19 sub-clusters and their position in the three-dimensional emotion space is presented in Figure 1 (the term in each subcluster with the highest prototypicality rating is presented in bold).

ALHCA for the Dutch emotion terms corresponded to the Indonesian ALHCA for the high order and for the basic level categories (see Figure 2). The first distinction was again between positive and negative emotions, accounting for 46% of the variance. All three criteria supported as optimal a solution with four clusters, namely, positive emotion, anger, fear, and sadness, accounting for 74% of the variance. In this dataset, a 20-cluster solution was supported by the three criteria at a lower order level, accounting for 95% of the variance (see Figure 2).

At the level of subclusters the two configurations show substantial similarities, but certain differences are also worth noting. *Malu* (''shame'') appears in the fear cluster in Indonesia and *bersalah* (''guilt'') in the sadness cluster. In The Netherlands *schaamte* (''shame'') and *schuld* (''guilt'') form one subcluster. At the level of subclusters and separate terms, *jengkel* (''irritation'') in Indonesia falls in a subcluster with a clearly positive position on the arousal dimension, while in the Dutch figure *irritatie* and *geprikkeldheid* (both translate

---

[7] In previous research (Fontaine et al., 1996; Shaver et al., 1987), the average linkage hierarchical cluster analyses were performed directly on the sorting data. However, the present data are at the ordinal level. Hierarchical cluster analyses require interval data. The results of the hierarchical cluster analysis are not robust under monotonic transformations of the dissimilarities (Everitt, 1980). As the distances in a three-dimensional geometric configuration, which are at internal level, account for (nearly) 90% of the variance in the sorting data in both cultures, they form a good and probably preferable alternative as input for the cluster analyses.

Basic And Lower-Order Emotion Clusters

Cluster / Terms	PLE	ARO	DOM
Positive Emotion	*1.94*	*-0.25*	*0.23*
tenteram [peacefulness]: aman [peacefulness], tenang [calmness], bebas [independence], nikmat [pleasantness], betah [feel at home]	1.90	-0.71	0.08
cinta [love]: sayang [love], ikhlas [resignation], tulus [honesty], kasih [affection], damai [peacefulness], rela [willingness]	1.40	-0.75	0.81
bahagia [happiness]: gembira [joy], girang [joy], senang [pleasure], riang [gaiety], suka sita [happiness], suka [joy]	2.85	-0.29	0.27
bangga [pride]: mantep [confidence], yakin [be sure], semangat [enthusiasm], optimis [optimism]	1.55	0.55	0.57
lega [relief]: plong [relief], puas [satisfaction], tersenjung [flattered], kagum [admiration], tertarik [attraction], terpesona [fascination]	1.90	0.11	-0.50
Anger	*-0.91*	*0.48*	*0.95*
benci [hate]: iri [jealousy], sirik [envy], dengki [envy], geram [fury], muak [disgust], sebal [annoyance], dendam [resentment], tidak suka [dislike], cemburu [jealousy]	-0.74	0.51	1.35
jengkel [irritation]: dongkol [annoyance], gondok [suppressed anger], kesal [annoyance], marah [anger], murka [fury], jijik [disgust]	-1.53	0.83	0.96
kecewa [disappointment]: sakit hati [hurt], terhina [insult], tersinggung [hurt]	-1.38	-0.19	0.63
jenuh [fed up]: jemu [fed up], bosan [fed up], suntuk [overtaken]	0.02	0.49	0.55
tercekam [fright]	-0.20	0.28	-0.32
Fear	*-0.59*	*0.97*	*-0.76*
malu [shame]: bimbang [doubt], ragu ragu [uncertainty], bingung [confusion], cemas [worry], kuatir [worry], was-was [suspicion], gelisah [nervousness], risau [worry], gugup [nervousness], rikuh [embarrassment], gundah [restlessness], resah [anxiety]	-0.89	0.80	-0.95
kikuh [awkwardness]: grogi [groggy], segan [diffidence], penasaran [suppressed anger], sungkan [reluctance]	0.06	0.89	-1.22
curiga [suspicion]: gusar [upset]	-0.84	0.88	0.19
takut [fear]: ngeri [terror], serem [terror], tegang [tenseness], terkejut [startle], panik [panic]	-0.40	1.45	-0.29
Sadness	*-0.64*	*-0.82*	*-0.34*
bersalah [guilt]: berdosa [sinfulness], pesimis [pessimism], menyesal [regret], rendah-diri [inferiority], minder [inferiority]	-1.07	-0.35	-1.07
sedih [sadness]: terasing [alienation], terkucil [isolation], duka [grief], frustasi [frustration], munung [melancholy], susah [worry], tertekan [dejection], pedih [pain], menderita [suffering], merana [misery], diabaikan [neglected], tertindas [oppression], putus asa [desperation], terpuluk [dejection]	-1.15	-0.89	-0.19
sendu [melancholy]: pilu [sorrow], kesepian [loneliness], sepi [loneliness], kehilangan [miss], hampa [emptiness], sunyi [loneliness], pasrah [resignation]	-0.39	-0.85	0.11
terharu [moved]: kasihan [compassion], iba [touched], tersentuh [touched]	0.45	-1.06	-0.93
rindu [homesickness]: kangen [longing], syahdu [quietness]	0.59	-1.06	0.01

PLE = Pleasantness
ARO = Arousal
DOM = Dominance
Note. Emotion words printed in italic have a translation-equivalent counterpart in Dutch.

Figure 1. Hierarchical cluster analysis on 120 Indonesian emotion terms and cluster position in a three-dimensional space.

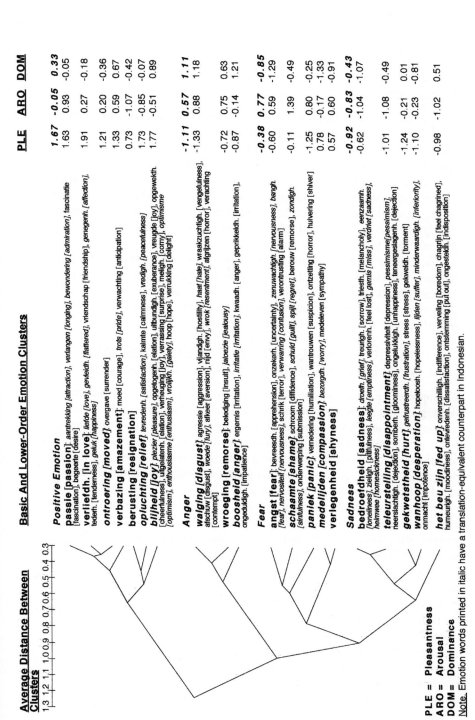

Average Distance Between Clusters

1.3 1.2 1.1 1.0 0.9 0.8 0.7 0.6 0.5 0.4 0.3

Basic And Lower-Order Emotion Clusters	PLE	ARO	DOM
Positive Emotion	*1.67*	*-0.05*	*0.33*
passie [passion]: *aantrekking [attraction], verlangen [longing], bewondering [admiration],* fascinatie [fascination], begeerte [desire]	1.63	0.93	-0.05
verliefdh. [in love]: *liefde [love], gevleidh. [flattered], vriendschap [friendship], genegenh. [affection],* tederh. [tenderness], geluk [happiness]	1.91	0.27	-0.18
ontroering [moved]: overgave [surrender]	1.21	0.20	-0.36
verbazing [amazement]: moed [courage], trots [pride], verwachting [anticipation]	1.33	0.59	0.67
berusting [resignation]	0.73	-1.07	-0.42
opluchting [relief]: tevredenh. [satisfaction], kalmte [calmness], vredigh. [peacefulness]	1.73	-0.85	-0.07
blijheid [joy]: plezier [pleasure], opgelogenh. [elation], uitbundigh. [exuberance], vreugde [joy], opgewekth. [cheerfulness], uitgelatenh. [elation], verheuging [joy], verrassing [surprise], meligh. [corny], optimisme [optimism], enthousiasme [enthusiasm], vrolijkh. [gaiety], hoop [hope], verrukking [delight]	1.77	-0.51	0.89
Anger	*-1.11*	*0.57*	*1.11*
walging [disgust]: agressie [aggression], vijandigh. [hostility], haat [hate], wraakzuchtigh. [vengefulness], atschuw [disgust], woede [fury], afkeer [aversion], nijd [envy], wrok [resentment], afgrijzen [horror], verachting [contempt]	-1.33	0.88	1.18
wroeging [remorse]: belediging [insult], jaloezie [jealousy]	-0.72	0.75	0.63
boosheid [anger]: ergernis [irritation], irritatie [irritation], kwaadh. [anger], geprikkeldh. [irritation], ongeduldigh. [impatience]	-0.87	-0.14	1.21
Fear	*-0.38*	*0.77*	*-0.85*
angst [fear]: bevreesdh. [apprehension], onzekerh. [uncertainty], zenuwachtigh. [nervousness], bangh. [fear], nervositeit [nervousness], schrik [terror], verwarring [confusion], veronrtrusting [alarm]	-0.60	0.59	-1.29
schaamte [shame]: schroom [diffidence], schuld [guilt], spijt [regret], berouw [remorse], zondigh. [sinfulness], onderwerping [submission]	-0.11	1.39	-0.49
paniek [panic]: vernedering [humiliation], wantrouwen [suspicion], ontzetting [horror], huivering [shiver]	-1.25	0.80	-0.25
medelijden [compassion]: bezongh. [worry], medeleven [sympathy]	0.78	-0.17	-1.33
verlegenheid [shyness]	0.57	0.60	-0.91
Sadness	*-0.92*	*-0.83*	*-0.43*
bedroefdheid [sadness]: droefh. [grief], treurigh. [sorrow], triesth. [melancholy], eenzaamh. [loneliness], zieligh. [pitifulness], leegte [emptiness], verlorenh. [feel lost], gemis [miss], verdriet [sadness], heimwee [homesickness]	-0.62	-1.04	-1.07
teleurstelling [disappointment]: depressiviteit [depression], pessimisme[pessimism], neerslachtigh. [dejection], somberh. [gloominess], ongelukkigh. [unhappiness], teneergeslagenh. [dejection]	-1.01	-1.08	-0.49
gekwetsheid [hurt]: gefrustreerdh. [frustration], stress [stress], gekweldh. [torment]	-1.24	-0.21	0.01
wanhoop [desperation]: hopeloosh. [hopelessness], lijden [suffer], minderwaardigh. [inferiority], onmacht [impotence]	-1.10	-0.23	-0.81
het beu zijn [fed up]: overschilligh. [indifference], vervelling [boredom], chagrijn [feel chagrined], humeurigh. [moodiness], ontevredenh. [dissatisfaction], onstemming [put out], ongestedh. [indisposition]	-0.98	-1.02	0.51

PLE = Pleasantness
ARO = Arousal
DOM = Dominance

Note. Emotion words printed in italic have a translation-equivalent counterpart in Indonesian.

Figure 2. Hierarchical cluster analysis on 120 Dutch emotion terms and cluster position in a three-dimensional space.

well as "irritation") belong to a subcluster that is slightly negative on the arousal dimension.

Discussion

Taking the results at face value, the same three dimensions of pleasantness, dominance and arousal adequately describe the cognitive space for both the Indonesian and Dutch students. Cluster analysis also reveals close correspondences, not only at a high level of inclusiveness (dichotomy between positive and negative terms), but also at the basic level of categorisation (four clusters: positive emotion, sadness, fear, and anger). When looking at the average coordinates of the clusters on the three dimensions, the correspondence is striking. Only at the level of subclusters were cross-cultural differences found that are likely to have some significance.

The present findings cannot be attributed to biased stimulus materials, or imposed (Western) categorisations. Culturally relevant emotion terms were gathered and evaluated in each cultural group separately by local judges. Moreover, no a priori ordering of emotion categories was imposed. Thus, the risk of cultural imposition is virtually nonexistent.

STUDY 3: INTEGRATION OF THE INDONESIAN AND DUTCH COGNITIVE EMOTION STRUCTURE

The apparent correspondences in the cognitive organisation of the emotion domain are not informative about the equivalence of separate terms. Moreover, we cannot say whether differences at subcluster level pertain to a single term, or to the subcluster as a whole. In addition, we have no means of expressing in a quantitative way how similar the basic and higher order clusters and the three dimensions are. To address such questions we undertook a further study in which a three-step sequence was followed.

First, to establish a connection between the two sets of emotion terms some common standard was needed across the two samples (Poortinga, 1989). For this purpose we collected information on the translation equivalence of the Indonesian and Dutch emotion terms.

Second, we investigated whether translation-equivalent emotion terms also demonstrated cognitive equivalence. As discussed in the Introduction, translation equivalence of a pair of terms does not necessarily guarantee cognitive equivalence. Any pair for which cognitive equivalence is questionable should be discarded as a common reference point.

Finally, we analysed the extent to which the cognitive emotion structures found for Indonesian and Dutch respondents in Study 2 could be represented by a single cognitive emotion structure without loss of information, using as a common reference pairs of terms that had met the criteria of both translation and cognitive equivalence.

Method

Nine independent sources were used to gather information on translation equivalence of the two sets of 120 terms, namely, three Indonesian-Dutch translations by bilinguals, an Indonesian-Dutch dictionary translation (Poerwadarminta & Teeuw, 1950), two Dutch-Indonesian translations by bilinguals, one Indonesian-English translation by a bilingual, an Indonesian-English dictionary translation and an English-Indonesian dictionary translation (Echols & Shadily, 1976, 1990). The English-Indonesian and Indonesian-English translations were included because English and Dutch are closely related languages (*The atlas of mankind*, 1982). The English-Dutch translation relied on the Van Dale dictionary (*Van Dale Groot Woordenboek Engels-Nederlands*, 1984; *Van Dale Groot Woordenboek Nederlands-Engels*, 1984).

Results

Translation equivalence. A pair of words was considered translation-equivalent when: (i) both terms were literally the same for at least 5 of the 9 sources; (ii) including at least 3 of the 6 Dutch-Indonesian and Indonesian-Dutch sources; and (iii) when all other translations could be considered synonyms. Of the 120 Indonesian and the 120 Dutch emotion terms, 50 pairs met these stringent criteria for translation equivalence (see emotion terms printed in italics in Figures 1 and 2).

Cognitive equivalence of translation-equivalent emotion terms. To investigate whether the 50 pairs of translation-equivalent emotion terms were also cognitively equivalent, we investigated whether such pairs of terms had the same position within a common emotion structure across the cultural groups. Except for sampling fluctuations, translation-equivalent terms that are also cognitively equivalent should fit a common or "consensus" configuration as well as they fit each of the two separate configurations. To compute a geometric representation for each of the two datasets separately we used Classical Multidimensional Scaling (CMDS; Borg & Groenen, 1997). For the computation of a single consensus solution for both sets simultaneously we used Replicated Multidimensional Scaling (RMDS; Borg & Groenen, 1997).

The three-dimensional consensus configuration with the 50 translation-equivalent terms explained 85% of the variance in the Indonesian data and 81% in the Dutch data, compared with 92% for the separate Indonesian configuration and 90% for the separate Dutch configuration (see Table 1). The high percentages accounted for by the three-dimensional consensus configuration indicated an overall high psychological similarity. However, scrutiny of individual pairs revealed a lack of fit for some pairs in the consensus configuration compared to the sample-specific configurations.

The identification of such apparently cognitively nonequivalent pairs was further investigated by means of an iterative procedure. In each step the pair was removed that showed the largest difference in RSQ between the consensus configuration and the two culture-specific configurations.[8] This procedure was repeated until a cut-off value of .15 had been reached. With this criterion eight pairs of terms were found to be cognitively nonequivalent (see Table 2). The consensus configuration for the remaining 42 terms had an RSQ of .88 for the Indonesian data and .90 for the Dutch data, while the culture-specific configurations showed an RSQ of .92 and .94, respectively, leaving only 4% unshared variance (see Table 1). Thus, the 42 pairs of terms are apparently not only translation-equivalent, but also cognitively equivalent.

In the three-dimensional consensus structure for the 42 equivalent pairs of terms the first dimension was a pleasantness dimension: "relief" and "pleasure" had high positive coordinates, whereas those with high negative coordinates included "disgust" and being "fed up". The second dimension was an arousal dimension. High positive coordinates included "panic" and "fury", and high negative coordinates were found for "sadness" and "compassion". For the third dimension, "hate" and "attraction" were among the terms with high positive coordinates, whereas "fear" and "desperation" showed high negative position. This dimension can therefore be interpreted as a dominance dimension.[9]

Consensus structure for all terms. We investigated whether the 42 translation-equivalent and cognitively equivalent pairs of emotion terms could be used as an empirically generated common standard for the entire emotion domain. Therefore, we examined whether an integrated structure including all 120 Indonesian and 120 Dutch emotion terms based on the 42 equivalent points could account for the cognitive structure of emotions found in each country separately without loss of information. For this we relied on Multidimensional Scaling (MDS) with partial overlap (Borg & Groenen, 1997). A geometrical representation was computed in which the equivalent terms had the same position for the two groups and in which no constraints were imposed on the other terms. Thus, the 42 cognitively equivalent pairs were each represented by a

---

[8] The Squared Correlation (RSQ) between the optimally transformed dissimilarities and the Euclidean distances computed under the model was taken as a measure of fit. This measure can also be computed for the separate emotion terms.

[9] When ALHCA was applied to the 42 cognitively equivalent pairs of emotion terms the various statistical indices supported a 4- and a 9-cluster solution as appropriate. The 4-cluster solution with positive emotion, fear, sadness, and anger accounted for 88% of the variance. In a 9-cluster solution, 94% was accounted for.

TABLE 2

Consensus, culture-specific, and difference RSQ for Indonesian and Dutch terms for iterative analysis of inequivalence

NT	English translation	Indonesian term	RSQIC	RSQII	DI	Dutch term	RSQDC	RSQDD	DD
50	worry	kuatir	.43	.91	-.48	bezorgdheid	.36	.82	-.46
49	sinfulness	berdosa	.78	.89	-.11	zondigheid	.09	.76	-.67
48	guilt	bersalah	.64	.96	-.32	schuld	.67	.86	-.19
47	shame	malu	.68	.81	-.13	schaamte	.23	.78	-.55
46	homesickness	rindu	.58	.88	-.30	heimwee	.80	.97	-.17
45	regret	menyesal	.77	.95	-.18	spijt	.74	.77	-.03
44	longing	kangen	.64	.75	-.11	verlangen	.71	.92	-.21
43	being hurt	tersinggung	.80	.98	-.18	gekwetsheid	.80	.92	-.12

Note: NT, Number of terms; RSQIC, RSQ of Indonesian term in consensus structure; RSQII, RSQ of Indonesian term in Indonesian structure; DI, Difference for Indonesian term; RSQDC, RSQ of Dutch term in consensus structure; RSQDD, RSQ of Dutch term in Dutch structure; DD, Difference for Dutch term.

single point in the emotion space. The remaining 78 Indonesian terms and 78 Dutch terms were represented by separate points.

The RSQ of the three-dimensional solution for these 198 points was .87 in the Indonesian and Dutch sample, against .90 and .88, respectively, for the specific configurations (see Table 1). As expected, the three dimensions could again be interpreted as pleasantness, arousal and dominance.[10]

Discussion

For 50 of the 120 emotion terms in each cultural group we found translation equivalence. It is important to note that these 50 pairs of terms stem from the whole emotion domain: Each underlying dimension and each higher order and basic cluster was represented. Thus, conceptually, these 50 terms formed an adequate basis for comparison. To what extent the 70 remaining terms in each language represent culturally similar or different meanings cannot be determined on the basis of the present study. Cognitive equivalence was not investigated for these terms, but among them are a large number of synonyms and near synonyms of the equivalent terms. We decided on strict criteria for translation equivalence in order to minimise the risk that the terms we used as a reference standard were in any way culturally biased. In the context of the present study, the exclusion of possibly equivalent terms appeared to be a less serious error than the inclusion of nonequivalent terms.

Forty-two of the 50 pairs of terms that met strict standards of translation equivalence also met our requirements for cognitive equivalence. Thus, invariance in the cognitive representation of emotion tended to generalise to the level of separate terms. For these 42 pairs, not only could identity of meaning be assumed, but also equivalence of the basic and higher order cluster structures.

Finally, the fact that the consensus structure over all terms only explained a few percentage points less of the variance in each sample than did the separate solutions for each sample is strong evidence that the 42 cognitively equivalent terms can be used as a common standard for the two cultural groups included in this study. Moreover, the overall structure of emotions can be considered to be virtually equivalent.

At the same time, there was evidence of cultural differences in meaning for eight pairs of translation-equivalent terms that did not meet the criterion

---

[10] A hierarchical cluster analysis on the distances between the 198 Indonesian, Dutch and Dutch-Indonesian emotion terms revealed the four 'basic' clusters mentioned above. A cluster solution with four clusters explained 71% of the variance in the distances between 198 terms in the joint emotion space. A full table is available on request from the first author.

for cognitive equivalence.[11] In part, this finding was followed up in our final study.

STUDY 4: POSITION OF GUILT AND SHAME WITHIN THE COMMON STRUCTURE

The results of the preceding studies formed the basis for a further exploration of the emotions of "shame" and "guilt" in the consensus structure. We found in Study 1 that "shame" received higher prototypicality ratings than "guilt" in both samples. In Study 2, *malu* ("shame") was part of the fear cluster, and *bersalah* ("guilt") part of the sadness cluster for the Indonesian sample, whereas in the Dutch sample *schuld* ("guilt") was part of a shame subcluster within the fear cluster. In Study 3, "shame" and "guilt" were both found to be translation-equivalent, but they did not meet the criteria for cognitive equivalence. To investigate further cross-cultural differences in location we collected ratings on the distance of guilt and shame to other emotion terms.

Method

Respondents.   The respondents were the same as those who participated in Study 1 (71 Indonesian and 89 Dutch students).

Procedure.   Respondents were asked to rate each of the emotion terms from the first study[12] with respect to its distance to "shame" and to "guilt". They used a 5-point scale, with the points labelled as follows: 1 (highly related in meaning), 2 (quite strongly related in meaning), 3 (somewhat related in meaning), 4 (not related in meaning), and 5 (opposite in meaning).

---

[11] There appears to be quite some correspondence between emotion terms that we identified as cognitively biased, and Indonesian terms that according to Heider (1991) had a different meaning than in the US. For example, he found that *takut* ("fear") was characterised by a strong secondary meaning of guilt. Although Heider did not find a guilt cluster, three emotion terms of our guilt cluster (*bersalah*, *berdosa*, and *menyesal*) were translation-equivalent, but not cognitively equivalent. Heider found that *tersinggung* ("being hurt") had a different meaning, as we did. The terms *rindu* ("homesickness") and *kangen* ("longing") formed a hallmark of Minangkabau culture; we found them to be cognitively nonequivalent (in a different Indonesian sample). On the other hand, sadness emotions had the highest prototypicality ratings in Heider's study. This was not replicated in our study. He also found that "jealousy" and "envy" were more related to sadness in the US and more to anger in Indonesia. We found no evidence for bias in the cognitive structure for the jealousy terms "*cemburu*" and "*jaloers*".

[12] The same sets of 153 Indonesian and 137 Dutch emotion terms that were presented in Study 1 were rated with respect to their relation with "guilt" and "shame".

Results

Analysis of the ratings was restricted to the 42 terms that had previously been found to be both cognitively equivalent and translation-equivalent. For reasons of clarity and stability, the focus of the analysis was on the four (basic) clusters, namely positive emotion, anger, sadness, and fear, rather than on the 42 separate pairs of terms.[13] In Figure 3 the average distance ratings are presented graphically. For the results to be reliable, individual differences in the distance ratings

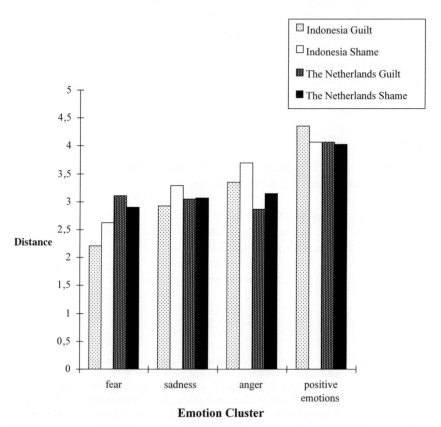

Figure 3. Average distance between "guilt", "shame", and the four basic emotion clusters in Indonesia and The Netherlands.

---

[13] "Inferiority" (*minderwaardigheid, rendah-diri*) was deleted because it was closely related to shame. In addition, "compassion" (*kasihan, medelijden*) and "moved" (*terharu, ontroering*) were deleted; they emerged in MDS configuration between the positive and negative emotion terms and might be poor examples of the sadness cluster. Thus, the construction of the 4 cluster scales was based on 39 terms.

should be consistent for terms within clusters. This was found to be the case; Cronbach's alpha was .78 on average and had a minimum value of .65.

Cross-cultural differences in the relationship between "guilt" and "shame" and the four emotion clusters were further analysed by means of a split-plot ANOVA design (Kirk, 1995). The average rating of the relationship between the terms in an emotion cluster and "shame" and "guilt", respectively, was the within-respondents variable. Country (i.e., Indonesia vs. The Netherlands) was the between-respondents variable. Testing at a .05 level, the main effect for country was not significant (see Table 3). This shows that respondents used the response scale in the same way across the two cultures. All other effects were significant, but only two explained a substantive amount of variance ($\hat{\omega}^2 = .370$ for the main effect of emotion cluster and $\hat{\omega}^2 = .054$ for the interaction between country and emotion cluster). Together: (i) the differences between "guilt" and "shame"; (ii) the interaction between country and the distance ratings for "guilt" and "shame", (iii) the differentiation in their relationship to the four clusters; and (iv) the second order interaction[14] explained only 2.6% of the variance. We therefore made no attempt to interpret these effects.

TABLE 3

Analysis of variance for relationship between "Guilt"/"Shame" and the four emotion clusters in Indonesia and The Netherlands

Source	df	SS	MS	F	$\hat{\omega}^2$
Between subjects					
Country	1	.48	.48	.30	.000
Error (S within country)	158	255.53	1.62		
Within subjects					
Emotion clusters	3	342.12	114.04	518.15**	.370
Guilt/Shame	1	4.19	4.19	19.17**	.004
Guilt/Shame × Emotion clusters	3	10.02	3.34	15.17**	.010
Country × Emotion clusters	3	50.32	16.77	76.20**	.054
Country × Guilt/Shame	1	3.06	3.06	13.88*	.003
Country × Emotion clusters × Guilt/Shame	3	8.59	2.86	13.10**	.009
Error (Guilt/Shame × Emotion clusters × S within country)	1106	243.42	.22		

Note: * $p < .05$; ** $p < .001$; S, subjects.

[14] To prevent any impression of selective presentation of evidence, it should be noted that this effect implied that in Indonesia "shame" (malu) was more distant from fear, sadness, and anger and less distant from positive emotions than "guilt" (bersalah), whereas in The Netherlands "guilt" (schuld) was as negative as "shame" (schaamte). Although this is inconsistent with the distinction between guilt and shame cultures, we found the effect to be too weak to be worth interpreting.

To explore the substantial effects further, the analysis was repeated for each of the two samples separately. In Indonesia pair-wise comparisons with Tukey's Studentised Range statistic showed that *bersalah* (''guilt'') and *malu* (''shame'') were significantly less distant from fear than from sadness ($p < .05$), less distant from sadness than from anger ($p < .05$), and less distant from anger than from positive emotion ($p < .05$). In The Netherlands, the distances of *schuld* (''guilt'') and *schaamte* (''shame'') from the fear, sadness, and anger clusters did not differ significantly ($p > .05$). As expected, the distance to the positive emotion cluster was larger than the distances to the negative emotion clusters ($p < .05$).

Discussion

A key finding from this last study is the replication that there is a difference between Indonesia and The Netherlands with respect to the position of the social emotions ''shame'' and ''guilt''. The distance ratings clearly showed that these two emotion terms have a negative meaning in both cultures (see Figure 3). Within this common pattern, the most notable difference is that in Indonesia both *malu* (''shame'') and *bersalah* (''guilt'') are somewhat less distant from fear and more distant from anger than are *schaamte* (''shame'') and *schuld* (''guilt'') in The Netherlands. The finding that *bersalah* (''guilt'') is close to fear in Indonesia is in line Heider's (1991) findings.

The fact that evidence of cognitive differences was replicated suggests that further research on this issue would be worthwhile. One tentative explanation accounting for all the present findings is based on differences between Indonesia and The Netherlands in the degree to which one is dependent on one's social group. With respect to material well-being this difference is evident; in The Netherlands there are elaborate social welfare systems that are virtually unknown in Indonesia. With respect to nonmaterial aspects such differences are also likely to exist. Thus, it could be that negative evaluation by one's own social group, be it in the form of social contempt (more-shame related) or in the form of social punishment for one's wrongdoing (more guilt-related), is more threatening in Indonesia than in The Netherlands. This could account for the higher prototypicality rankings for both *malu* and *bersalah* in Indonesia than for *schaamte* and *schuld* in The Netherlands. The finding that *malu* and *bersalah* are closer to fear in Indonesia compared to the location of the linguistically equivalent terms in The Netherlands is also compatible with such an interpretation.

Perhaps the most relevant finding from this final study is the absence of the hypothesised differentiation between ''guilt'' and ''shame''. The Indonesian terms for both emotions were rated as more prototypical and more related to ''fear'' and less to ''anger'' than the Dutch terms. This lack of cross-cultural differentiation between guilt and shame casts doubt on the traditional distinction between guilt and shame cultures.

GENERAL DISCUSSION AND CONCLUSIONS

Current theoretical discussions of the relation between culture and emotions continue to focus on the contrasts between relativist and universalist conceptualisations (e.g., Kitayama & Markus, 1994). The fruitfulness of such a dichotomy can be questioned (Mesquita, Frijda, & Scherer, 1997; Poortinga, 1997), but such questioning does not in itself offer a solution. One of the difficulties is that an empirical juxtaposition of the two approaches is problematic. First, it is often unclear what the criteria are for the demarcation between invariance (as observable evidence supporting universality) and cross-cultural variation; depending on their orientation, researchers either emphasise similarities or cross-cultural differences (Poortinga, 1998). Proponents of either approach tend to focus on different aspects of emotions and to present different types of empirical evidence. Comparative, universalistic studies tend to report more data based on instruments and stimuli that originate from one culture, whereas relativistic accounts are mainly based on descriptive analyses within a single cultural group (cf. Mesquita & Frijda, 1992). This focus on different aspects of emotion raises the possibility that the empirical findings may be compatible, but that theoretical positions hinder their integration. In the present studies the demarcation and integration of what is culture-common and what is culture-specific was treated as an empirical question. The approach followed was meant to allow explicitly for the emergence of culture-specific trends in the data that would be more compatible with a relativistic orientation, as well as trends more compatible with a universalistic viewpoint. In this way we tried to avoid the criticism of cultural imposition that often is raised against culture-comparative research (e.g., Greenfield, 1997).

Empirical support for the essential invariance of the overall cognitive structure of emotions and a number of separate emotion terms was established for Indonesian and Dutch students. For the terms found to be equivalent, this outcome strongly restricts the scope for treating emotions as culturally constructed meanings. At the same time, the body of findings creates an empirically anchored reference standard within which remaining differences (qualitative or quantitative) can be further analysed. As well as linguistic and cognitive invariance for 42 pairs of terms, (some degree of) cultural specificity was found for eight pairs of terms, while many other terms still remain unexamined. A separate investigation of the cultural specificity of two emotions, namely "shame" and "guilt" helped to identify some consistent differences in the position of these terms in the cognitive maps of Indonesian and Dutch students and points to the need for further cross-cultural research into these emotions.

Manuscript received 12 September 1999
Revised manuscript received 2 November 2000

REFERENCES

Benedict, R. (1946). *The chrysanthemum and the sword: Patterns of Japanese culture*. Boston, MA: Houghton Mifflin.

Borg, I., & Groenen, P. (1997). *Modern multidimensional scaling: Theory and applications*. New York: Springer.

Boucher, J.D. (1979). Culture and emotion. In A.J. Marsella, R.G. Tharp, & T.V. Ciborowski (Eds.), *Perspectives on cross-cultural psychology* (pp. 159–178). San Diego, CA: Academic Press.

Brandt, M.E., & Boucher, J.D. (1986). Concepts of depression in emotion lexicons of eight cultures. *International Journal of Intercultural Studies, 10*, 321–346.

Breugelmans, S.M., Poortinga, Y.H., Philippot, P., Ambadar, Z., Sriewijono, A., Setiadi, B., & Vaca J. (2000). *Cross-cultural comparisons of body sensations with emotions in Belgium, Indonesia and Mexico*. Manuscript in preparation.

Brislin, R.W. (1980). Translation and content analysis of oral and written material. In H.C. Triandis & J.W. Berry (Eds.), *Handbook of cross-cultural psychology* (Vol. 1, pp. 389–444). Boston: Allyn & Bacon.

Brislin, R.W. (1986). The wording and translation of research instruments. In W.J. Lonner & J.W. Berry (Eds.), *Field methods in cross-cultural research* (pp. 137–164). Newbury Park, CA: Sage.

Church, A.T., Katigbak, M.S., Reyes, J.A.S., & Jensen, S.M. (1998). Language and organization of Filipino emotion concepts: Comparing emotion concepts and dimensions across cultures. *Cognition and Emotion, 12*, 63–92.

Creighton, M.R. (1990). Revisiting shame and guilt cultures: A forty-year pilgrimage. *Ethos, 18*, 279–307.

Davison, M.L. (1983). *Multidimensional scaling*. New York: Wiley.

Echols, J.M., & Shadily, H. (1976). *Kamus Ingris Indonesia*. Jakarta, Indonesia: Gramedia.

Echols, J.M., & Shadily, H. (1990). *Kamus Indonesia Ingris* (3rd ed.). Jakarta, Indonesia: Gramedia.

Ekman, P. (1973). Cross-cultural studies of facial expression. In P. Ekman (Ed.), *Darwin and facial expression* (pp. 169–222). New York: Academic Press.

Everitt, B. (1980). *Cluster analysis* (2nd ed.). New York: Halstead Press.

Fehr, B., & Russell, J.A. (1984). Concept of emotion viewed from a prototype perspective. *Journal of Experimental Psychology: General, 113*, 464–486.

Fontaine, J.R.J., Poortinga, Y.H., Setiadi, B., & Suprapti, S.M. (1996). The cognitive structure of emotions in Indonesia and The Netherlands: A preliminary report. In H. Grad, A. Blanca, & J. Geogras (Eds.), *Key issues in cross-cultural psychology: Selected papers from the Twelfth International Congress of the International Association for Cross-Cultural Psychology* (pp. 159–171). Lisse, The Netherlands: Swets & Zeitlinger.

Frijda, N.H. (1986). *The emotions*. Cambridge, UK: Cambridge University Press.

Frijda, N.H. (1987). Emotion, cognitive structure, and action tendency. *Cognition and Emotion, 1*, 115–143.

Geertz, H. (1961). *The Javanese family*. New York: Free Press.

Greenfield, P.M. (1997). Culture as process: Empirical methods for cultural psychology. In J.W. Berry, Y.H. Poortinga, & J. Pandey (Eds.), *Handbook of cross-cultural psychology* (2nd ed., Vol.1, pp. 301–346). Boston, MA: Allyn & Bacon.

Heider, K.G. (1991). *Landscapes of emotion: Mapping three cultures of emotion in Indonesia*. New York: Cambridge University Press.

Izard, C.E. (1977). *Human emotions*. London: Plenum.

Keeler, W. (1983). Shame and stage fright in Java. *Ethos, 11*, 152–165.

Kirk, R.E. (1995). *Experimental design: Procedures for the behavioral sciences* (3rd ed.). New York: Books/Cole.

Kitayama, S., & Markus, H. R. (Eds.). (1994). *Emotion and culture: Empirical studies of mutual influence*. Washington, DC: APA.

Kruskal, J.B., & Wish, M. (1978). *Multidimensional scaling.* London: Sage.

Lazarus, R. (1991). *Emotion and adaptation.* New York: Oxford University Press.

Levy, R.I. (1984). The emotions in comparative perspective. In K.R. Scherer & P. Ekman (Eds.), *Approaches to emotion* (pp. 397–412). Hillsdale, NJ: Erlbaum.

Lindsay-Hartz, J., De Rivera, J., & Mascolo, M.F. (1995). Differentiating guilt and shame and their effects on motivation. In J.P. Tangney & K.W. Fischer (Eds.), *Self-conscious emotions: The psychology of shame, guilt, embarrassment, and pride* (pp. 274–300) New York: Guilford Press.

Lutz, C. (1988). *Unnatural emotions: Everyday sentiments on a Micronesian atoll and their challenge to western theory.* Chicago, IL: University of Chicago Press.

Lutz, C., & White, G.M. (1986). The anthropology of emotions. *Annual Review of Anthropology, 15,* 405–436.

Markam, S.S. (undated). *Lekseikon dantaksonomi emosi.* Unpublished report, Universitas Indonesia, Jakarta, Indonesia.

Mesquita, B., & Frijda, N.H. (1992). Cultural variations in emotions: A review. *Psychological Bulletin, 112,* 179–204.

Mesquita, B., Frijda, N.H., & Scherer, K.R. (1997). Culture and emotion. In J.W. Berry, P.R. Dasen, & T.S. Saraswathi (Eds.), *Handbook of cross-cultural psychology* (2nd ed., Vol. 2, pp. 255–297). Boston, MA: Allyn & Bacon.

Osgood, C.E., May, W.H., & Miron, M.S. (1975). *Cross-cultural universals in affective meaning.* Urbana, IL: University of Illinois Press.

Piers, G., & Singer, M.B. (1953). *Shame and guilt: A psychoanalytic and a cultural study.* Springfield, IL: Charles Thomas.

Poerwadarminta, W.J.S., & Teeuw, A. (1950). *Indonesisch-Nederlands woordenboek.* Groningen, The Netherlands: Wolters.

Poortinga, Y.H. (1989). Equivalence of cross-cultural data: An overview of basic issues. *International Journal of Psychology, 24,* 737–756.

Poortinga, Y.H. (1997). Towards convergence? In J.W. Berry, Y.H. Poortinga, & J. Pandey (Eds.), *Handbook of cross-cultural psychology* (2nd ed., Vol. 1, pp. 347–387). Boston, MA: Allyn & Bacon.

Poortinga, Y.H. (1998). Cultural diversity and psychological invariance: Methodological and theoretical dilemmas of (cross-)cultural psychology. In J.G. Adair, D. Belanger, & K.L. Dion (Eds.), *Advances in psychological science: Vol. 1. Social, personal, and cultural aspects* (pp. 229–245). Hove, UK: Psychology Press.

Poortinga, Y.H., & Van de Vijver, F.J.R. (1987). Explaining cross-cultural differences: Bias analysis and beyond. *Journal of Cross-Cultural Psychology, 18,* 259–282.

Reisenzein, R., & Schimmack, U. (1999). Similarity judgements and covariations of affects: Findings and implications for affect structure research. *Personality and Social Psychology Bulletin, 5,* 539–555.

Rimé, B., Mesquita, B., Philippot, P., & Boca, S. (1991). Beyond the emotional event: Six studies on the social sharing of emotion. *Cognition and Emotion, 5,* 435–465.

Rosaldo, M. (1980). *Knowledge and passion: Ilongot notions of self and social life.* Cambridge, UK: Cambridge University Press.

Rosch, E. (1978). Principles of categorization. In E. Rosch & B.B. Lloyd (Eds.), *Cognition and categorization* (pp. 27–48). Hillsdale, NJ: Erlbaum.

Russell, J.A. (1983). Pancultural aspects of the human conceptual organization of emotions. *Journal of Personality and Social Psychology, 45,* 1281–1288.

Russell, J.A. (1991). Culture and the categorization of emotions. *Psychological Bulletin, 110,* 426–450.

Russell, J.A., Lewicka, M., & Niit, T. (1989). A cross-cultural study of a circumplex model of affect. *Journal of Personality and Social Psychology, 57,* 848–856.

SAS/STAT user's guide, Version 6 (1994). Cary, NC: SAS Institute.

Scherer, K.R. (1984). Emotion as a multicomponent process: A model and some cross-cultural data. In P. Shaver (Ed.), *Review of personality and social psychology* (Vol. 5, pp. 37–63). Beverly Hills, CA: Sage.

Shaver, P., Schwartz, J., Kirson, D., & O'Connor, C. (1987). Emotion knowledge: Further exploration of a prototype approach. *Journal of Personality and Social Psychology, 52,* 1061–1086.

Shaver, P., Wu, S., & Schwartz, J.C. (1992). Cross-cultural similarities and differences in emotion and its representation: A prototype approach. In M. S. Clark (Ed.), *Review of personality and social psychology: Vol. 13. Emotion* (pp. 175–212). Newbury Park, CA: Sage.

Tangney, J.P. (1990). Assessing individual differences in proneness to shame and guilt: Development of the Self-Conscious Affect and Attribution Inventory. *Journal of Personality and Social Psychology, 59,* 102–111.

The atlas of mankind: The story of peoples of the world, their origins, cultures and beliefs (1982). London: Mitchell Beazley.

Triandis, H.C. (1988). Collectivism versus individualism: A reconceptualization of a basic concept of cross-cultural psychology. In G.K. Verma & C. Bagley (Eds.), *Cross-cultural studies of personality, attitudes and cognition* (pp. 60–95). London: Macmillan.

Triandis, H.C., Leung, K., Villareal, M., & Clack, F.L. (1985). Allocentric versus idiocentric tendencies: Convergent and discriminant validation. *Journal of Research in Personality, 19,* 395–415.

Van Dale Groot Woordenboek Engels-Nederlands (1984). Antwerp, Belgium: Van Dale Lexicografie.

Van Dale Groot Woordenboek Nederlands-Engels (1984). Antwerp, Belgium: Van Dale Lexicografie.

Van de Vijver, F., & Leung, K. (1997). Methods and data analysis of comparative research. In J.W. Berry, Y.H. Poortinga, & J. Pandey (Eds.), *Handbook of cross-cultural psychology* (2nd ed., Vol. 1, pp. 257–300). Boston: Allyn & Bacon.

Van Hemert, D.A., Van de Vijver, F.J.R., Poortinga, Y.H., & Georgas, J. (2001). *Structural and functional equivalence of the Eysenck Personality Questionnaire within and between countries.* Manuscript submitted for publication.

Van Herk, H. (2000). *Equivalence in cross-national context: Methodological and empirical issues in marketing research.* Unpublished doctoral dissertation, Tilburg University, Tilburg, the Netherlands

Young, F.W., & Lewyckyj, R. (1979). *ALSCAL user's guide* (3th ed.). Unpublished manuscript, University of North Carolina at Chapel Hill.

COGNITION AND EMOTION, 2002, *16* (1), 87–101

Crying and mood change: A cross-cultural study

Marleen C. Becht and Ad J.J.M. Vingerhoets

Tilburg University, The Netherlands

Correspondence should be addressed to Marleen C. Becht, Department of Clinical Health Psychology, Tilburg University, P.O. Box 90.153, 5000 LE Tilburg, The Netherlands; e-mail: m.c.becht@kub.nl

The authors wish to express their gratitude to the following colleagues, who participated as collaborators in the ISAC study. This means translating, copying, and administering questionnaires, and the coding and processing of the answers in order to provide useful data: Cyndy Gallois and Matthew Jones, University of Queensland, Australia; Harrald Wallbott, University of Salzburg, Austria; Filip de Fruyt and Anette Cathrin Nilsen, University of Ghent, Belgium; Pierre Philippot, Bernard Rimé, and Emmanuelle Zech, University of Louvain, Louvain-la-Neuve, Belgium; Ana Cristina Limongi and Juan Perez-Ramos, Universidade de São Paulo, Brazil; Elka Todorova, Institute of Sociology, Sofia, Bulgaria; Eugenia Vinet, Universidad de La Frontera, Temuco, Chile; Sun Yuming, Nanjing Normal University, Nanjing, China; Zheng Xue, South China Normal University, Guangzhou, China; Samir Farag, Institute for Strategic Sciences, Cairo, Egypt; Ahmed El Azayem, Abou El Azayem Institute, Cairo, Egypt; Jukka Tontti, University of Helsinki, Finland; Irmela Florin and Stefanie Glaessel, Philipps University, Marburg/Lahn, Germany; Charity Akotia, University of Ghana, Legon Accra, Ghana; Tanya Anagpostopolou, Aristotle University, Thessaloniki, Greece; Aikaterina Gari, University of Crete, Rethymnon, Greece; Imre Janszky, Semmelweis University of Medicine, Budapest, Hungary; Suzanne Kulcsar and Janos Nagy, Eötvos Loránd Tudományetem Bölcsészettudományi Kar, Budapest, Hungary; Fridrik Jonsson & Jakob Smari, University of Iceland, Reykjavik, Iceland; Y. Bhushan, Sandhya Karpe, Narsee Monjee Institute of Management Studies, Bombay, India; H.L. Kaila, S.N.D.T. Women's University, India; Yulia Ayriza, Gadjah Mada University, Yogyakarta, Indonesia; Shulamith Kreitler and Shiri Nussbaum, Tel Aviv University, Israel; Pio Enrico Ricci Bitti, University of Bologna, Italy; Mary Richardson and Susan Anderson, University of the West Indies, Jamaica; Josiah Oketch-Oboth, University of Nairobi, Kenya; Rytis Orintas, Kaunas Academic Clinics, Lithuania; Cynthia Joseph, Universiti Sains Malaysia, Penang, Malaysia; Shishir Subba, Tribhuvan University, Kathmandu, Nepal; Mary-Anne Mace, University of Canterbury, Christchurch, New Zealand; Akinsola Olowu, Obafemi Awolowo University, Ile-Ife, Nigeria; Alegria Majluf, Universidad Peruana Cayetano heredia, Lima, Peru; Joanna Kossewska, Pedagogical University, Krakow, Poland; Felix Neto, Faculdade de psicologia, Porto, Portugal; Adriana Baban, University of Cluj, Cluj-Napoca, Romania; Chon Kyum Koo, Taegu University, South-Korea; Jose Bermudez, Fac. Psicologia, Madrid, Spain; Töres Theorell, National Institue for Psychosocial Factors and Health, Stockholm, Sweden; Ulf Lundberg, Stockholm University, Sweden; Janique Sangsue, University of Geneva, Carouge, Switzerland; Ferda Aysan, Faculty of Education at Buca, Izmir, Turkey; Moira Macquire, University of Luton, Bedfordshire, UK; Randolph Cornelius, Vassar College, Poughkeepsie, NY, USA.

http://www.tandf.co.uk/journals/pp/02699931.html   DOI:10.1080/02699930143000149

This study was designed to determine the influence of crying-related variables and country characteristics on mood change after crying. It was hypothesized that mood improvement would be positively associated to crying frequency, Individualism-Collectivism, and the extent of gender empowerment in a country. Masculinity-Femininity and shame were expected to have a negative relation with mood change. Self-report data were collected in 30 countries (1680 male and 2323 female students). Although bivariate associations yielded inconsistent results, in a regression analysis Masculinity-Femininity, national income, shame, and crying frequency emerged as significant predictors of mood change, all in the anticipated direction. The results suggest that how one feels after a crying episode depends on how common crying is in one's culture and on general feelings of shame over crying. It also seems that (perceptions of) role patterns may play an important part in the experience of mood change.

Although recent research has taught us much about the antecedents and consequences of emotions and emotional behaviour (cf. Frijda, 1986; Scherer, Matsumoto, Wallbott, & Kudoh, 1988; Scherer, Wallbott, & Summerfield, 1986), surprisingly little is known about crying. To date, basic questions concerning the nature, context, and functions of crying remain largely unanswered (see Vingerhoets, Cornelius, Van Heck, & Becht, 2000). The popular press and clinicians have congruent assumptions about crying resulting in catharsis, mood improvement, and even better health (cf. Cornelius, 1986; Vingerhoets & Scheirs, 2001). In the scientific literature it is not difficult to find authors who share this conviction and the following are a few examples. Menninger, Mayman, and Pruyser (1964) noted that crying may be considered as "perhaps the most human and universal of all relief measures" (p. 138); Mills and Wooster (1987) speak of crying as "a vital part of a healing or growing process, that should not be hindered" (p. 125); and Solter (1995) characterises crying as an inborn healing mechanism. Thus, it appears that the connection between crying and catharsis is deeply embedded in Western folk psychology, as well as in some more formal psychological theories (Cornelius, 1997, 2001).

Whereas some theorists consider crying as a mechanism serving detoxification of the body (Frey, 1985), others regard it as a mere epiphenomenon, having no causal relationship with relief or mood improvement (e.g., Efran & Spangler, 1979). According to Frijda (1986), crying is the ultimate sign of powerlessness. In addition, several authors emphasise the communicative aspects of crying, signalling distress and the need for help (e.g., Kottler, 1996; Melinand, 1902; Murube, Murube, & Murube, 1999; Roes, 1990). The facilitation of attachment is also emphasised, because crying strengthens mutual bonds (Bekker & Vingerhoets, 2001; Zeifman, 2001) and induces social support.

Concerning the effects of crying on mood, empirical research has yielded some noteworthy discrepancies (see Cornelius, 1997 for a review). Retrospective studies in which subjects were asked to remember a recent crying episode generally suggest that crying improves mood (e.g., Bindra, 1972; Frey,

Hoffman-Ahern, Johnson, Lykken, & Tuason, 1983; Kraemer & Hastrup, 1986). In contrast, laboratory studies in which participants are exposed to sad films consistently show that those who have cried feel worse and have more negative moods than those who have not shed any tears (e.g., Choti, Marston, Holston, & Hart, 1987; Gross, Fredrickson, & Levenson, 1994; Martin & Labott, 1991). The reasons for this discrepancy are unclear. Because positive effects of crying are generally expected, people's recollections of their own experiences may be biased. Alternatively, Cornelius (1997) has suggested that mood improvement after crying may be mediated by the reactions of the social environment. If others react positively with comfort, social support, and perhaps even the removal of the source of the distress, mood improvement is a very likely result. In addition, there are speculations about psychobiological processes (e.g., the release of endorphins; cf. Vingerhoets & Scheirs, 2001) that may be held responsible for the positive effects of crying. These processes may need some time to manifest themselves, or may only be operational if one cries with a certain intensity, which could explain why these positive effects are not found in laboratory studies.

Mood change may also be related to crying frequency. Schlosser's (1986) findings revealed that those persons who cry more frequently are most likely to report mood improvement. Labott and Teleha (1996) further demonstrated that frequent (female) criers felt more happy with the instruction to let their tears flow, whereas women who reported crying only seldom felt better in the condition in which they where requested to withold their tears. The findings reviewed above suggest a positive relationship between crying frequency and positive mood change after crying.

We further hypothesise that the effects of crying on mood are mediated by cultural factors. As has been made clear by several authors (e.g., Georges, 1995; Wellenkamp, 1995), in some cultures the expression of intense emotions, such as crying, is disapproved of, or only allowed in very specific and well-defined situations. For example, the Balinese are not allowed to cry during the whole period of mourning after the death of a loved one (Rosenblatt, Walsh, & Jackson, 1976).

Georgas, Van de Vijver, and Berry (2000) have identified country specific ecosocial indices that represent the cultural background according to the eco-cultural model of Berry, Poortinga, Segall, and Dasen (1992). These indices appear to be closely related to psychological variables when analysing scores stemming from several cultures, and offer more possibilities to determine the nature of cultural differences than just a comparison across nations, as is often the case in cross-cultural research. However, in order to be able to use country-level variables (forming one value per country) appropriately, one should be aware that the psychological measures should also be at the country level. The sample should therefore consist of quite a range of cultures, which is often not the case.

One important country-level variable is Masculinity-Feminity (Hofstede, 1980, 1983). In countries scoring high on masculinity, men are expected to feel more ashamed of their crying than in countries scoring low on masculinity. Consequently, we expect less mood improvement in masculine countries compared to more feminine countries.

In collectivistic societies like Indonesia and Japan (Hofstede, 1980), in which common interests prevail over individual goals, the display of intense emotions is regarded as less appropriate than it is in individualistic cultures (Matsumoto, 1990). It can thus be hypothesised that people from collectivistic countries report less mood improvement after crying than people from individualistic societies.

In countries favouring stereotypic gender roles, more substantial sex differences in crying are expected. The extent to which a country favours sex-stereotypical roles is reflected by the extent of women's participation in political and economical life, which is represented by the Gender Empowerment Measure (GEM; United Nations Development Programme, 1998).

Additional country characteristics measured in the present study are national income and mean annual temperature. Wealthier countries appear to be more individualistic (Georgas et al., 2000), so national income should also contribute to positive mood change, paralleling the effect of individualism. The choice of temperature as a possible relevant variable was prompted by Pennebaker, Rimé, and Blankenship (1996), who found that a warm climate promotes the expression of emotions. However, rather than finding higher crying frequencies in warmer countries, the opposite appears to be true: Crying frequency is negatively related to average annual temperature (Becht, Poortinga, & Vingerhoets, 2001). In the present study we will expand on these relationships by focusing on the relationship with mood change.

To summarise, the objectives of the present study are to obtain insight into cultural differences in self-reported mood change after crying. It is generally expected that the more people cry, the more they report a positive mood change after crying. However, this relation is assumed to be mediated by (expectations about) the reactions from the social environment. Thus, the more people feel ashamed of crying, the less positive should be their mood change. This implies that people from collectivistic and masculine countries and from countries with a low GEM will show less mood improvement after crying than people from individualistic and feminine countries, and from countries with a high GEM. Finally, we will explore the relationship between mood change after crying and national income and mean annual temperature.

METHOD

Respondents

This study formed part of the International Study on Adult Crying (ISAC), a large continuous international study in which several aspects of crying are investigated. The ISAC project started in 1996. In every country an attempt was made to obtain data of at least 50 male and 50 female respondents, mainly students. For the analyses reported here, data were available from 2181 men and 2915 women living in 35 countries. To improve sample homogeneity, only young adults aged between 16 and 28 years were included in the data analyses. Moreover, only data from countries with at least 30 participants of each sex were included. Fifty-four respondents indicated they had not cried since they were 17 years of age. Because they comprised only 1.3% of the sample, scattered over many countries, their data were removed from the sample and not further considered. The final dataset consisted of 4003 respondents from 30 countries (2323 women, 1680 men), with a mean age of 21.3 years (men 21.9; women 20.8). Sample information per country is summarised in Table 1.

Measures

The ISAC questionnaire (Vingerhoets, 1995) is based on several existing questionnaires (e.g., the Weeping Frequency Scale, Labott & Martin, 1987; the Crying Frequency Scale, Kraemer, & Hastrup, 1986; Crying Questionnaire, Williams, 1982; Williams & Morris, 1996), and has been further extended in consultation with the international collaborators. The aim was to develop a relatively context-free instrument, which means that it uses concepts that are universally applicable, as far as can be established (Berry et al., 1992). The basic questionnaire was written in English. To produce translations into different languages, the collaborators from non-English-speaking countries were instructed to use the back-translation procedure described by Brislin (1980). The following variables included in this questionnaire were used to address the present research questions:

Mood change was assessed using a scale including the following seven mood states: (1) relaxed, (2) in control, (3) happy, (4) relieved, (5) tense, (6) depressed, and (7) sad. The respondents indicated whether they *generally* experienced more, the same, or less of the specified mood after a crying episode, as compared to before. For each mood indicator, a positive change was scored with +1 ("more" for mood states 1 to 4, "less" for mood states 5–7), no change was scored as 0, and a negative change was scored as −1. The scale yields a total score (Mood Change Score: MCS) ranging between −7 and +7, with −7 indicating a maximum deterioration of one's mood after crying, and +7 a maximum mood improvement. Cronbach's alpha for this scale was .77.

Shame was assessed by the extent to which the respondent agreed with the following item: "I feel ashamed when I am crying". A 7-point Likert scale yielded a minimum score of 1 (I do not agree) and a maximum of 7 (I agree).

Estimated Crying Frequency (ECF) is the (recollected) number of times the respondent has cried in the last four weeks. Most of the respondents cried between zero and 10 times; the responses of the 2.7% of respondents who reported crying more than 10 times were discarded from analyses.

TABLE 1
Sample size and mean age per country

Country	Women		Men		Total	
	N	Mean age	N	Mean age	N	Mean age
1. Australia	174	19.0	59	20.3	233	19.7
2. Belgium	125	28.5	31	33.6	156	31.0
3. Brazil	178	27.5	145	23.7	323	25.6
4. Bulgaria	32	30.5	32	29.5	64	30.0
5. Chile	52	21.4	52	22.1	104	21.7
6. China	92	21.8	56	22.2	148	22.0
7. Finland	31	27.5	39	26.9	70	27.2
8. Germany	45	22.2	32	24.3	77	23.3
9. Ghana	40	27.1	39	27.6	79	27.4
10. Greece	76	21.5	34	22.9	110	22.2
11. Iceland	154	24.7	126	24.4	280	24.6
12. India	85	25.7	116	28.3	201	27.0
13. Indonesia	105	21.3	36	27.0	141	24.2
14. Israel	48	22.1	47	23.3	95	22.7
15. Italy	78	20.1	35	19.7	113	19.9
16. Kenya	71	22.2	85	21.1	156	21.7
17. Lithuania	135	19.7	53	19.9	188	19.8
18. Malaysia	48	21.9	39	21.5	87	21.7
19. Nepal	45	22.8	49	23.4	94	23.1
20. Netherlands	75	21.1	82	22.6	157	21.9
21. Nigeria	36	19.8	51	22.0	87	20.9
22. Peru	48	21.0	43	21.2	91	21.1
23. Poland	56	19.4	52	20.6	108	20.0
24. Portugal	59	23.0	60	23.1	119	23.1
25. Romania	90	21.9	69	21.8	159	21.8
26. Spain	50	20.2	49	20.6	99	20.4
27. Sweden	30	26.8	28	27.9	58	27.4
28. Switzerland	59	21.9	40	25.4	99	23.6
29. Turkey	50	21.6	50	22.1	100	21.8
30. USA	156	18.4	51	18.4	207	18.4
Total	2323	20.8	1680	21.9	4003	21.3

Apart from these questionnaire variables, we made use of the following country characteristics:

Individualism-Collectivism and *Masculinity-Femininity* are country characteristics distinguished by Hofstede (1980, 1983). In his operationalisation, Individualism-Collectivism refers to free time and freedom and independency from the organisation one is affiliated to. Masculinity-Femininity refers to the importance of material and status aspects of the job and the company and the relative unimportance of social relations between colleagues and secondary aspects like living area. Unfortunately, Hofstede did not report data for 10 of the countries included in our dataset. To avoid the loss of data, we followed Fischer and Manstead (2000) by using Taiwanese data for China, West African data for Ghana and Nigeria, East African data for Kenya, Norwegian data for Iceland, and (former) Yugoslavian data for Lithuania, Romania, Poland, and Bulgaria.

The *Gender Empowerment Measure* (GEM) of the United Nations Development Program (1996) is an index of the degree of participation of women in economic and political life. It tracks the percentage of women in parliament and in administration and management, the percentage of female professional and technical workers, and women's earned income share as a percentage of that of men. Data for five specific countries were lacking, namely, Ghana, Kenya, Lithuania, Nepal, and Nigeria. For these countries values were substituted from the closest neighbouring country (Togo, Sudan, Estonia, India, and Cameroon, respectively).

National income is operationalised by using the Gross Domestic Product per capita (GDPpc), which is a calculation of the buying power of a country per capita in US dollars, derived from the World Factbook (CIA, 1998). The figures were mostly based on the year 1996, except for the countries Bulgaria, China, Finland, Malaysia, Peru, Poland, Romania, and Turkey, for which estimates from 1998 were used.

Mean Annual Temperature (MAT) was retrieved from the database of Georgas (see Georgas et al., 2000). Data for Lithuania and Iceland were missing and were substituted by Polish and Norwegian data, respectively.

Procedure

The procedure of data collection varied somewhat among countries. In some countries (e.g., the Netherlands) the questionnaire was taken home to be completed. Elsewhere (e.g., Greece), it was administered during lectures. At some universities, students were requested to cooperate, in other cases they participated in order to fulfil course requirements or to earn a small sum of money, and in still other cases cooperation was entirely on a voluntary basis. Data collected from more than one location within a country (e.g., Belgium, Brazil, Greece, India) were pooled. Data entry, coding, and analyses were carried out at Tilburg University (The Netherlands).

RESULTS

Crying frequency

Estimated crying frequency (ECF) differed significantly between the sexes. Men reported having cried 1.0 times on average in the previous four weeks, whereas women reported an average of 2.7 times ($F(1, 3663) = 437.9, p \leq .001, \eta^2 = .10$).

Differences were also found among countries $(F(29, 3663) = 5.5, p \leq .001)$. The USA scored on average 2.7, whereas China scored 0.9 (see Table 2 for the means of all countries). The eta squared for country was .04, and for the (significant) interaction between country and sex .02 $(F(29, 3663) = 2.3, p \leq .001)$.

TABLE 2
Average country scores for mood change, estimated crying frequency, and shame

Country	MCS		ECF		Shame	
	Men	Women	Men	Women	Men	Women
	M (SD)	M (SD)	M (SD)	M (SD)	M (SD)	M (SD)
Australia	2.7 (3.6)	2.7 (3.4)	1.5 (1.7)	2.8 (2.2)	4.5 (1.9)	3.8 (2.0)
Belgium	4.0 (2.4)	3.7 (2.9)	1.3 (2.2)	3.3 (2.6)	4.4 (1.7)	4.5 (1.9)
Brazil	3.3 (2.9)	4.2 (2.6)	1.0 (1.5)	3.1 (2.6)	4.2 (2.0)	3.4 (2.1)
Bulgaria	2.4 (2.8)	2.8 (3.0)	0.3 (0.6)	2.1 (2.0)	4.0 (2.5)	3.3 (1.9)
Chile	4.5 (2.4)	4.1 (2.4)	1.2 (1.4)	3.6 (2.3)	3.5 (2.0)	3.2 (1.7)
China	3.0 (2.7)	3.6 (2.5)	0.4 (0.6)	1.4 (1.5)	3.4 (2.1)	3.0 (2.0)
Finland	4.7 (2.4)	4.9 (2.5)	1.4 (2.2)	3.2 (2.5)	2.9 (1.8)	3.0 (1.9)
Germany	3.7 (2.7)	3.8 (2.3)	1.6 (1.9)	3.3 (2.6)	2.8 (1.8)	3.4 (1.9)
Ghana	2.5 (2.8)	4.2 (2.5)	0.7 (1.4)	1.7 (2.1)	3.7 (2.2)	3.6 (1.7)
Greece	3.6 (2.2)	3.7 (2.7)	1.1 (1.5)	2.8 (2.5)	4.1 (2.2)	3.9 (2.2)
Iceland	3.6 (2.9)	4.6 (2.7)	0.6 (1.4)	1.9 (1.9)	3.9 (2.0)	3.7 (1.9)
India	3.6 (2.8)	3.1 (3.4)	1.0 (2.0)	2.5 (2.2)	3.8 (2.1)	3.4 (2.0)
Indonesia	2.4 (3.3)	3.8 (2.8)	1.0 (1.4)	2.1 (2.0)	4.8 (2.4)	4.2 (1.9)
Israel	2.8 (3.2)	2.7 (3.1)	1.3 (1.5)	2.7 (2.3)	3.5 (2.1)	3.2 (1.7)
Italy	2.9 (3.5)	3.1 (2.5)	1.7 (2.7)	3.2 (3.2)	4.1 (2.0)	3.6 (2.2)
Kenya	3.9 (3.5)	3.9 (3.3)	1.3 (1.9)	2.1 (2.2)	4.8 (2.4)	3.7 (2.5)
Lithuania	3.0 (3.0)	4.5 (2.0)	0.8 (1.2)	3.1 (2.7)	4.1 (2.1)	3.5 (2.0)
Malaysia	2.3 (2.8)	3.8 (3.0)	0.6 (1.0)	2.1 (2.1)	4.9 (2.2)	3.9 (1.8)
Nepal	2.0 (3.0)	1.3 (3.2)	1.9 (2.9)	2.0 (2.4)	4.3 (2.2)	4.5 (2.1)
Netherlands	4.4 (2.3)	4.3 (2.3)	0.9 (1.6)	3.4 (2.4)	4.9 (2.0)	4.5 (1.6)
Nigeria	1.9 (3.5)	3.0 (3.6)	1.0 (2.1)	1.4 (2.4)	4.8 (2.4)	3.9 (2.4)
Peru	1.7 (4.5)	3.1 (4.5)	0.6 (1.0)	1.6 (2.1)	4.3 (1.9)	4.5 (1.5)
Poland	2.3 (2.5)	3.5 (2.9)	0.9 (1.8)	3.1 (2.3)	4.5 (2.2)	4.4 (2.0)
Portugal	3.9 (2.4)	3.6 (2.7)	0.6 (1.1)	2.3 (2.1)	3.6 (2.1)	3.6 (2.0)
Romania	2.7 (3.2)	3.8 (2.8)	0.9 (1.4)	2.4 (2.5)	4.0 (2.2)	3.5 (2.1)
Spain	3.8 (2.9)	3.6 (2.3)	0.6 (1.1)	2.8 (2.3)	3.7 (2.1)	3.2 (2.0)
Sweden	4.4 (2.3)	4.9 (2.2)	0.8 (1.2)	2.8 (1.9)	3.3 (1.7)	3.5 (1.7)
Switzerland	2.8 (3.2)	3.5 (2.9)	0.7 (1.4)	3.3 (2.9)	4.8 (2.0)	4.7 (2.1)
Turkey	3.2 (2.7)	3.3 (2.8)	1.1 (1.6)	3.6 (3.1)	4.4 (2.4)	3.4 (2.2)
USA	2.7 (3.4)	3.0 (3.1)	1.9 (2.2)	3.5 (2.8)	3.9 (2.3)	3.7 (2.0)
Total	3.3 (3.0)	3.7 (2.9)	1.0 (1.7)	2.7 (2.5)	4.1 (2.2)	3.7 (2.0)

Note: MCS = Mood Change Score; ECF = Estimated Crying Frequency; Shame = feeling ashamed when crying.

Mood change after crying

Both men and women indicated that they generally felt better after crying ($M =$ 3.3 and 3.7, respectively; $F(1, 3722) = 18.4$, $p \leq .001$), with sex hardly explaining any variance ($\eta^2 < .01$). Differences among countries were also found ($F(29, 3722) = 5.6$, $p \leq .001$, $\eta^2 = .04$), with Finnish respondents scoring highest ($M = 4.8$) and Nepalese lowest ($M = 1.7$; see Table 2 for the means of all countries). There was a small interaction effect between sex and country ($F(29, 3722) = 1.5$, $p = .052$, $\eta^2 = .01$).

Shame

Men felt more ashamed while crying than women did ($M = 4.1$ and 3.7, SD $= 2.1$ and 2.0, respectively; $F(1, 3870) = 21.5$, $p \leq .001$), but the percentage of variance explained by sex was low ($\eta^2 < .01$). Feelings of shame while crying were also significantly different among countries ($F(29, 3870) = 5.8$, $p \leq .001$; $\eta^2 = .04$). The lowest average score was found in Finland, the highest in Switzerland (see Table 2). There was no significant interaction between sex and country.

Crying frequency, mood change, and shame

For each country, means and standard deviations were calculated for the male and female samples separately. These aggregated scores were used in succeeding analyses. MCS at country level was negatively associated with shame, but significantly so only for men ($r = -.45$, $p \leq .05$, for men; $r = -.27$, n.s., for women). ECF related neither to MCS ($rs = .07$ and .21, n.s., for men and women, respectively), nor to shame ($rs = -.07$, and $-.05$, n.s., for men and women, respectively).

Mood change, crying-related variables, and country characteristics

Pearson's correlations between MCS, ECF, shame (all aggregated), and the country characteristics are shown in Table 3. Significant associations for women were found between MCS and GEM and MF, and between ECF and IC, GDPpc, and MAT. For men, significant links were found between MCS and GDPpc, GEM, and MAT, between shame and MAT, and between ECF and IC, MF, and GDPpc.

Finally, a stepwise regression analysis was performed with MCS as the dependent variable and sex, shame, ECF, and the country indices as independent variables. Significant predictors were ECF, shame, and the country indices MF and GDPpc (see Table 4). This indicates that in more feminine and wealthier countries, and in countries were the average crying frequency is relatively high and feelings of shame are relatively low, crying generally results in a (reported) mood improvement.

TABLE 3

Correlations between country-level variables and mood change, shame, and crying frequency

	IC	MF	GDPpc	GEM	MAT
Women					
MCS	−.01	−.53**	.18	.37*	−.23
Shame	.10	.20	.05	−.02	.12
ECF	.56***	.09	.58***	.43*	−.46*
Men					
MCS	.35	−.32	.38*	.42*	−.42*
Shame	−.14	.14	−.22	−.33	.38*
ECF	.50**	.47**	.32	.00	−.07

Note: MCS = Mood Change Score; Shame = feeling ashamed when crying; ECF = Estimated Crying Frequency; IC = Individualism-Collectivism; MF = Masculinity-Femininity; GDPpc = Gross Domestic Product per capita; GEM = Gender Empowerment Measure; MAT = Mean Annual Temperature.
*$p <= .05$; **$p <= .01$; ***$p <= .001$.

TABLE 4

Summary of stepwise regression of mood change on scores averaged per country for each sex ($n = 60$)

Variable	B	SE B	Beta	p
Shame	−.402	.160	−.275	*
MF	−.019	.005	−.417	**
GDPpc	.000024	.000	.243	*
ECF	.187	.092	.226	*

Note: $R^2 = .423$; Shame = feeling ashamed when crying; MF = Masculinity-Femininity; GDPpc = Gross Domestic Product per capita; ECF = Estimated Crying Frequency.
*$p <= .05$; **$p <= .001$.

DISCUSSION

The aim of the present study was to obtain more insight into the determinants of mood change after crying. We proposed that—independent of post-crying whether mood change is a principally socially determined effect, or has a more biological basis—it can be expected that it is strongly affected by social and cultural factors. To investigate the role of these factors, we focused on associations between certain country characteristics and mood change.

The present study revealed significant differences both between sexes and between countries for crying frequency, shame over crying, and mood change after crying. Corroborating previous findings (see Vingerhoets & Scheirs, 2000 for an overview) women reported crying more frequently. In addition, they reported less shame over crying and a slightly better mood after crying than men, but these differences were hardly relevant. Generally, for both men and women in all countries, a positive mood change after crying was found.

The main focus of the present study was on the relationship between mood change after crying and country characteristics. In order to examine these relationships, we calculated bivariate correlations between the variables and performed a regression analysis with mood change as the dependent variable and crying-related variables and country characteristics as predictors. These two types of analyses yielded dissimilar findings, which reflects the relatively strong interrelations between the predictors. One therefore needs to be careful when interpreting the extent to which our hypotheses were supported.

Focusing on the bivariate findings, a negative association between shame and mood change was anticipated, but this association was only significant for men. Contrary to expectations, no significant relation between mood change and crying frequency was revealed. In addition, the associations with the country characteristics were not always as anticipated. In correspondence with our hypotheses was the positive association between mood change and the extent to which women participated in public life. However, the data failed to show a connection between Individualism-Collectivism and mood change. The negative association of mood change with Masculinity-Femininity was in line with our hypothesis, but was only significant for women. For men there was a positive relation between mood change and national income, but not for women. Contrary to expectations, a positive mood change appeared to be negatively associated with mean annual temperature, but only so for men. In summary, the pattern of findings of the bivariate relationships only partially supported our hypotheses. In the regression analysis, we found a significant influence of crying frequency and shame on mood change, and Masculinity-Femininity and national income emerged as important country variables. These associations were all in accordance with our expectations. Moreover, sex did not appear to make a significant difference.

Recapitulating, the analyses at bivariate level produced inconclusive results. Multivariate analyses yielded a clearer pattern of results: In more feminine and wealthier countries where one cries relatively often and one experiences little shame over crying, people generally report more mood improvement after crying. Although some slight sex differences were found, the general pattern of findings was consistent for both men and women. As the Masculinity-Femininity dimension is not directly related to differences between men and women, but rather to constructs created by experiences and expectations (Fischer, Becht, Bekker, Vingerhoets, & Manstead, in press), our findings suggest that it is the perception of role patterns which influences post-crying mood change, rather than the actual status of women in society or biologically based sex differences. In particular, the idea that crying is not appropriate for the masculine repertoire seems important. Even if crying were to result in mood improvement (e.g., as a consequence of neurophysiological processes), other experienced or anticipated consequences (e.g., loss of face) may have a counter-effect, possibly nullifying or at least reducing any positive change.

The present results are in line with the notion that the degree to which one reports relief or mood improvement after crying depends on sociocultural factors. The present macrolevel data indirectly lend support to Cornelius' (1997) hypothesis that mood improvement after crying is a consequence of how the social environment reacts to the crying. From the psychological point of view, it is important to examine whether the associations reported here also hold at the microlevel. Until now, little research has been done, but the preliminary data reported by Cornelius (1997), and the findings of Labott and Teleha (1996) and Schlosser (1986) in addition to the findings presented here, emphasise the need to examine mood change after crying in relation to experienced shame, the presence of others, and how appropriate crying in that specific situation is perceived by oneself and one's peers.

The fact that experienced mood change is also dependent on cultural factors does not necessarily imply that psychobiological factors have no role to play. In several other psychobiological phenomena, including premenstrual syndrome and "maternity blues", a complex interaction between biological and socio-cultural factors has been suggested (e.g., Eugster, Horsten, & Vingerhoets, 2001), showing that such an interaction is by no means exceptional. Apart from paying more attention to person characteristics, specific context variables, and the broader sociocultural setting, we also argue that the investigation of psy-chobiological processes should not be neglected in future studies of crying and mood change.

For an adequate evaluation of the findings of cross-cultural studies, one needs to be aware of the possible role of confounds and bias. The present study is vulnerable to the same general problems as those outlined by Scherer (1997) in his cross-cultural ISEAR project. First, it is entirely based on self-reports, which are (besides their well-known general weaknesses) especially vulnerable to response bias. If respondents in some countries tend to score high on all measures and participants in other countries generally obtain low scores, this will result in positive correlations between variables. A replication of the findings reported here using observational methods would be highly desirable. Second, the samples (university students) are, of course, not representative of the general population of the respective countries. There can even be cross-cultural differences in the representativeness of students for a national population. On the other hand, as Scherer (1997) has pointed out, the use of student samples makes the datasets more homogeneous across countries, and thus more appropriate for purposes of comparison. It should also be noted that by using one (averaged) score per country, the sample size for analyses becomes relatively small, although aggregated data are generally more stable than data from individual cases. A further limitation of the present study is the substitution of country characteristics when certain information about a specific country was missing. Data from neighbouring countries concerning weather indices are likely to be reasonably valid, but whether psychocultural characteristics can be substituted as easily from one country to another is more debatable. Finally, there is the issue of whether a single index can adequately represent the wide variety of cultural groups within some countries.

Despite these weaknesses, the present study has yielded some intriguing findings that should help to promote the development of more specific hypotheses about the role of cultural factors in crying and its relation to health and well-being. The present data suggest that how one feels after a crying episode is influenced by how crying is appraised and what the (expected) reactions from the social environment are. If crying is considered an adequate or justified reaction, others may offer comfort and emotional support; however, if the shedding of tears is regarded as inappropriate, it is more likely to lead to disapproval and anger. Such reactions, which may in turn be determined by whether or not cultural (display) rules are violated or complied with, may be important determinants of how one feels after a crying episode. Whatever the case, crying appears to be a universally strong social stimulus which seldom leaves one's own mood and behaviour, and that of others, unaffected. Future studies should seek to unravel the factors that exert an influence on crying behaviour and its effect on mood in specific situations.

Manuscript received 15 November 1999
Revised manuscript received 12 January 2001

REFERENCES

Becht, M.C., Poortinga, Y.H. & Vingerhoets, A.J.J.M. (2001). Crying across countries. In A.J.J.M. Vingerhoets & R.R. Cornelius (Eds.), *Adult crying: A biopsychosocial approach* (pp. 135–158). Hove, UK: Brunner-Routledge.

Bekker, M.H.J., & Vingerhoets, A.J.J.M. (in press). Male and female tears: Swallowing versus shedding? The relationship between crying, biological sex and gender. In A.J.J.M. Vingerhoets & R.R. Cornelius (Eds.), *Adult crying: A biopsychosocial approach* (pp. 91–113). Hove, UK: Brunner-Routledge.

Berry, J.W., Poortinga, Y.H., Segall, M.H., & Dasen, P.R. (1992). *Cross-cultural psychology: Research and applications.* Cambridge, UK: Cambridge University Press.

Bindra, D. (1972). Weeping: A problem of many facets. *Bulletin of the British Psychological Society, 25,* 281–284.

Brislin, R.W. (1980). Translation and content analysis of oral and written material. In H.C. Triandis & J.W. Berry (Eds.), *Handbook of cross-cultural psychology: Vol. 2. Methodology* (pp. 389–444). Boston, MA: Allyn & Bacon.

CIA (1998, March). *The World Factbook 1997.* Internet: http://www.odci.gov/cia/publications/factbook.

Choti, S.E., Marston, A.R., Holston, S.G., & Hart, J.T. (1987). Gender and personality variables in film-induced sadness and crying. *Journal of Social and Clinical Psychology, 5,* 535–544.

Cornelius, R.R. (1986). *Prescience in the pre-scientific study of weeping? A history of weeping in the popular press from the mid-1800's to the present.* Paper presented at the 57th Annual meeting of the Eastern Psychological Association, New York.

Cornelius, R.R. (1997). Toward a new understanding of weeping and catharsis? In A.J.J.M. Vingerhoets, F.J. Van Bussel, & A.J.W. Boelhouwer (Eds.), *The (non)expression of emotions in health and disease* (pp. 303–322). Tilburg, The Netherlands: Tilburg University Press.

Cornelius, R.R. (2001). Crying and catharsis. In A.J.J.M. Vingerhoets & R. R. Cornelius (Eds.), *Adult crying: A biopsychosocial approach* (pp. 199–211). Hove, UK: Brunner-Routledge.

Efran, J.S., & Spangler, T.J. (1979). Why grown-ups cry: A two-factor theory and evidence from The Miracle Worker. *Motivation and Emotion, 3,* 63–72.

Eugster, A., Horsten, M., & Vingerhoets A.J.J.M. (2001). Menstrual cycle, pregnancy, and crying. In A.J.J.M. Vingerhoets & R.R. Cornelius (Eds.), *Adult crying: A biopsychosocial approach* (pp. 177–198). Hove, UK: Brunner-Routledge.

Fischer, A.H., Becht, M.C., Bekker, M.H.J., Vingerhoets, A.J.J.M. & Manstead, A.S.R. (in press). Femininity, masculinity, and the riddle of crying. In I. Nyclicek, L. Temoshok, & A.J.J.M. Vingerhoets (Eds.), *Emotions, well-being and health.* Hove, UK: Brunner-Routledge.

Fischer, A.H., & Manstead, A.S.R. (2000). The relation between gender and emotions in different cultures. In A.H. Fischer (Ed.), *Gender and emotions: Social psychological perspectives* (pp. 71–96). Cambridge, UK: Cambridge University Press.

Frey, W.H. (1985). *Crying: The mystery of tears.* Minneapolis, MN: Winston Press.

Frey, W.H., Hoffman-Ahern, C., Johnson, R.A., Lykken, D.T., & Tuason, V.B. (1983). Crying behavior in the human adult. *Integrative Psychiatry, 1,* 94–100.

Frijda, N.H. (1986). *The emotions.* New York: Cambridge University Press.

Georgas, J., Van de Vijver, F.J.R., & Berry, J.W. (2000). *Ecosocial indices and psychological variables in cross-cultural research.* Manuscript submitted for publication.

Georges, E. (1995). A cultural and historical perspective on confession. In J.W. Pennebaker (Ed.), *Emotion, disclosure and health* (pp. 11–24). Washington, DC: APA.

Gross, J.J., Fredrickson, B.L., & Levenson, R.W. (1994). The psychophysiology of crying. *Psychophysiology, 31,* 460–468.

Hofstede, G. (1980). *Culture's consequences.* Beverly Hills, CA: Sage.

Hofstede, G. (1983). National cultures in four dimensions: A research based theory of cultural differences among nations. *International Studies of Man & Organisations, 8,* 46–74.

Kottler, J.A. (1996). *The language of tears.* San Francisco, CA: Jossey-Bass.

Kraemer, D.L., & Hastrup, J.L. (1986). Crying in natural settings: Global estimates, self-monitored frequencies, depression and sex differences in an undergraduate population. *Behaviour Research and Therapy, 24,* 371–373.

Labott, S.M., & Martin, R.B. (1987). The stress-moderating effects of weeping and humor. *Journal of Human Stress, 13,* 159–164.

Labott, S.M., & Teleha, M.K. (1996). Weeping propensity and the effects of laboratory expression or inhibition. *Motivation and Emotion, 20,* 273.

Martin, R.B., & Labott, S.M. (1991). Mood following emotional crying: Effects of the situation. *Journal of Research in Personality, 25,* 218–244.

Matsumoto, D. (1990). Cultural similarities and differences in display rules. *Motivation and Emotion, 14,* 195–214.

Mélinand, C. (1902, June). Why do we cry? The psychology of tears. *Current Literature, 32,* 696–699.

Menninger, K., Mayman, M., & Pruyser, P. (1964). *The vital balance.* New York: Viking.

Mills, C.K., & Wooster, A.D. (1987). Crying in the counseling situation. *British Journal of Guidance and Counseling, 15,* 125–131.

Murube, J., Murube, L., & Murube, A. (1999). Origin and types of emotional tearing. *European Journal of Ophthalmology, 9,* 77–84.

Pennebaker, J.W., Rimé, B., & Blankenship, V.E. (1996). Stereotypes of emotional expressiveness of northerners and southerners: A cross-cultural test of Montesquieu's hypotheses. *Journal of Personality and Social Psychology, 70*, 372–380.

Roes, F. (1990). Waarom huilen mensen? [Why do people cry?]. *Psychologie, 10*, 44–45.

Rosenblatt, P.C., Walsh, R.P., & Jackson, D.A. (1976). *Grief and mourning in cross-cultural perspective.* New Haven, CN: HRAF Press.

Scherer, K.R. (1997). The role of culture in emotion-antecedent appraisal. *Journal of Personality and Social Psychology, 73*, 902–922.

Scherer, K.R., Matsumoto, D., Wallbott, H. G., & Kudoh, T. (1988). Emotional experience in cultural context: A comparison between Europe, Japan, and the United States. In K. R. Scherer (Ed.), *Facets of emotion: Recent research* (pp. 5–30). Hillsdale, NJ: Erlbaum.

Scherer, K.R., Wallbott, H.G., & Summerfield, A.B. (1986). *Experiencing emotion: A cross-cultural study.* Cambridge, UK: Cambridge University Press.

Schlosser, M.B. (1986, August). *Anger, crying, and health among females.* Paper presented at the Annual Meeting of the American Psychological Association, Washington, DC.

Solter, A. (1995). Why do babies cry? *Pre- and Perinatal Psychology Journal, 10*, 21–43.

United Nations Development Programme (UNDP, 1998). *Gender empowerment measure.* Internet: http://www.undp.org/hdro

Vingerhoets, A.J.J.M. (1995). *The ISAC Questionnaire.* Department of Psychology, Tilburg University, the Netherlands.

Vingerhoets, A.J.J.M., Cornelius, R.R., Van Heck, G.L., & Becht, M.C. (2000). Adult crying: A model and review of the literature. *Review of General Psychology, 4*, 354–377.

Vingerhoets, A.J.J.M., & Scheirs, J.G.M. (2000). Sex differences in crying: Empirical findings and possible explanations. In A.H. Fischer (Ed.), *Gender and emotion. Social psychological perspectives.* (pp. 143–165). Cambridge, UK: Cambridge University Press.

Vingerhoets, A.J.J.M., & Scheirs, J.G.M. (2001). Crying and health. In A.J.J.M. Vingerhoets & R.R. Cornelius (Eds.), *Adult crying: A biopsychosocial approach* (pp. 227–246). Hove, UK: Brunner-Routledge.

Wellenkamp, J. (1995). Cultural similarities and differences regarding emotional disclosure: Some examples from Indonesia and the Pacific. In J.W. Pennebaker (Ed.), *Emotion, disclosure and health* (pp. 293–312). Washington, DC: APA.

Williams, D.G. (1982). Weeping by adults: Personality correlates and sex differences. *Journal of Psychology, 110*, 217–226.

Williams, D.G., & Morris, G.H. (1996). Crying, weeping or tearfulness in British and Israeli adults. *British Journal of Psychology, 87*, 479–505.

Zeifman, D.M. (2001). Developmental aspects of crying: Infancy and childhood. In A.J.J.M. Vingerhoets & R.R. Cornelius (Eds.), *Adult crying: A biopsychosocial approach* (pp. 37–53). Hove, UK: Brunner-Routledge.

COGNITION AND EMOTION, 2002, *16* (1), 103–125

Cultural dimensions, socioeconomic development, climate, and emotional hedonic level

Nekane Basabe, Dario Paez, and Jose Valencia
University of the Basque Country, San Sebastian, Spain

Jose Luis Gonzalez
University of Burgos, Spain

Bernard Rimé
University of Louvain, Belgium

Ed Diener
University of Illinois, Champaign, USA

A research synthesis was conducted with four studies which correlated national mean self-ratings of affect balance (positive minus negative affect) and subjective well-being with the nations' cultural characteristics (individualism, masculinity, uncertainty avoidance, and power-distance national scores on Hofstede's dimensions), socioeconomic development (Human Development Index), and climate (absolute latitude). A *meta-analysis* of these collective level cross-cultural studies shows that individualism correlates positively with affect balance and subjective well-being, controlling for socioeconomic development, cultural femininity, power-distance, uncertainty avoidance, and climate. Similar results were found for individual-level data. The meaning of collective-level or national means of individual self-reports of affect balance is discussed.

Cross-cultural differences in the experience and expression of emotion are an important topic not only in current social psychology, but also in classic and modern philosophy. The present paper examines various ideas concerning the differences in emotion between nations from the perspective of current

---

Correspondence should be addressed either to Dario Paez or Nekane Basabe, Departmento de Psicología Social y Metodología, Universidad del Pais Vasco, Avda. de Tolosa 70, San Sebastian 20009, Spain; e-mail: pspparod@ss.ehu.es, or pspbaban@vf.ehu.es

This study was supported by the following Basque Country University Research Grants (UPV 109.231-G56/98).

empirical research, with the aim of integrating the results of large-scale cross-cultural studies. Between nations differences in emotional life were analysed in the past as an aspect of "national character". Classical and Enlightenment philosophers frequently derived "national character" from climate. Climate includes a range of what are currently termed ecological factors (Jahoda, 1992). At the same time, Classical and Enlightenment philosophers pointed out the weaknesses involved in advocating a purely climatic interpretation. Factors, such as social institutions, were combined with climatic determinism. Hume thought that ecological causes, including climate, were relatively unimportant for explaining differences in national character: He attributed differences in emotional experience to "moral" causes, that is, what Jahoda would term social and economic factors (Jahoda, 1977). Current cross-cultural social psychology also combines ecological, social, and cultural determinism (Jahoda, 1992). Empirical differences across countries in affect balance, subjective well-being, and emotions are related to differences in subjective culture (e.g., values) and socioeconomic factors (Diener, Diener, & Diener, 1995).

Culture and emotional hedonic level

We will examine theory and data regarding the relationships between cultural factors and a basic dimension in emotion: pleasantness-unpleasantness, or hedonic level. The frequency, and to a lesser extent the intensity, of positive and negative emotions are the basis of hedonic level. Subjective well-being (SWB) is related to people's affect balance (e.g., relative frequency of positive and negative emotions), and to affective (e.g., global happiness appraisals) and cognitive evaluations of their lives (e.g., life satisfaction appraisals, contentment or degree to which an individual perceives his/her aspirations as having been met). SWB scores, particularly affect balance scores, could be conceived of as measures of emotional hedonic level, and different studies have shown that SWB is related to social and cultural factors (Diener & Larsen, 1993). Culture is conceived of as a set of denotative (what is, or beliefs), connotative (what should be, or attitudes, norms, and values), and pragmatic (how things are done or procedural rules) knowledge, shared by a group of individuals who have a common history and who participate in a social structure. Shared values play a key role in the individuals' psychological functioning and emotional experience. Core cultural values are reflected in key collective texts and collective behaviour, which together constitute cultural plots or scripts (Inkeles & Levinson, 1969; Schooler, 1996; Triandis, 1995). Inkeless and Levinson (1969) concluded that there is a series of basic problems that all cultures have to deal with: (a) the relation with authority; (b) the concept of the self or person (which includes the relationship between the person and society and the person's concept of masculinity and femininity); and (c) conflicts and their resolution (expression vs. inhibition of emotions, including the control of aggression).

Hofstede (1991) conducted a seminal survey on work values and empirically identified, by means of collective factor analyses using nations as units and means as scores, a four-dimensional solution, which fits with Inkeless and Levinson's basic social problems. Using survey data collected in the 1970s from IBM employees in 53 nations and regions, Hofstede derived four dimensions along which dominant values in different nations could be expressed. Following Inkeless and Levinson's social tasks model, Hofstede labelled these dimensions: Individualism-Collectivism, Power-Distance, Masculinity-Femininity, and Uncertainty Avoidance. Despite the fact that the survey was conducted more than 20 years ago, Hofstede's scores have shown high concurrent validity in current cross-cultural research (Bond & Smith, 1996; Fernandez, Carlson, Stepina, & Nicholson, 1997; Miller-Loesi, 1995). Moreover, the chapter on cross-cultural issues in the fourth edition of the *Handbook of Social Psychology* concludes that individualism and power-distance stand out as two important cultural dimensions affecting psychological processes (Fiske, Markus, Kitayama, & Nisbett, 1998). Other authors have empirically established that cultural femininity and uncertainty avoidance are two dimensions that correlate strongly with higher emotional intensity (Paez & Vergara, 1995) and negative affect (Arrindell et al., 1997; Lynn & Martin, 1995).

The individualism-collectivism dimension (IDV) refers to the priority given to the person or to the group or collective (often the extended family). Examples of collectivist countries are Guatemala, Indonesia, and Taiwan. Examples of individualistic countries are the USA and the countries of Western Europe. Cultural individualism fosters an independent social representation of the person. Collectivist cultures emphasise relatedness (Fiske et al., 1998; Hofstede, 1991; Kagitçibasi, 1994; Markus, Kitayama, & Heimain, 1996; Smith & Bond, 1998). Individualistic cultures promote introspection and focus attention on inner experience. In contrast, collectivist cultures do not encourage attention to the inner self. Most salient features of emotional experience are external and interactional (i.e., how one's actions affect others). Evidence suggests that emotional experience is perceived and expressed more intensely in individualistic than in collectivist cultures (Markus & Kitayama, 1991; Matsumoto, 1991; Scherer, 1988). Individualism, by way of the higher relevance attributed to individual mental life and well-being, correlates with higher levels of affect. At the same time, individualistic cultures afford freedom to pursue individual goals and feel satisfaction, creating situations which elicit positive emotions. In contrast, feelings of social support and associated SWB might be greater in collectivist societies. However, studies confirm that cultural individualism correlates with subjective well-being when income, human rights and equality are controlled (Diener et al., 1995).

Power-distance (PDI) refers to the extent to which national cultures expect and accept that power is distributed unequally in society. Examples of low power-distance countries are Denmark and New Zealand. Examples of high power-distance countries are Malaysia and Guatemala. In high power-distance societies an important emotional distance separates subordinates from authorities. Respect and formal deference for higher status people (e.g., parents, elders, etc.) are valued. Matsumoto (1989) reported that participants from high power-distance cultures gave lower intensity ratings to negative emotions (anger, fear or sadness) displayed by an individual in a photograph, in comparison to participants from lower power-distance cultures. Suppressing status-threatening emotions is maximised in high power-distance societies because status differences are important (Matsumoto, 1991). Strong social differences that are typical of high power-distance societies (e.g., Guatemala and Malaysia) probably cause high stress and negative emotional situations. Arrindell et al. (1997) found, at a collective level, that power-distance was associated with unpleasantness of emotional experience (i.e., lower SWB).

The masculinity-femininity dimension (MAS) refers to the extent to which cultures strive for ego-goals and competitiveness. Masculine cultures stress stereotypical gender behaviour, and the dominant values are success, money, competition, and assertiveness. Feminine cultures do not emphasise gender role differences, are not competitive, and value cooperation and concern for the weak. Examples of masculine countries are Japan, Austria, and Mexico. Examples of feminine countries are Scandinavia, the Netherlands, Chile, and Costa Rica (Hofstede, 1991; Smith & Bond, 1998). One important potential consequence of the cultural values of femininity is the perceived obligation to provide emotional support. Social support is probably higher in feminine cultures and provides the individual with a strong network in times of distress. Arrindell et al. (1997) found that more affluent feminine cultures show higher pleasantness of emotional experience (i.e., higher SWB).

Uncertainty avoidance (UAI) defines the extent to which people feel threatened by an ambiguous situation, which they try to avoid by means of strict codes and beliefs. High uncertainty avoidance nations, such as Greece and Portugal, are emotional, and security-seeking. Nations with low uncertainty avoidance cultures, for instance Jamaica and Denmark, are more relaxed, and accept more risks. Strong uncertainty avoidance cultures stress formal rules and social control. A high need for predictability and anxiety characterise such cultures, which usually tend to be more anxious and expressive. In weak uncertainty avoidance cultures anxiety is relatively low—people do not need to worry about predicted behaviour or avoid ambiguities. Previous studies confirm that uncertainty avoidance is related to high anxiety and to lower well-being or unpleasantness of emotional experience (Arrindell et al., 1997; Hofstede, 1991).

Ecological and economic factors involved in cultural dimensions and their influence on emotions

Cultural dimensions are partly associated with ecological and economic factors. Higher latitude (i.e., cold climate) correlates with lower power-distance, along with higher purchase power. Individualism is strongly related to both economic development and higher geographical latitude (i.e., countries with moderate and cold climates tend to be individualistic cultures, while countries with hot climates tend to be collectivist cultures). Hofstede's (1991) longitudinal data suggest that increasing economic development causes individualism. When a country's wealth increases, people have access to resources that allow them to have more privacy and individual choices, reinforcing individualism. Unlike individualism and power-distance, cultural femininity-masculinity and uncertainty avoidance are both unrelated to a country's level of economic development and geo- graphical latitude. This implies that the influence of cultural femininity and uncertainty avoidance on emotional experience is relatively independent of ecological and economic factors (Hofstede, 1991). With regard to the influence of socioeconomic development and the subjective experience of emotion, Wallbott and Scherer (1988) found that lower income was related to higher intensity of emotional experience. As Wallbott and Scherer (1988) suggest, more intense, longer-lasting emotional reactions to events, and more attribution to less controllable causes, are common features of the members of poorer countries. In less developed countries social life is more uncontrollable and social stress is higher, all of which is linked to more intense emotional reactions, and at the same time to lower pleasantness of emotional experience. Two collective-level studies show that high income was related to SWB, when other sociocultural factors were taken into account (Arrindell et al., 1997; Diener et al., 1995). Theories of geographical determinism and stereotypes suggest that climate influences emotional intensity and frequency. During the first century BC Poseidonos' writings contrasted the Norse (Germanic or Celtic tribes living in a cold climate), characterised by an excess of thymus or emotionality, with the Mediterranean or southerners (living in a moderate climate), governed by logos or emotional control and reflection. In the eighteenth century, Montesquieu posited a reverse climate theory for emotional experience: Warmer climates made southerners more sensitive to emotion (Jahoda, 1992). Moreover, in the tradition running from Montesquieu to the Romantic authors, recent ''Mediterranean'' anthro- pology holds that among Southern Europeans, in comparison to Northern ones, an emotional (e.g., violent and passionate) culture prevails (Fernández, 1987; Gilmore, 1990; Llobera, 1987). Violent crime studies support the hypothesis that a warm climate promotes aggression (Anderson, 1989, quoted in Pennebaker, Rimé, & Blankenship, 1996). Anderson and Anderson's (1996) collective-level analysis suggests that both warm climate or heat and an index of Honour Culture correlates with higher Southern violence rates in the USA, and are probably related to negative affect and aggression. Southern European nationalities (French, Spanish, Italians and Greeks) are perceived as scoring at the "loose" end of Peabody's Tight-Loose dimension, which contrasts high versus low Impulse Control and low versus high Affiliation and Impulse Expression (Peabody, 1999). Pennebaker et al. (1996) found, at a within-country level, that people living in the South reported being more emotionally expressive than those living in more Northern regions—in the "Old World", and in the Northern Hemisphere. Finally, a recent review of various surveys conducted on frequency of sexual intercourse in stable couples confirmed that Northern European countries have lower means, both for men and women, than Southern European countries. This confirms "the cultural stereotype that people in relatively warmer climates are more passionate" (Hubert, Bajos, & Sandfort, 1998, p.125). Briefly, the available data suggest that there is a "kernel of truth" regarding the ste-reotype that southerners are highly emotional. At the individual level, higher temperatures have been found to increase hostile affect and cognition, and to decrease positive affect (in laboratory settings, Anderson et al., 1995, quoted in Smith & Bond, 1998). A warm climate is supposed to make individuals more attentive to internal states (Pennebaker et al., 1996), to increase the frequency of interaction and thereby to make it more likely that people are in emotional situations, reinforcing emotional intensity and frequency. However, because of the association between cold climate, individualism and socioeconomic development, cold climate should probably be associated with SWB and positive affect balance (Church & Lonner, 1998).

In sum, the available data and a theoretical analysis of cultural dimensions support the assumption that pleasantness of emotional experience is higher in individualistic, low power-distance and feminine cultures, and in developed countries. Both theory and available data suggest that uncertainty avoidance is associated with unpleasantness of emotional experience. There is limited evi-dence supporting the association between warm climate and emotional intensity. Cold climate is probably associated with higher pleasantness of emotional experience.

METHOD

Procedure and Measures

Predictor variables

Cultural factors. Hofstede (1991) reports individualism-collectivism, power-distance, masculinity-femininity, and uncertainty avoidance scores for 53 nations and regions. Hofstede's scores and Schwartz's (1994) rating of culture-level value types show strong concurrent validity: IDV correlates positively with affective and intellectual autonomy: $r(23) = .46$ and $r(23) = .53$, $p \leq .05$ respectively, negatively with conservatism: $r(23) = -.56$, $p \leq .05$), and hierarchy: $r(23) = -.51$, $p \leq .05$ and positively with egalitarian commitment: $r(23) = .51$, $p \leq .05$). Hofstede's PDI correlates positively with conservatism and negatively with affective autonomy: $r(23) = .45$, and $r = -.45$, $p \leq .05$, respectively. Hofstede's MAS correlates positively with mastery: $r(23) = .56$, $p \leq .05$, and UAI correlates positively with harmony: $r = .43$, $p \leq .05$ (see Schwartz, 1994, p.109). A conceptual replication of Hofstede's research conducted by Fernandez et al. (1997) provides standardised scores for Russia and China that were included in the present data. Because these latter scores are as yet unvalidated, data analyses were run with and without the Chinese and Russian scores. High scores represent high IDV, PDI, MAS, and UAI (see Table 1 for the nations' cultural, social, and ecological scores).

Socio-economic factors. The human development index (HDI) measures national well-being and trends by combining three basic components of human development: longevity (mean life expectancy in the nation); knowledge (rate of literacy and school population); and standard of living (Gross National Product per person). HDI is the best known measure of development. It is better than the limited purchase power and per capita measures (Cordelier & Didiot, 1997).

TABLE 1
Hofstede's cultural dimensions and ecological and social variables

Country	IDV	PDI	MAS	UAI	HDI	LAT	LE	HR
Argentina	46	49	56	86	.885	−34	72.9	
Australia	90	36	61	51	.929	−22	78.2	4.42
Austria	55	11	79	70	.928	48	77.0	5.65
Bahrain	38	80	53	68	.866	26	72.9	
Belgium	75	65	54	94	.929	51	77.2	4.46
Brazil	38	69	49	76	.796	−22	66.8	7.18
Canada	80	39	52	48	.951	55	79.0	4.97
Chile	23	63	28	86	.882	−34	74.9	11.62
China	17	82	90	72	.609	39	69.8	12.58
Colombia	13	67	64	80	.840	3	70.4	10.25
Croatia	27	76	21	88	.760	46	72.6	
Cuba	12	81	73	76	.726	21	75.7	10.96
Denmark	74	18	16	23	.924	55	75.7	4.46
Egypt	38	80	53	68	.611	30	66.3	10.86
Finland	63	33	26	59	.935	60	76.8	4.43
France	71	68	43	86	.935	47	78.1	4.54
Germany	67	35	66	65	.920	50	77.2	4.58
Ghana	20	77	46	54	.467	5	60.0	

(Continued overleaf)

TABLE 1
(Continued)

Country	IDV	PDI	MAS	UAI	HDI	LAT	LE	HR
Greece	35	60	57	112	.909	38	78.1	4.85
Hong Kong	25	68	57	29	.909	22	78.5	
India	48	77	56	40	.436	17	62.6	8.81
Indonesia	14	78	46	48	.641	−3	65.1	
Iran	41	58	43	59	.754	35	69.2	
Ireland	70	28	68	35	.919	53	76.3	5.71
Israel	54	13	47	81	.908	31	77.8	7.01
Italy	76	50	70	75	.914	42	78.2	6.03
Japan	46	54	95	92	.938	32	80.0	5.03
Korea (S)	18	60	39	85	.886	37	72.4	9.17
Malaysia	26	104	50	36	.826	3	72.0	10.94
Mexico	30	81	69	82	.845	24	72.2	9.55
The Netherlands	80	38	14	53	.938	52	77.9	4.42
New Zealand	79	22	58	49	.927	−41	76.9	4.42
Nigeria	77	77	46	54	.400	9	50.1	10.20
Norway	69	31	8	50	.937	59	78.1	4.88
Pakistan	14	55	50	70	.442	33	64.0	
Panama	11	95	44	86	.859	8	73.6	6.31
Peru	16	64	42	87	.694	−12	68.3	
Philippines	32	94	64	44	.665	14	68.3	4.87
Portugal	27	63	31	104	.878	39	75.3	5.01
Russia	3	105	53	112	.804	55	66.6	11.37
Singapore	20	74	48	8	.881	11	77.1	9.57
South Africa	65	49	63	49	.649	−33	54.7	11.08
Spain	51	57	42	86	.933	37	78.0	5.10
Sweden	71	31	5	29	.933	59	78.5	4.41
Switzerland	68	34	70	58	.926	47	78.6	4.96
Taiwan	17	58	45	69		25		
Tanzania	27	64	41	52	.364	−6	47.9	10.76
Thailand	20	64	34	64	.832	13	68.8	9.01
Tunisia	38	80	53	68	.727	36	69.3	
Turkey	37	66	45	85	.711	37	69.0	10.97
United Kingdom	89	35	66	35	.924	54	77.2	4.84
USA	91	40	62	46	.940	38	76.7	4.58
Yugoslavia	27	76	21	88	.857	44	72.8	9.57
Zimbabwe	65	49	63	49	.534	−17	44.1	

Note: IDV, Individualism; PDI, Power-distance; MAS, Masculinity; UAI, Uncertainty avoidance; HDI, Human development index; LAT, Latitude; LE, Life expectancy at birth (years); HR, Human rights. A high score for each variable denotes a high degree of the construct in question, except for human rights where a low number reflects greater rights.

Latitude: Mean latitude refers to the North-South midpoint of the country: Positive scores refer to degrees above the Equator, negative scores refer to degrees below the Equator.

Data: Hofstede (1991); (Cuba = Venezuela; Tunisia and Bahrein = Arab countries; Tanzania = East Africa; Nigeria and Ghana = West Africa); Life expectancy (PNUD, 1999, pp. 134–137); Human rights (Diener et al., 1995, p. 856), *n* = 54 countries.

HDI scores for each nation were obtained from the United Nations Program for Development (UNPD).

Climatic factors.   Absolute latitudes as provided in Pennebaker et al.'s study were used. Lower absolute latitude reflects warmer climates. Confirming the validity of absolute latitude as an index of climate, cross-cultural research has found a first factor of climate variables which is a direct reflection of a country's distance from the equator. Countries with high scores in this factor have short days, high overall temperatures, and massive rainfall during a short period (Scherer, 1997). These results suggest that distance from the Equator (absolute latitude) is a good climatic index.

Structural collective-level variables

In order to contrast the validity of mean levels of self-reported well-being and affect balance, culture-level measures of well-being (life expectancy) and affect balance (human rights) were used. These data allow us to contrast the relationship between "objective" and structural collective-level measures, with both predictors and macropsychological indexes (e.g., national means of affect balance and SWB, or aggregated individual measures). Even if the two collective variables are related, they are supposed to tap different domains (see below).

Life expectancy.   As a collective-level measure of national well-being we use mean life expectancy in the nation (PNUD, 1999). Because of the relationship between fulfilment of basic needs and general life satisfaction, life expectancy is supposed to represent collective-level well-being.

Human rights.   As a collective-level measure of positive affect we use the Gupta et al. (1994, quoted in Diener et al., 1995) score regarding the degree in which a nation possesses 40 different human rights. Human rights scores were used (i.e., no searches without warrant, independent courts, innocent until proven guilty, no secret trials, freedom to teach ideas, and no arbitrary seizure of property). The scores for each country are shown in Table 1. A low score represents more rights. Because of the associations between interpersonal trust, good social climate, respect for human rights, human rights violations, aggression and negative affect, this measure is supposed to be a collective-level index of affect balance (positive minus negative affect).

Dependent measures: Subjective well-being and affect balance

Subjective well-being.   Diener et al.'s (1995) study provides SWB scores for 43 nations on the basis of random and student samples. SWB scores refer to the mean standardised value of four surveys: three national surveys plus one student survey. Diener et al. included surveys of both happiness (related to the presence of positive affect and the absence of negative affect) and life satisfaction (more cognitive measures emphasising judgements of life domains). Happiness scores correlated positively with income ($r=.43$) and with individualism ($r=.40$), satisfaction scores correlated positively with income ($r=.57$) and with individualism ($r=.59$), and SWB correlated positively with income ($r=.65$) and with individualism ($r=.58$), suggesting that SWB overestimated the relationship between socioeconomic and cultural factors with affect (see Diener et al., 1995, for national means). The 42 nations included in the present research are those in Diener et al.'s study for which we were able to find cultural and socioeconomic information. The final sample comprised 67439 participants (ranging from 91 in Colombia to 9961 in the Philippines).

Inglehart's subjective well-being measure. Inglehart's (1998) study analysed the results of the World Values Study Group from 1990 to 1991 and provides SWB scores for 43 nations on the basis of random samples. Inglehart's SWB measure was the average of two different indexes. The first index comprised the percentage of very happy people minus the percentage of those unhappy. A second index was created by subtracting the percentage of people with low life satisfaction from the percentage of people reporting high life satisfaction (see Inglehart, 1998, p. 471, for national means). The 29 nations studied here are those included in Inglehart's research for which we were able to find cultural and socioeconomic variables. The final sample comprised 40,341 participants (samples ranging from 588 in Finland to 2792 in Belgium).

Bradburns positive and negative affect scale. We re-analysed the results of the World Values Study Group on positive and negative affect. National means as measured by Bradburn's affect balance scale were used. Macintosh (1998) describes the general methodology used in this research. Data were collected in 38 nations, using large random samples (ranging from 303 in Ireland to 4000 in Spain). Five items measured positive affect and another five items measured negative affect. The average inter-item correlation was .46 for positive affect and .53 for negative affect, showing moderate reliability. Using the nonsignificance of χ^2-test at $p \le .01$ as a criterion, a confirmatory factor analysis confirmed the structural validity of the negative affect scale in 74% of the 38 samples. The results were worse for the positive scale (Macintosh, 1998). The 26 nations studied here are those from the Macintosh's study for which we were able to find cultural and socioeconomic information (see Macintosh, 1998, for national means).

Self-ratings of frequency of positive and negative emotions or Diener's affect balance. A self-rating of the frequency of four negative emotions (anger, fear, sadness, and guilt) and four positive emotions (pride, joy, contentment, and affection) was used. Frequency ratings are supposed to reflect common practices in a culture or society, or descriptive norms. Participants rated the frequency with which they experienced the emotions and feelings ("During the past month, how often have you felt each emotion?") scored from 1 = never to 7 = always. The alpha coefficient on a collective level for the four items assessing the frequency of emotion was .87 for negative emotions and .83 for positive emotions. An affect balance score was created by subtracting frequency of negative emotions from frequency of positive emotions (Andrews & Robinson, 1991). Suh, Diener, Oishi, and Triandis (1998) describe the general methodology used in this study (see Basabe et al., 2000, for national means). The 32 nations studied here are those included in the Suh et al. study for which we were able to find cultural and socioeconomic information. The final sample comprised 6099 students (70% female) with a mean age of 21.26 (SD = 6.3 years).

Results

Concurrent and criterion validity of the hedonic scores at a collective level. To check the construct validity of the collective-level hedonic scores, a series of correlations was performed between the standardised scores of the four types of measures (SWB as assessed by Diener et al., 1995, and by Inglehart, 1998, and affect balance as assessed by Bradburn's measure (Macintosh, 1998) and by Diener et al., 1995). Diener et al.'s SWB scores correlate significantly, and as expected (see Table 3), with other measures (weighted mean correlation was $r_w = .72$). Mean weighted correlation was $r_w = .69$ for Inglehart's score, $r_w = .52$ for Bradburn's affect balance measure, and $r_w = .53$ for Diener's affect balance measure. Using nations as units of analysis and means as scores, the correlations between aggregated psychological indexes of hedonic level and culture-level affect balance (human rights) and SWB (life expectancy) scores were also performed to assess the criterion validity of subjective emotional scores at the collective level (see Table 2). Life expectancy was related to a greater aggregated self-reported well-being: weighted $r_w(71) = .63$. Finally, violation of human rights correlated with lower aggregated reporting of well-being: weighted $r_w(72) = -.57$, and with lower aggregated reporting of positive versus negative affect: weighted $r_w(49) = -.38$. These results confirm the concurrent and criterion validity of the nation's affect balance and SWB means.

Cultural dimensions, socioeconomic development, climate, and hedonic level: Collective level analysis. The relationship between predictor factors and emotion measures at the collective level was examined. Table 3 shows the correlation between each of the predictors (dimensions of national culture, HDI, and climate). Hofstede's IDV and PDI indexes are usually interrelated, and both are associated with climate and socioeconomic development (see Table 3). Our

TABLE 2
Intercorrelations of well-being measures across nations

Measure	1	2	3	4	5	6
1. Diener's SWB						
2. Inglehart's SWB	.59**					
3. Bradburn's affect balance	.85**	.53**				
4. Diener's affect balance	.61**	.53**	.40*			
5. Life expectancy	.51**	.78**	.10	−.03		
6. Human rights	−.46**	−.80**	−.34	−.42*	−.65**	
r_w [a]	.72**	.69**	.52**	.53**	.63**	.53**
χ^2 [b]	5.06[c]	6.60[c]	0.58[c]	0.47[c]	3.69[d]	8.26[e]
df	2	2	2	2	1	3

Note: Pearson product-moment coefficients across nations. A high number on each variable denotes a high score on the termed variable, except for human rights on which a low number indicates greater rights. Collective level analysis (n = 44–17 countries).

[a] r_w = weighted average of the correlations after Fisher z transformation; [b] $\chi^2(df)$ = measure of homogeneity (a set may be interpreted to be homogeneous if the χ^2-value is not significant $p \leq .01$); df (degrees of freedom) = number of studies minus 1; all χ^2-values are not significant at $p \leq .01$; [c] Correlations between SWB (subjective well-being) measures (1–4 variables); [d] Correlations between SWB (1), Inglehart SWB (2), and life expectancy (5); [e] Correlations between SWB measures (1–4) and human rights (6).

TABLE 3
Intercorrelations of cultural, social, and ecological variables across nations

Measures	1	2	3	4	5
1. IDV					
2. PDI	−.74**				
3. MAS	.00	.07			
4. UAI	−.35**	.26**	.07		
5. HDI	.46**	−.46**	−.11	.07	
6. LAT	.57**	−.55**	−.23***	.10	.52**

Note: Pearson product-moment coefficients across nations. A high number on each variable denotes a high score on the variable in question. IDV, Individualism; PDI, Power-distance; MAS, Masculinity; UAI, Uncertainty avoidance; HDI, Human development index; LAT, Absolute latitude. n = 52 countries.

*$p \leq .05$; **$p \leq .01$; ***$p \leq .10$ (two-tailed).

114

52 countries sample results point to the need to control for interdependence between cultural factors. IDV was related to low power-distance, low uncertainty avoidance, cold climate, and socioeconomic development at the collective level. Finally, high power-distance and uncertainty avoidance were associated. Using the country score on HDI, absolute latitude, and Hofstede's scores, a series of Pearson correlations at the collective level were performed in order to assess relationships between cultural dimensions, human development index, climate, and national differences in hedonic level (affect balance and SWB).

In order to control for correlations among the predictors, multiple regressions were computed and standardized beta weights were used as an index of specific influence. To integrate results, a meta-analysis was performed on the main measures. To assess the statistical heterogeneity of the four size estimates, we computed the associated Fisher r–z and weighted mean effect size (r_w). Effect size was weighted by degrees of freedom or $N-3$, whereas N was the number of nations on which each r or β was based. To take into account the high variance or error estimation in small sample size studies, effect size was also weighted by the total sample size of each study (Rosenthal, 1991). The statistical significance of the rs heterogeneity was obtained using the following formula: $\Sigma[(N_i-3)$ $(Z_{ri}-\text{mean } Z_r)^2]$, distributed as χ^2 with number of studies minus 1 as degrees of freedom. Effect size was estimated with both bivariate correlations and beta weights (see Table 4). IDV was positively related with SWB and the affect balance measure. The mean correlation (weighted and unweighted) was $r = .56$. The beta coefficients from the four studies did not differ significantly. The IDV effect size using multivariate coefficients was homogeneous, positive, and significant. The effect size did not change when the Chinese and Russian IDV scores were excluded. PDI was negatively, homogeneously, and significantly related with SWB and affect balance measure. The mean correlation (weighted and unweighted) was $r = -.60$. The PDI effect size using multivariate coefficients was negative, significant but heterogeneous. The significant heterogeneity was due to the higher correlation of PDI with Diener's affect balance measure. The effect size did not change when the PDI scores for China and Russia were excluded.

MAS was negatively related with SWB and affect balance. The unweighted mean correlation for cultural masculinity was $r = -.34$, while the weighted mean correlation was $r_w = -.31$. The effect size using multivariate coefficients was negative and significant. The heterogeneity contrast was significant, due to the higher correlation of MAS with Diener's affect balance measure. Excluding the Chinese and Russian MAS scores did not change the effect size. UAI was associated negatively with SWB and affect balance. The unweighted mean correlation was $r = -.43$ and the weighted mean correlation was $r_w = -.42$. The multivariate estimated effect size was negative, significant but heterogeneous. The beta weights for the four datasets vary significantly because of the positive

TABLE 4
Cultural-social-ecological variables on national levels of subjective well-being and
affect balance (multiple regression analysis)

	SWB (1) Diener		SWB (2) Inglehart		Affect balance Bradburn (3)		Affect balance Diener (4)	
	R	β	r	β	r	β	r	β
IDV	.64**	.30	.77**	.32	.49*	−.01	.23	.18
PDI	−.59**	−.10	−.77**	−.21	−.57**	−.23	−.41*	−.73**
MAS	−.20	−.09	−.29	−.16	−.30	−.15	−.56**	−.66**
UAI	−.53**	−.38*	−.47*	−.18	−.61**	−.45*	−.05	.30
HDI	.57**	.50*	.69**	.51*	.19	.09	.13	−.11
LAT	.25	−.24	.54*	−.16	.28	−.00	.07	−.67**

	IDV	PDI	MAS	UAI	HDI	LAT
$r_w^{\,a}$	.56**	−.60**	−.31**	−.42**	.44**	.30**
$\chi^2(3)^b$	9.45*	4.68	3.84	5.16	8.43*	9.16*
$\beta_w^{\,a}$	.22*	−.34**	−.24**	−.20*	.29**	−.30*
$\chi^2(3)^b$	1.82	12.90*	8.13*	9.32*	10.06*	10.0*

Note: Pearson product-moment coefficients across nations and standardised beta coefficients. A high number on each variable denotes a high score on the variable in question. IDV, Individualism; PDI, Power-distance; MAS, Masculinity; UAI, Uncertainty avoidance; HDI, Human development index; LAT, Absolute latitude. Collective level analysis $n=42$ (1), 29 (2), 26 (3), 32 (4).

$^a r_w$ and β_w = weighted average of the correlations (and beta standardised coefficients) after Fisher z-transformation; $^b \chi(\mathrm{df})$ = measure of homogeneity (a set may be interpreted to be homogeneous if the χ^2-value is not significant, $p \leq .05$); df (degrees of freedom) = number of studies minus 1.

$^*p \leq .05$; $^{**}p \leq .01$ (two-tailed).

beta coefficient between UAI and Diener's affect balance measure, which is probably due to multicollinearity. Excluding the Chinese and Russian UAI scores did not change the effect size. HDI was related to SWB and affect balance. The unweighted and weighted mean correlations were $r = .42$ and $r_w = .44$, respectively, both $p \leq .01$. The effect size using multivariate coefficients was positive, significant, and heterogeneous. Diener's and Inglehart's SWB scores show medium to high correlations, but Bradburn's and Diener's affect balance measures show nonsignificant and low correlations. Cold climate was associated with SWB and affect balance. The unweighted and weighted mean correlations were $r = .31$ and $r_w = .30$, respectively. However, the multivariate effect size was negative. Moreover, the heterogeneity contrast was significant. The fact that the multivariate effect size was negative is probably due to multicollinearity arising from the strong correlation of cold climate with socioeconomic development and IDV.

In summary, a *meta-analysis* conducted with four collective-level studies show that IDV was related with SWB and positive affect balance, when other cultural factors (MAS, PDI, and UAI), socioeconomic development, and climate were taken into account. UAI and PDI also show a unique but heterogeneous negative association with SWB and affect balance. Finally, socioeconomic development shows a unique association with SWB, but not with affect balance.

Cultural dimensions, socioeconomic development climate, and affect balance: Individual-level analysis.   The relationship between predictor factors and hedonic measures at the individual level was examined in order to check that collective-level associations are similar to individual-level relationships. This analysis included all participants in the respective studies. Individual-level data were available for the Bradburn and Diener et al. measures of affect balance. The results are shown in Table 5 and Figures 1 and 2.

The results show that the association between cultural dimensions and individual hedonic responses is similar to what was found at the collective level. Specifically, the results are similar with respect to PDI and MAS in the case of Diener's affect balance measure: High power-distance and masculinity were related to lower affect balance at both the individual and collective levels. In the

TABLE 5
Cultural-social-ecological variables on affect balance
(multiple regression analysis-individual level)

	Affect balance Bradburn (1)		Affect balance (Diener (2)	
	r	β	r	β
IDV	.18**	.06**	.10**	.09**
PDI	−.18**	−.01	−.12**	−.05*
MAS	−.04**	−.01	−.18**	−.18**
UAI	−.17**	−.14**	−.02	.05*
HDI	.07**	.06**	.05*	.01
LAT	.10**	.03**	.02	−.05*
$R(R^2)$		.22 (.05)		.22 (.05)

Note: Pearson product-moment coefficients across nations and standardised beta coefficients; $R(R^2)$ = Multiple R (adjusted R^2). A high number on each variable denotes a high score on the termed variable. IDV, Individualism; PDI, Power-distance; MAS, Masculinity; UAI, Uncertainty avoidance; HDI, Human development index; LAT, Absolute latitude. Individual level analysis $n_1 = 40341$, $n_2 = 6099$.
   $*p \leq .01$; $**p \leq .001$ (two-tailed).

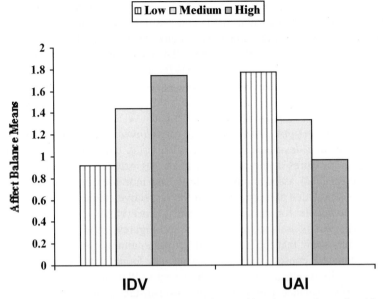

Figure 1. IDV (Individualism) and UAI (Uncertainty avoidance) groups by tertiles. Means of Bradburn's Affect Balance ($n = 40341$).

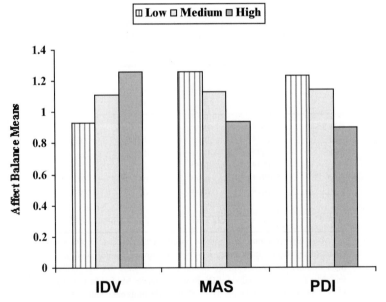

Figure 2. IDV, Individualism; PDI, Power-distance; MAS, Masculinity groups by tertiles. Means of Diener's Affect Balance ($n = 6099$).

case of Bradburn's affect balance measure the results for UAI were similar at an individual and collective level: High uncertainty avoidance was related to lower affect balance. Nevertheless, the effects associated with UAI, PDI, and MAS were heterogeneous and unstable. When climate, socioeconomic development, and other cultural dimensions were controlled, participants living in more individualistic countries had higher affect balance than did those living in more collectivist societies, for both Diener's and Bradburn's affect balance measures. This analysis reflects at an individual level the same associations found for individualism at the collective level, suggesting that at least for the reported hedonic level, collective and psychological processes are parallel—even if the individual level correlations are lower than those found at the collective level. Individualism explained around 5% of the variance at the collective level, whereas at the individual level the same dimension explained less than 1% of the variance. Finally, participants living in more developed countries show higher affect balance than do people living in less developed societies. Individual-level climate effects were positive for Bradburn's affect balance measure, but negative for Diener's affect balance—probably due to multicollinearity problems between latitude, socioeconomic development, and individualism. Nevertheless, the results for Bradburn's affect balance measure at the individual level suggest that both warm climate and sociocultural factors (lower socioeconomic development, collectivism, and higher uncertainty avoidance) correlate with lower affect balance.

DISCUSSION AND CONCLUSION

The findings reported above allow us to answer a "classical" question: What is the relation between emotional well-being and cultural dimensions, social development, and climate? The results allow us to understand how cultural dimensions are related to the hedonic level of emotional experience: affect balance, or positive minus negative emotions, and SWB as a complementary index of hedonic level. The relative influence of sociocultural factors on affect balance was also examined at the individual level. The findings are consistent with classic Weberian and Durkheimian hypotheses: Culture determines emotional experience. Hofstede's (IDV, and to a lesser extent UAI) cultural dimensions are associated in a congruent manner with emotional hedonic level. The evidence also shows that high socioeconomic development is related to well-being. This suggests that an increase in quality of life, privacy, and social resources, related to the level of earning, education, and expectancy of life, result in a more positive emotional experience. Finally, the results show that socioeconomic and cultural factors are more important predictors of affect balance and SWB than is climate. Thus, the evidence supports Hume's assumption that climatic effects on the subjective experience of emotions disappear, or are weakened, when social and cultural factors are taken into account.

We will now discuss, in order of importance, the influence of cultural dimensions. Next, the influence of socioeconomic and climatic factors will be examined. Finally, the significance and potential of aggregated self-report affect balance and SWB will be discussed.

Individualism and hedonic level. Individualism shows a homogeneous medium-sized positive association with emotional pleasantness, explaining approximately 5% of the variance at a collective level and 0.5% at the individual level. Previous studies suggest that individualism is associated with positive SWB (Arrindell et al., 1997; Diener et al., 1995). With respect to affect balance, the results show that hedonic level is better in individualistic cultures. This probably reflects greater personal freedom, which allows people to satisfy needs and individual strivings. Frequency of unpleasant emotions was negatively related to individualism in the Suh et al. (1998) study. In other terms, individualism offers protection against difficult events, probably because it provides material comfort and quality of life. However, individualism did not correlate significantly with the frequency of positive emotions. These results suggest that individualistic cultures do not facilitate situations that elicit positive emotions; indeed, suicide and divorce are higher in individualistic cultures than in collective ones (Bellah, Madsen, Sullivan, Swidler, & Tipton, 1985; Levine, 1997; Seligman, 1988). On the other hand, in the Suh et al. (1998) study IDV was associated with higher intensity and social desirability or public acceptance of emotional expression. This could also explain why individualistic cultures had higher affect balance, because higher social desirability and higher intensity of positive emotions correlate with SWB (Basabe et al., 2000).

Uncertainty avoidance and hedonic level. UAI shows an heterogeneous medium-sized positive association with emotional unpleasantness, explaining 4% of the variance at a collective level and 2% at an individual level in one study on affect balance. People living in high UAI cultures tend to experience higher levels of anxiety, neuroticism, and negative emotions, or low SWB, in this and other studies (Arrindell et al., 1997). Because it is probably a stressful society, a high uncertainty avoidance culture reinforces the frequency of anger, fear, and sadness, and in this way provokes low well-being (Basabe et al., 2000). Data are congruent with Hofstede's statement that cultures with strong avoidance uncertainty (e.g., Greece) are emotional whereas cultures with weak uncertainty avoidance (e.g., Denmark) are less emotional and more relaxed (Hofstede, 1986, quoted in Arrindell et al., 1997).

Power-distance and hedonic level. The meta-analysis found a heterogeneous medium-sized negative association of power-distance with emotional unpleasantness, explaining 12% of the variance at the collective level and 0.3%

at the individual level in one study on affect balance. Multivariate effect sizes were heterogeneous because of a higher similar sign association of power-distance with Diener's index of affect balance. Arrindell et al. (1997) found that high power-distance emerged as an independent predictor of unpleasantness of emotional experience or low SWB of nations, when controlling for other cultural dimensions and social factors. In different studies, power-distance was associated with lower SWB and negative affect balance, probably because strong social differences related to high power-distance societies cause stress.

Cultural femininity and hedonic level. Cultural masculinity shows a negative, small, and heterogeneous association with emotional unpleasantness, explaining 6% of variance at a collective level and 3% at the individual level in one study on affect balance. The results obtained in these studies suggest that feminine cultures are more likely to be positive emotional societies, with a general dominance of positive emotion experience. Previous studies also show, at least partially, that SWB is higher in feminine cultures (Arrindell et al., 1997). Cultural femininity was associated with a higher frequency of positive emotions, such as joy, and to a lower frequency of negative emotions, such as anger and sadness. These results are convergent with Hofstede's assumption: Feminine cultures are more likely to be welfare, cooperative societies, which accentuate interpersonal relationships, sympathy, and concern for the weak (Hofstede, 1991).

Ecological, socioeconomic factors, and hedonic level. Cold climate was related to greater well-being and pleasantness of affect, with a heterogeneous low-to-medium bivariate effect size. Contrary to the romantic view of warm climates as a hedonistic paradise, the results show that SWB and affect balance are higher in cold climates—which are usually more developed countries. Nevertheless, the multivariate effect size was negative and heterogeneous, probably due to the multicollinearity of cold climate with socioeconomic development and IDV. Climate is not a stable predictor of emotional life. The results support partially the more positive well-being of developed societies. However, associations were very heterogeneous and suggest that social development was more related to life satisfaction (SWB as assessed by Inglehart and Diener et al.) than to affect balance scores (affect balance as assessed by Bradburn and Diener's measures).

Culture-level measures of hedonic level self-reports: Limitations and possibilities as measures of emotional climate. The results reported in this article are based on self-reports, and analyses were performed at a collective level. Individual level analysis does not necessarily yield the same relationships and it is incorrect to assume that an association found among aggregated variables will also be found at the psychological or individual level of measure (i.e., the ecological or aggregate fallacy). Nevertheless, empirical analyses using collective scores as contextual variables and individual-level measures of affect balance confirm our results at the psychological level, particularly for individualism. On the other hand, what is the meaning and validity of the aggregated self-report of SWB and affect balance? Some authors criticise the use of aggregated psychological measures and propose that only structural global culture-level measures are meaningful. Structural properties refer to relationships between individuals within a group, such as power, status, communication, and division of labour. Global properties refer to the social products of a group, such as laws, arts, folklore, and language (Liska, 1990). For instance, Bond (1994) criticises the idea that national means of values are a satisfactory index of country-level collectivism, power-distance, and so on. For such authors, only scores related to structural and global national characteristics (observation of human rights, references to freedom in the constitution, proportion of women in the workforce, murder rates, etc.) make sense. Nevertheless, other authors argue that aggregated psychological or macro-psychological measures are meaningful aggregates of individual experiences, reflecting sociopsychological processes. Capitalism, a structural variable, could be measured as an aggregate, such as the national rate of entrepreneurship or the national average of "protestant work ethic" attitudes (Liska, 1990). The aggregation of individual perceptions of the organisational setting has been used to represent social climate (Gonzalez-Romá, Peiró, Lloret, & Zornoza, 1999). Studies using aggregated or averaged data from individuals to represent the organisational-level variables have shown stronger correlations at the collective level compared with the individual level (Ostroff, 1993). Our results confirm that SWB and affect balance macropsychological scores show concurrent validity with structural and global collective-level measures. Hedonic emotional scores also show stronger correlations at the collective than at a contextual-individual level (see Katona, 1979 for the meaning of macropsychology; Florin, Giamartino, Kenny, & Wandersman, 1990, and Liska, 1990, for the methodological and conceptual problems of aggregation). This suggests that aggregated affect balance and SWB self-report measures can be interpreted as meaningful emotional measures of societies as a whole, probably as indexes of emotional climate. Emotional climate (EC) is regarded as more variable than emotional culture, but more stable than specific emotional episodes, and describes the mood of a cultural group. It affects not only how one feels, but also what can and cannot be done. EC is related to the perceived stable dominance of a group of emotions (e.g., positive over negative emotions) in the collective or group in an historical period of time in a given group or society (De Rivera, 1992). In other terms, country means of affect balance are a satisfactory measure of a collective construct, such as EC, because it is reasonable to believe that individual hedonic level should be shared with others, expressed as a social tendency, and should have an impact on social climate.

Some studies (e.g., Suh et al., 1998) used nonrepresentative samples, and this can be seen as a methodological weakness. However, nonrepresentative samples (e.g., student samples) can reflect the position of the cultural group relative to a similar (e.g., another student sample) samples in other cultural groups (Bond, 1991). Moreover, student sample affect means (SWB) have been found to correlate well with means based on representative samples (Diener et al., 1995). Construct validity across cultures is a more serious problem, although some convergent construct validity for the measures used was found in this and other studies (see Suh et al., 1998, for Diener's measures). Despite of these methodological limitations, some of our results were triangulated by being replicated across the four datasets.

Another criticism with respect to our data is that pertaining to the historical evolution of countries. Hofstede's scores are based on data collected in the 1970s. Available data suggests that some countries (e.g., Chile) have increased their level of individualism since then (Fernandez et al., 1997). However, the trend towards high individualism is a general one. Furthermore, the subjective emotional data of the young and adult samples were collected in the 1980s and 1990s (see Lynn & Martin, 1995). This means that the respondents were socialised during the years in which Hofstede's scores were collected. Moreover, these scores show convergent validity with current surveys of values and with current cross-cultural studies (Schwartz, 1994; Smith & Bond, 1998). Finally, differences between nations can be attributed to differential response styles, such as extremity ratings (e.g., Asians tended to choose moderate items). However, we used differential scores (positive affect minus negative affect) as one measure, and this type of measure, like intra-individual standardisation, controls for unwanted cross-cultural differences due to response sets.

Taken as a whole, the present results show that some cultural dimensions are important determinants of self-reports of emotional hedonic level, with an influence similar to socioeconomic factors and greater than climatic factors.

Manuscript received 31 September 1999
Revised manuscript received 7 November 2000

REFERENCES

Anderson, C.A., & Anderson, K.B. (1996). Violent crime rate studies in philosophical context: A destructive testing approach to heat and southern culture of violence effects. *Journal of Personality and Social Psychology, 70,* 740–756.

Andrews, F.M. & Robinson, J.P. (1991). Measures of subjective well-being. In J.P. Robinson, P.R. Shaver, & L.S. Wrightsman (Eds.), *Measures of personality and social psychological attitudes* (pp. 61–114). San Diego, CA: Academic Press.

Arrindell, W.A., Hatzichristou, Ch., Wensink, J., Rosenberg, E., van Twillert, B., Stedema, J., & Meijer, D. (1997). Dimensions of national culture as predictors of cross-national differences in subjective well-being. *Personality and Individual Differences, 23,* 37–53.

Basabe, N., Paez, D., Valencia, J., Rimé, B., Pennebaker, J., Diener, E., & Gonzalez, J.L. (2000). Sociocultural factors predicting subjective experience of emotion. *Psicothema, 12*, 55–69.

Bellah R.N., Madsen R., Sullivan W.M., Swidler, A., & Tipton, S.M. (1985). *Habits of the heart.* New York: Harper & Row.

Bond, M.H. (1991). Chinese values and health: a cultural-level examination. *Health Psychology, 5*, 137–152.

Bond, M.H. (1994). Into the heart of collectivism: A personal and scientific journey. In U. Kim, H.C. Triandis, Ç. Kagitçibasi, S. Choi, & G. Yoon (Eds.), *Individualism and collectivism: Theory, methods and applications* (pp. 66–76). Thousands Oaks, CA: Sage.

Bond, M.H., & Smith, P.B. (1996). Cross-cultural social and organizational psychology. *Annual Review of Psychology, 47*, 205–235.

Church, A.T., & Lonner, W.J. (1998). The cross-cultural perspective in the study of personality. *Journal of Cross-Cultural Psychology, 29*, 32–62.

Cordelier, S., & Didiot, B. (1997). *The world: Annual world review of economy and geopolitics.* Paris: La Decouverte.

De Rivera, J. (1992). Emotional climate: social structure and emotional dynamics. In K.T. Strongman (Ed.), *International review of studies on emotion* (Vol.2, pp.197–202). Chichester, UK: Wiley.

Diener, E., Diener, M., & Diener, C. (1995). Factors predicting the subjective well-being of nations. *Journal of Personality and Social Psychology, 69*, 851–864.

Diener, E., & Larsen, R.J. (1993). The experience of emotional well-being. In M. Lewis & J. Haviland (Eds.), *Handbook of emotions* (pp. 405–415). New York: Guilford Press.

Fernandez, D.R., Carlson, D.S., Stepina, L.P., & Nicholson, J.D. (1997). Hofstede's country classification 25 years later. *Journal of Social Psychology, 137*, 43–54,

Fernandez, J.W. (1987). Fieldwork in Southwestern Europe. *Critique of Anthropology, 7*, 83–99.

Fiske, A.P., Markus, H.R., Kitayama, S., & Nisbett, R.E. (1998) The cultural matrix of social psychology. In D. Gilber, S. Fiske, & G. Lindzey (Eds.), *The handbook of social psychology* (4th ed., pp. 915–981). Boston, MA: McGraw Hill.

Florin, P., Giamartino, G.A., Kenny, D.A., & Wandersman, A. (1990). Levels of analysis and effects: Clarifying group influences and climate by separating individual and group effects. *Journal of Applied Social Psychology, 20*, 881–900.

Gilmore, D. (1990). On Meditarraneanist studies. *Current Anthropology, 31*, 395–396.

Gonzalez-Romá, V., Peiró, J.M., Lloret, S., & Zornoza, A. (1999). The validity of collective climates. *Journal of Occupational and Organizational Psychology, 72*, 25–40.

Hofstede, G. (1991). *Cultures and organizations. Software of the mind.* London: McGraw–Hill.

Hubert, M., Bajos, N., & Sandfort, T. (1998). *Sexual behavior and Aids in Europe.* London: UCL Press.

Inglehart, R. (1991). *Culture shift in advanced industrial society.* Princeton, NJ: Princeton University Press.

Inglehart, R. (1998). *Modernización y posmodernización. El cambio cultural, económico y político en 43 sociedades* (No. 161). Madrid: CIS.

Inkeles, A. & Levinson, D.J. (1969). National character: The study of modal personality and sociocultural systems. In G. Lindzey & E. Aronson (Eds.), *The handbook of social psychology* (2nd ed.), (Vol. 4, pp. 418–506). Menlo Park, CA: Addison-Wesley.

Jahoda, G. (1977). Cross-cultural perspectives. In H. Tajfel & C. Fraser (Eds.), *Introducing social psychology.* Hardmonstworth, UK: Penguin.

Jahoda, G. (1992). *Crossroads between culture and mind.* New York: Harvester/Wheatsheaf.

Kagitçibasi, Ç. (1994). A critical appraisal of individualism and collectivism: Toward a new formulation. In U. Kim, H.C. Triandis, Ç. Kagitçibasi, S. Choi, S., & G. Yoon (Eds.), *Individualism and collectivism: Theory, methods and applications* (pp. 52–65). Thousands Oaks, CA: Sage.

Katona, J. (1979). Toward a macropsychology. *American Psychologist, 34*, 118–126.

Levine, R. (1997). *A geography of time.* New York: Basic Books.

Lynn, R., & Martin, T. (1995). National differences for thirty-seven nations in extraversion, neuroticism, psychoticism and economic, demographic and other correlates. *Personality and Individual Differences*, *19*, 403–406.

Liska, A.L. (1990). The significance of aggregate dependent variables and contextual independent variables for linking macro and micro theories. *Social Psychology Quarterly*, *53*, 292–301.

Llobera, J.R. (1987). The anthropology of Southwestern Europe: The way forward. *Critique of Anthropology*, *7*, 101–108.

Macintosh, R. (1998). A confirmatory factor analysis of the affect balance scale in 38 nations: A research note. *Social Psychology Quarterly*, *61*, 83–91.

Markus, H.R., & Kitayama, S. (1991). Culture and the self: Implications for cognition, emotion, and motivation. *Psychological Review*, *98*, 224–253.

Markus, H.R., Kitayama, S., & Heimain, R.J. (1996). Culture and basic psychological principles. In E.T. Higgins & A.W. Kruglanski (Eds.), *Social psychology: Handbook of basic principles* (pp. 857–913). New York: Guilford Press.

Matsumoto, D. (1989). Cultural influences on the perception of emotion. *Journal of Cross-Cultural Psychology*, *20*, 92–105.

Matsumoto, D. (1991). Cultural influences on facial expression of emotion. *Southern Communication Journal*, *56*, 128–137.

Miller-Loesi, K. (1995). Comparative social psychology: Cross-cultural and cross-national. In K.S. Cook, G.A. Fine, & J.S. House (Eds.), *Sociological perspectives on social psychology* (pp. 396–420). Boston, MA: Allyn & Bacon.

Ostroff, C. (1993). Comparing correlations based on individual-level and aggregated data. *Journal of Applied Psychology*, *78*, 569–582.

Paez, D. & Vergara, A. (1995). Culture differences in emotional knowledge. In J.A. Russel, J.M. Fernández-Dols, A.S.R. Manstead, & J.C. Wellenkamp (Eds.), *Everyday conceptions of emotion* (pp. 415–434). Dordrecht: Kluwer.

Peabody, D. (1999). Nationality characteristics: dimensions for comparison. In Y.T. Lee, C.R. McCauley, & J.G. Draguns (Eds.), *Personality and person perception across cultures* (pp. 65–84). Hillsdale, NJ: Erlbaum.

Pennebaker, J.W., Rimé, B., & Blankenship, V.E. (1996). Stereotypes of emotional expressiveness of northerners and southerners: A cross-cultural test of Montesquieu's hypotheses. *Journal of Personality and Social Psychology*, *70*, 372–380.

PNUD (1999). *Informe sobre desarrollo humano 1999* [World development report, 1999]. Madrid: PNUD-Mundiprensa.

Rosenthal, R. (1991). *Meta-analytic procedures for social research*. Newbury Park, CA: Sage.

Scherer, K. (1988). *Facet of emotion: Recent research*. Hillsdale, NJ: Erlbaum.

Scherer, K. (1997). The role of culture in emotion-antecedent appraisal. *Journal of Personality and Social Psychology*, *73*, 902–922.

Schooler, C. (1996). Cultural and social structural explanations of cross-cultural psychological differences. *Annual Review of Sociology*, *22*, 323–49.

Schwartz, S.H. (1994). Beyond individualism/collectivism: New cultural dimensions of values. In U. Kim, H.C. Triandis, Ç. Kagitçibasi, S. Choi, S., & G. Yoon (Eds.), *Individualism and collectivism: Theory, methods and applications* (pp. 85–119). Thousands Oaks, CA: Sage.

Seligman, M.E.P. (1988). Boomer blues. *Psychology Today*, October, 50–55.

Smith, P.B., & Bond, M.H. (1998). *Social psychology across cultures* (2nd ed.). London: Prentice Hall.

Suh, E., Diener, E., Oishi, S., & Triandis, H. (1998). The shifting basis of life satisfaction judgements across cultures: emotions versus norms. *Journal of Personality and Social Psychology*, *74*, 482–493.

Triandis, H.C. (1995). *Individualism and collectivism*. Boulder, CO: Westview.

Wallbott, H.G. & Scherer, K. (1988). Emotion and economic development. *European Journal of Social Psychology*, *18*, 267–273.

COGNITION AND EMOTION, 2002, *16* (1), 127–141

Different emotional lives

Batja Mesquita

Wake Forest University, Winston-Salem, NC, USA

Mayumi Karasawa

Tokyo Woman's Christian University, Japan

Cultural differences in daily emotions were investigated by administering emotion questionnaires four times a day throughout a one-week period. Respondents were American students, Japanese students living in the United States, and Japanese students living in Japan. Americans rated their emotional lives as more pleasant than did the Japanese groups. The dimension of emotional pleasantness (unpleasant-pleasant) was predicted better by interdependent than independent concerns in the Japanese groups, but this was not the case in the American group where the variance predicted by interdependent and independent concerns did not significantly differ. It is argued that cultural differences in the concerns most strongly associated with pleasantness are related to differences in ideals, norms, and practices of what it means to be a person. Cultural differences in the concerns are assumed to implicate differences in the nature of emotional experience.

Emotions are contingent on concerns. Concerns are dispositions "to desire occurrence or nonoccurrence of a given kind of situation" (Frijda, 1986, p.335). A situation that was desired will elicit pleasant or good feelings and a situation that was undesired will elicit unpleasant or bad feelings when its occurrence was undesired (Descartes, 1647; Frijda, 1986; Maslow, 1970; Skinner, 1971; Spinoza, 1677/1979). We will assume universality of the relationship between emotions and concerns in this most general form.

This study started from the idea that concerns vary across cultures, because being a person in the world can be a markedly different task in distinct cultural

Correspondence should be addressed to Batja Mesquita, Wake Forest University, Department of Psychology, Box 7778 Reynolda Station, Winston-Salem, NC 27109, USA; e-mail: mesquita@wfu.edu, or to Mayumi Karasawa, Department of Communication, College of Culture and Communication, Tokyo Woman's Christian University, 2-6-1 Zempukuji, Suginami-ku, Tokyo, 167-8585, Japan; e-mail: mayumik@twcu.ac.jp

The authors want to thank Phoebe Ellsworth, Will Fleeson, Hazel Markus, Shinobu Kitayama, and Bob Zajonc for their help and suggestions.

http://www.tandf.co.uk/journals/pp/02699931.html   DOI:10.1080/0269993014000176

contexts.[1] The "selfways" of different cultures—the characteristic ways in which an individual participates in the culture—are different (Markus, Mullally, & Kitayama, 1997).[2] Cultural differences in the ways selves are constructed and lived imply differences in central concerns. What is good or pleasant and what is bad or unpleasant will differ along with the ideals, norms, and examples of personhood.

The hypothesis was tested that the types of concerns associated with emotions differ as a function of culturally different selfways. As given concerns are more focal to the cultural selfways, they are expected to have a relatively greater effect on felt pleasantness or unpleasantness. This hypothesis was tested by comparing differences in concerns underlying the daily emotions of Japanese and American college students.

Differences between American and Japanese selfways

American selfways have been characterised as independent, Japanese selfways as interdependent (Markus & Kitayama, 1991). Independence is marked by promotion of one's own goals, personal accomplishment, distinction from others, realisation of internal attributes, and expression of the individual self. On the other hand, interdependence motivates the desires to fit in or belong, to occupy one's proper position, to engage in appropriate action and to promote common aims and others' goals.

Research has also suggested that American selves are relatively more agentic and focused on achieving a positive self, whereas Japanese are relatively more adjusting to the social environment and focused on the avoidance of a negative self and negative relationships (Heine, Lehman, Markus, & Kitayama, 1999; Karasawa, 2001; Kitayama, Markus, Matsumoto, & Norasakkunkit, 1997; Lewis, 1995; Morling & Kitayama, 1999; Weisz, Rothbaum, & Blackburn, 1984). American selfways favour self-esteem, achievement or ability, and primary control as concerns, whereas Japanese selfways include avoiding relational disruption, breaches of harmony, and the loss of face. Note that independent American selfways are about achieving positive end states and that interdependent Japanese selfways are about avoiding negative outcomes.

---

[1] By cultural contexts we mean any set of conditions with specific meanings and practices. Cultural contexts are, therefore, not contingent on national boundaries. However, some national boundaries do seem to correspond to a distinct set of meanings and practices.

[2] Selfways are distinguished from individual selves in that they are the cultural template not the individual instantiation of self (Markus et al., 1997). An individual will be likely to adopt the concerns of his/her culture, although it goes without saying that there will be some within-culture variation in selves, and thus in the guiding concerns and salient questions (Markus et al., 1997; Mesquita & Ellsworth, 2001). When we talk about cultural differences in selves and concerns, we mean that on the average the concerns of individuals differ from one culture to the next (or also that the mode is different in different cultures).

The experience of being American or Japanese can thus be very different. Yet, both independent and interdependent concerns appear in American and Japanese contexts. One of the ways to characterise the difference between American and Japanese selfways is by different degrees of focality of different types of concerns. The relative importance of independent and interdependent concerns is likely to vary across cultural contexts in ways that converge with the different selfways. There is some evidence supporting this notion. For example, self-esteem was found to be a concern for both Japanese and Americans, but more so for Americans (Heine et al., 1999; Kitayama et al., 1997). Japanese and Americans were both concerned with primary control in some occasions, but Americans more so; the reverse was true for secondary control (Morling & Kitayama, 1999; Weisz et al., 1984). Finally, relational closeness naturally is important across cultures, but it seemed more central to the functioning of the Japanese self than it is to the functioning of the American self (e.g., Lebra, 1994; Markus et al., 1997). Situations that are relevant to concerns of the independent self thus supposedly have greater impact in an American context, whereas situations that are relevant to concerns of the interdependent self will be more salient in a Japanese context.

Emotion-eliciting situations sampled in this study illustrate differences in the salience of independent versus interdependent concerns across cultural contexts. Generally, independent concerns permeated many descriptions of the antecedent events reported by Americans in this study, whereas interdependent concerns constituted the core of Japanese antecedent events. Following are instances of unpleasant situations that involve others.

American female:

I was late for a sorority function. My friends came to pick me up and I was not even close to being ready. I had to throw on some outfit and finish my make-up as I walked out the door. It was not a good start of the night [for me].

Japanese female (United States):

I was eating dinner with my Japanese friend and her roommate in the cafeteria. I sat down at the table last. While I was still eating, everyone else was waiting for me. So I felt bad for them. I could have told them not to worry about me and go ahead and leave, but I could not even say that.

The American example reflects an emphasis on the independent concern of control by relating the respondent's difficulty in meeting a self-set goal. The situation is about unpleasant consequences that are strictly of personal concern, rather than of relational concern. The Japanese situation on the other hand reveals interdependent concerns: The emotion is about the unpleasant consequences of the respondent's late arrival for others, about the social uneasiness that it creates, and about the respondent's inability to reinstate social harmony.

These self-reports illustrate that American and Japanese emotion antecedents may be permeated with different types of concern.

Cultural concerns as salient dimensions of emotional life

Concerns that are central to cultural selfways can be assumed salient evaluative dimensions. They are self-relevant and cannot leave the individual indifferent. Thus, the relevance of a situation to culturally salient concerns will more likely lead to an evaluation of pleasantness or unpleasantness, and thus to emotions. The process may be conscious, but need not be (Ellsworth & Scherer, in press).

Of central interest to this research was the relative impact of independent and interdependent concerns in everyday emotional life. We were interested in the *practice* of emotional life, aiming to compare the typical associations between concerns and emotion. The prediction was that independent concerns would typically be more associated with pleasantness in an American context, whereas interdependent concerns would be more commonly associated with pleasantness in a Japanese context.

It is important to underline the distinction between everyday emotional potential and emotional practice (Mesquita, Frijda, & Scherer, 1997). Emotional potential consists of the responses that are available to the individual in principle, whereas emotional practices are the combined responses that actually or typically occur in specific contexts. The aim of the current study was to test for typical patterns of association. A different enterprise all together would have been to test for potential associations. Even if pleasantness tends to reflect independent concerns in the American context, sometimes feelings of pleasantness may be induced by interdependent concerns. Conversely, the existence of a typical Japanese scenario in which pleasantness reflects changes in interdependent concerns, does not rule out the possibility that pleasantness is at times tied to independent concerns. This study aims at finding the rule, not the exception.

THIS STUDY

This study was designed to test cultural differences in concerns underlying *everyday* emotions. Everyday emotions were collected, by asking respondents to complete emotion questionnaires four times a day for about a week. The method allowed us to get at the dimensions of daily experiences of emotion that were salient to a person at the moment of experience or right after. We studied the emotions of three cultural groups: American students, Japanese students in Japan, and Japanese exchange students in the United States.

Our first hypothesis was that, on the whole, Americans would evaluate emotional events as more pleasant than the Japanese. From the American tendency to strive for positive selves and positive outcomes in general (Kitayama et al., 1997), we inferred that Americans focus on aspects of the situation that could make them feel good. On the other hand, we did not expect a bias towards pleasantness on the part of the Japanese. The Japanese have been described as paying attention to both good and bad aspects of the situation and the self, in order to maintain harmony and balance (e.g., Heine et al., 1999).

Our second hypothesis was that the relationship of independent and inter-dependent concerns with the dimension of pleasantness would differ across cultures. More specifically, we hypothesised that within the American group, independent concerns would be more associated with the dimension of plea-santness than interdependent concerns, and that within the Japanese groups interdependent concerns would be more more associated with the dimension of pleasantness than would independent concerns.

METHOD

Sample

The respondents were 53 American college students (A), 27 men and 26 women; 46 Japanese college students, 23 men and 23 women, who were temporarily studying at an American university (JUS); and 50 Japanese college students, 21 men and 29 women, in Japan (JJ). Of the JUS sample, 87% had been abroad for less than five years (mode: less than a year; median: 1–2 years). The mean age differed across the three groups, $F(2, 131) = 5.4$, $p <. 001$; A: $M = 19.0$, SD = 4.9; JUS: $M = 24.4$, SD = 4.9; JJ: $M = 21.3$, SD = 2.3.

The American students were all undergraduates at Wake Forest University who were enrolled in the Introductory Psychology course, and who participated in this study as part of the course requirement. The Japanese students in the Unites States were exchange students at Wake Forest University and neigh-boring universities (Guilford College Greensboro, Duke University, University of North Carolina at both Greensboro and Chapel Hill, and North Carolina State University at Raleigh). The Wake Forest exchange students received a present for their participation, the other students received US$20. Japanese students in Japan were undergraduates at Shirayuri College, Tokyo, and at Kyoto Uni-versity. Shirayuri students participated in the study as part of a course requirement. Kyoto students were compensated with the equivalent of US$15.

Questionnaires

A demographic questionnaire asked about sex and age, as well as the time that the participants had spent abroad (less than a year; 1–2 years; 2–5 years; 5–10 years; more than 10 years).

An emotion questionnaire was administered four times a day. The ques-tionnaires started by asking the participants whether they had experienced any emotion during the past three hours. If so, the respondents were asked to report the last emotion they had experienced and to describe its antecedent event (the examples in the introduction were taken from these descriptions). Respondents rated the *pleasantness* of the event on a 5-point scale ranging from *very unpleasant* to *very pleasant*.

In this study, the independent and interdependent concerns were represented as separate sets of questions. The questions representing independent concerns all have to do with the central notions of being in control and being a unique and successful person. The items pertained to *self in control* [scale from not at all (1) to totally (5)], *ability to cope* [scale from total certainty unable to cope (1) to total certainty able to cope (5)], and *self-esteem* (scale from very harmful to self-esteem (1) to very beneficial to self-esteem (5)]. In contrast, interdependent concerns were reflected in questions about relational closeness, as well as questions about the fit of one's own and other people's behaviour in the relationship. Respondents rated situations on *social distance: closer to or further away from other people* [scale from a lot further (1) to a lot closer (5)], *face loss* (scale from not at all (1) to lost face a lot (3)], and *other people's behaviour signalling a bad relationship: somebody else's immoral/improper behaviour* [scale from not immoral at all (1) to very immoral (5)]. Respondents were able to answer pleasantness and concerns by checking "not applicable".

The questionnaires were designed in English, and translated into Japanese. As a check on the translation, we had the questionnaire back-translated into English. Few differences appeared, and the two Japanese translators agreed on how to resolve those differences. Americans received the English questionnaire, and both Japanese groups received the Japanese version of the questionnaire.

Procedure

In all cultural groups, the participants met with a researcher, who administered the demographic questionnaire. By mistake, the Kyoto students did not fill out the questionnaire. For all but one student the sex could be tracked down, but their ages are missing.

The researcher also explained the experience-sampling questionnaire, articulating the different components of emotions referred to in the questionnaire. The participants were told that they had to complete the questionnaire four times a day (at 12 am, 3 pm, 6 pm, and 9 pm) for eight consecutive days starting on the day of the meeting.[3] It was emphasised to the respondents that they should complete the questionnaire at or around the indicated time, because we were interested in "on-line reports" of emotions. Participants were

---

[3] The study lasted only seven days for students at Kyoto University. We decided to reduce the duration of the study after the Japanese students at Shiyuri College had indicated that the study was very demanding on their time. As it turned out Japanese students in Japan had the highest completion rates, which may be one of the reasons why they were the only group complaining about the load of the study.

encouraged to skip the questionnaire if they could not complete it within an hour of the designated time.

Questionnaires were collected every other day, partly to maintain the participants' involvement, and partly to ensure participants did not complete all the questionnaires at the same time. At the end of eight days the students were debriefed and told about the cross-cultural character of the study.

Measures of association

Respondents were asked to complete the questionnaire four times a day, for eight days. The reported instances of emotion constituted multiple measurement points for each respondent. For each measurement point we conducted six regressions, with pleasantness as the dependent variable and one of the six concern questions as the predictor variable. The unstandardised betas from these regression analyses were then averaged within each respondent. In this way we arrived at the within-respondent means of six unstandardised betas (self in control, ability to cope, self-esteem, social distance, face loss, and immoral/improper behaviour). The mean association between pleasantness and independent concerns was subsequently calculated by averaging the three unstandardised betas from the regressions of the independent concerns on to pleasantness (self in control, ability to cope, self-esteem). The mean association between pleasantness and independent concerns was calculated by first changing the sign of the betas for face loss and immoral/improper behaviour, and then averaging the three unstandardised betas from the regressions of the interdependent concerns on to pleasantness (social distance, face loss, and immoral/improper behaviour).

Response rates

Four respondents, all male students in the JUS group, were excluded from further analyses because they had completed fewer than 10 questionnaires. On average, the American students completed 30 questionnaires (n of questionnaires = 1568), Japanese students in the United States completed 25 questionnaires (n of questionnaires = 1065), and Japanese in Japan completed 29 questionnaires (n of questionnaires = 1462).

No emotions

The questionnaire had the option to report "no emotion" in the past three hours. This option was not equally used in the three cultures, $F(2, 142) = 29.8, p < .001$. On average, 4 of the questionnaires reported no emotions in the American sample (n = 53), 3 of the questionnaires in the JUS sample (n = 45), and 11 of the questionnaires in the JJ sample.

An additional nine respondents were excluded from data analysis, because they reported fewer than 10 instances of emotions, and their regressions were thus relatively unreliable.[4] This group included one JUS man, one JJ woman, and seven JJ men. The final analyses include all 53 American respondents (27 men and 26 women), 41 JUS respondents (19 men and 23 women), and 42 JJ respondents (13 men, 28 women, and 1 gender missing).

RESULTS

General analytic trategy

All analyses were conducted using the aggregate variables per respondent. Culture and sex served as between-subject factors for all the analyses reported. None of the analyses yielded culture by sex interactions, and only one yielded a significant sex difference. Only this significant result will be reported. As the cultural groups differed in age, all analyses were also conducted with age as a covariate. Controlling for age did not change the hypothesised cultural differences, but the missing data of the Japanese who failed to complete a demographic questionnaire did reduce the number of respondents included in the analyses even further. In order to include the maximum number of respondents in the analyses to be presented, we chose to present the results uncontrolled for age.

Hypothesis 1: Differences in pleasantness.   Consistent with our hypothesis, a univariate analysis of variance yielded cultural differences in the average level of pleasantness, $F(2, 133) = 3.5, p < .05$; A: $M = 3.22$, SD $= 0.36$, JUS: $M = 3.04$, SD $= 0.49$, JJ: $M = 2.99$, SD $= 0.43$. Pleasantness also significantly differed between the sexes, $F(1, 133) = 5.6, p < .05$; Women: $M = 3.17$, SD $= 0.46$, Men: $M = 3.00$, SD $= 0.43$). A planned contrast confirmed that Americans rated emotional events in their lives, on average, as more pleasant than did the Japanese in either Japan or the United States, $t(133) = -2.7, p < .01$. Furthermore, in the American group the average appraisal of the situation was pleasant (i.e., positively different from neutral: $t(52) = 4.4, p < .001$), but neither the Japanese in the United States nor the Japanese in Japan appraised the emotional situations as significantly different from neutral, JUS: $t(40) = .6$, $p > .1$; JJ: $t(41) = -.2, p > .1$.

Hypothesis 2: Independent and interdependent concerns.   We also found support for cultural differences in the relative importance of independent and interdependent concerns as predictors of pleasantness. A repeated measures analysis of variance with the standardised betas of independent and

---

[4] The patterns of average unstandardised betas did not change by removing the respondents who reported fewer than 10 instances of emotions. Yet, the correlations with other, nonreported measures increased significantly, suggesting that removal of respondents with fewer than 10 reports of emotion made the results more reliable.

interdependent concerns as within-subject factors and sex and culture as between-subject factors yielded a significant interaction between the types of concerns (independent, interdependent) and culture, $F(2, 129) = 5.5$, $p < .01$. Thus, the cultures varied in the extents to which independent and interdependent concerns contributed to pleasantness. Further analyses suggested differences between the American group and the two Japanese groups. The Japanese groups were not significantly different from each other, $F(1, 81) = 1.6$, $p > .1$.

Furthermore, we hypothesised that within the American group, independent concerns would be more predictive of pleasantness than interdependent concerns and that within the Japanese groups interdependent concerns would be more predictive of pleasantness than would independent concerns. The means of the unstandardised betas of independent and interdependent concerns by culture are displayed in Figure 1. Paired t-tests confirmed that interdependent concerns were more predictive of pleasantness than independent concerns in the Japanese groups, JUS: $t(41) = -3.5$, $p < .01$; JJ: $t(42) = -4.9$, $p < .001$. However, contrary to our predictions, independent concerns in the American group were not more predictive of pleasantness than interdependent concerns, A: $t(52) = -1.07$, $p > .1$.

We explored to what extent the contribution of independent concerns to pleasantness was related to the contribution of interdependent concerns, by calculating Pearson's correlations by culture between the mean unstandardised

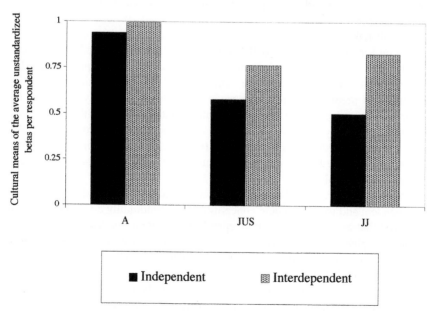

Figure 1.   Independent and interdependent concerns as predictors of pleasantness.

slopes for independent and interdependent concerns. Significant correlations were found for the A and JUS groups (A: $r = .3, p < .05$; JUS: $r = .3, p < .05$), but the betas for independent and interdependent concerns were uncorrelated in the JJ group ($r = 0, p > .1$). Thus, pleasant events in the American and JUS groups tend to reflect independent and interdependent concerns at the same time, but in the JJ group this is not the case.

DISCUSSION

This study followed the daily emotions of Japanese and American students throughout a one-week period. We found remarkable differences in the profiles of everyday emotional lives. The first finding was that, compared to Americans, the Japanese in Japan reported more often that they had experienced no emotions at all. This was an unpredicted finding. Furthermore, as predicted, we found that American emotional life was judged more positively than was the Japanese: On average, Americans appraised emotional events as somewhat pleasant, whereas the Japanese appraised emotional events as "neutral". Consistent with our predictions, independent and interdependent concerns predicted pleasantness to a different extent in the American group than they did in the Japanese. In the Japanese groups independent concerns were more reflected in pleasantness than interdependent concerns. Contrary to our predictions, the pattern was not reversed in the American group: No differences were found in the extent to which independent and interdependent concerns were underlying the dimension of pleasantness.

The different patterns of correlations suggest that different processes may be going on for the American and JUS groups, on the one hand, and the JJ group, on the other. Where independent and interdependent concerns appear to predict pleasantness in related ways in the American and JUS groups, they seem to be independent predictors of pleasantness in the JJ group. This may mean that for Americans and Japanese living in the United States a situation that is pleasant because it makes you feel unique is also a situation in which you feel socially OK. When interdependent concerns (e.g., relational closeness) underlie pleasantness in the JJ group, they are not usually associated with a sense of self-esteem and control.

Whereas the strength of associations between pleasantness and the individual independent and interdependent concerns are cross-culturally different, it should be noted that in all cultures both independent and interdependent concerns were related to pleasantness. Thus, in all three cultures pleasantness was strongly related to such concerns as self-esteem and control, as well as to interdependent concerns such as social closeness and face loss.

In sum, the most important finding of the study is that pleasantness and unpleasantness, when they occur, are typically related to different concerns in the two cultures (see Kitayama, Markus, & Kurokawa, 2000, for convergent findings). Although both independent and interdependent concerns figure in the emotional lives in all cultures, the focal concerns appear to be related to the cultural selfways. That is, emotions in interdependent groups depend largely on interdependent concerns that are focal to the interdependent selfways. The impact of interdependent and independent concerns on emotions were not found to be different in the American group. One of the explanations may be that the effects of independent and interdependent concerns on pleasantness were correlated in this group. Indeed, independent and interdependent concerns themselves were most correlated in the American group too (A: $r = .5, p < .01$; JUS: $r = .4, p < .05$; JJ: $r = .3, p < .05$).

It should be noticed that the established relations between type of concerns and pleasantness are based on within-person averages of regression outcomes. This means that the cultural differences are in part differences in psychological tendencies. When an individual in an interdependent culture encounters events that are relevant to interdependent concerns, he/she is more likely to have emotions than when the events are relevant to interdependent concerns. This is not true for the psychology of individuals in interdependent cultures. The data thus point to differences in psychological mechanisms.

Explaining unexpected findings

We had hypothesised that, in the American group, independent concerns would be more predictive of the dimension of pleasantness than interdependent concerns. The findings did not support this hypothesis. Still, there is reason to assume that interdependent concerns work differently for Americans than they work for the Japanese. First, both the mean means and the mean standard deviations of interdependent concerns were significantly lower in the American group than they were in the Japanese groups.[5] These findings can be interpreted to mean that interdependent concerns were not perceived to be relevant very often in the American group as opposed to the Japanese. The betas for the American group, then, supplement this picture to suggest that interdependent concerns infrequently play a role in everyday American lives; yet, *when* they are recognised as relevant, they affect pleasantness markedly.

It is not clear that in those cases the interdependent items meant the same to the American as to the Japanese group. Given the medium-sized correlation between the betas for independent and interdependent concerns in the American group, and the zero correlation in the Japanese group, interdependent concerns may mean something different in an American context. Interestingly, this would be true for all those living in an American context, Americans and Japanese

---

[5] For interdependent concerns the data were as follows: American: M ($n = 53$) = 1.9, SD = 0.20; Japanese: M ($n = 93$) = 2.2, SD = 0.40; Levene's $F = 14.87, p < .001$; independent samples $t(141.8) = 6.2, p < .001$.

alike. One hypothesis is that pleasant feelings in the United States context stem from congruency with the dominant independent selfways—to be unique and in control—and that perceived relational closeness and fit reflects the social value that this congruence with selfways buys you. The meaning of relational closeness and fit may thus differentiate between American and Japanese contexts. Items differentiating between American interdependence and Japanese interdependence may bring clarity in this issue.

Not only the ratio between the betas of independent and interdependent concerns varied across cultures, but also the absolute level. We suspect that the higher betas in the American group are due to the larger variance that was established in the dimension of pleasantness, as compared to the variance in the Japanese groups. Alternatively, it might be assumed that Japanese pleasantness has other powerful predictors that were not captured by the concern questions.

Differences in cultural concerns: Implications for experience

Do our data imply that emotional experience is different or simply that the reasons for emotions are different across cultures? Although the data are not conclusive in this regard, we are led to think that the emotional experience itself must be different when it is an answer to such markedly distinct questions as "Am I on top of things?" or "Are social relationships OK?" For one thing, the agency in these questions is importantly different. Appraisal theories have argued that matters of agency do influence the subjective experience of emotions (e.g., Smith & Ellsworth, 1985).

Another important reason is that situations that touch mostly on independent or mostly on interdependent concerns give rise to very different coping possibilities (cf. Frijda & Zeelenberg, 2001). Situations affecting independent concerns would logically lead one to try to be more effective or competent, or to gain more control if this is lacking. Situations that touch on interdependent concerns would not benefit in the same way from primary control or agency. Instead, the help of others is needed to improve relationships and restore harmony if this is wanting. The primary coping responses will be those of primary control in the independent context and of secondary control in the interdependent context. Thus, differences in the major cultural concerns appear to have significant impact on secondary appraisal and coping, which have been identified as defining elements of emotional experience (Lazarus, 1991).

Differences in the salience of concerns are thus assumed to have an effect on appraisal and coping style, both in the moment itself and in the long run. We believe, therefore, that concerns affect emotions beyond their occurrence to shape the very experience. As the anthropologist Rosaldo stated: "Instead of viewing culture as an 'arbitrary' source of 'contents' that are processed by our universal minds, it becomes necessary to ask how 'contents' may themselves affect the 'form' of mental process'' (Rosaldo, 1984, pp.137–138).

Questions for future research

The present study poses many questions for future research. Why did Japanese respondents report fewer emotions than Americans? One reason may be that the Japanese in Japan focus less on subjective phenomena than do Americans, and therefore have a lower tendency to report emotions. By contrast, an essential part of independent American selfways, one defining of a "good person", seems to be to work out how one feels. Americans may, therefore, be more inclined to recognise and label inner states as emotions, or indeed as anything that is more outspoken, than are the Japanese. Another, related reason may be that Japanese restrict their definition of emotions to situations involving others (cf. Levenson, Ekman, Heider, & Friesen, 1992). Thus, the range of situations qualifying as emotional may be larger for Americans than for Japanese living in Japan. Furthermore, the Japanese have been reported to place empathy before their personal emotions (Lebra, 1994; Tatara, 1998). Emotions, such as anger, should be controlled, for the sake of others who might be negatively affected by them. Emotional inhibition may sometimes take the form of a *post-hoc* regulatory mechanism, but it is equally possible that the emotional inhibition affects the emotional experience itself, in which case participants are likely to report "no emotion" (Mesquita, in press). Finally, the preferred states for Americans and Japanese may differ. Whereas Americans seem to strive for positive emotion, the lack of negative and disturbing emotions may be the desired state among Japanese. "No emotion" may stand for a lack of disturbance that is sought after by Japanese. Whatever the reason for the lower rate of reports of emotions, this reason seems no longer applicable to Japanese who have been living in the United States for less than two years.

A second question posed by the data is the following: What exactly is the reason that the Japanese (both in the United States and in Japan) evaluate their emotional lives as neutral on average, whereas Americans rate their lives as overall somewhat pleasant? The first reason for the differences might of course be that American life *is* somewhat more pleasant than Japanese life, possibly because independent selfways are primarily about making life pleasant for the individual (Kitayama et al., 1997). A second reason might be that American appraisals are biased towards positivity, whereas Japanese appraisals are not (Kitayama et al., 1997). Yet a third possibility is that Japanese ratings should be read as "neither pleasant and unpleasant". The pleasant and unpleasant characteristics of an event may be seen as balancing each other out. Cognition research shows that East Asians are less inclined to classify in mutually exclusive categories (Nisbett, Peng, Choi, & Norenzayan, 2001), which in this case could mean that they are less inclined than Americans to consider an event as *either* good *or* bad. Finally, "good" may have different meanings for Japanese and Americans. Previous research has suggested that "good" in Japanese life means that there is a nice balance between positive and negative characteristics, whereas "good" in American life is identified with exclusively positive characteristics (Heine et al., 1999).

In conclusion, this study has suggested that, as a consequence of the cultural differences in selfways, many interesting and consequential differences are to be found in the daily emotional experiences that people from distinct cultural contexts have. Naturally, the consequences of the culturally different focal concerns for different types of emotional responses should be investigated, rather than assumed. Questions about culture-specific patterns of emotional responses as related to differential central concerns should be addressed in future research.

Manuscript received 3 November 1999
Revised manuscript received 8 November 2000

REFERENCES

Descartes, R. (1970). *Les passions de l'âme.* Amsterdam: Elsevier. (Original work published 1647.)

Ellsworth, P.C., & Scherer, K.R. (in press). Appraisal processes in emotion. In R.J. Davidson, H. Goldsmith, & K.R. Scherer (Eds.), *Handbook of the affective sciences.* Oxford: Oxford University Press.

Frijda, N.H. (1986). *The emotions.* Cambridge, UK: Cambridge University Press.

Frijda, N.H., & Zeelenberg, M. (2001). Appraisal: What is the dependent? In K.R. Scherer, A. Schorr, & T. Johnstone (Eds.), *Appraisal processes in emotion: Theory, methods, research* (pp. 141–155). New York: Oxford University Press.

Heine, S.J., Lehman, D.R., Markus, H.R., & Kitayama, S. (1999). Is there a universal need for positive self-regard? *Psychological Review, 106,* 766–794.

Levenson, R.W., Ekman, P., Heider, K., & Friesen, W.V. (1992). Emotion and autonomic nervous system activity in the Minangkabau of West Sumatra. *Journal of Personality and Social Psychology, 62,* 972–988.

Karasawa, M. (2001). Nihonnjinnni okeru jitano ninnshiki:jikohihan baiasuto tasyakouyou baiasu [A Japanese mode of self-making: Self-criticism and other-enhancement]. *Japanese Journal of Psychology, 72,* 198–209.

Kitayama, S., Markus, H.R., & Kurokawa, M. (2000). Culture, emotion, and well-being: Good feelings in Japan and the United States. *Cognition and Emotion, 14,* 93–124.

Kitayama, S., Markus, H.R., Matsumoto, H., & Norasakkunkit, V. (1997). Individual and collective processes in the construction of the self: Self-enhancement in the United States and self-criticism in Japan. *Journal of Personality and Social Psychology, 72,* 1245–1267.

Lazarus, R. (1991). *Emotion and adaptation.* New York: Oxford University Press.

Lebra, T.S. (1994). Mother and child in Japanese socialization: A Japan–U.S. comparison. In P. Greenfield & R.R. Cocking (Eds.), *Cross-cultural roots of minority child development* (pp. 259–274). Hillsdale, NJ: Erlbaum.

Lewis, C.C. (1995). *Educating hearts and minds.* New York: Cambridge University Press.

Markus, H.R., & Kitayama, S. (1991). Culture and the self: Implications for cognition, emotion and motivation. *Psychological Review, 96,* 224–253.

Markus, H.R., Mullally, P.R., & Kitayama, S. (1997). Selfways: Diversity in modes of cultural participation. In U. Neisser & D. Jopling (Eds.), *The conceptual self in context* (pp. 13–61). New York: Cambridge University.

Maslow, A.H. (1970). *Motivation and personality* (2nd ed.). New York: Harper.

Mauro, R., Sato, K., & Tucker, J. (1992). The role of appraisal in human emotions: A cross-cultural study. *Journal of Personality and Social Psychology, 62*, 301–317.

Mesquita, B. (in press). Emotions as dynamic cultural phenomena. In R. Davidson, H. Goldsmith, & P. Rozin (Eds.), *The handbook of affective sciences*. New York: Oxford University Press.

Mesquita, B., & Ellsworth, P. (2001). The role of culture in appraisal. In K.R. Scherer & A. Schorr (Eds.), *Appraisal processes in emotion: Theory, methods, research* (pp. 233–248). New York: Oxford University Press.

Mesquita, B. & Frijda, N.H. (1992). Cultural variations in emotions: A review. *Psychological Bulletin, 112*, 179–204.

Mesquita, B., Frijda, N.H., & Scherer, K.R. (1997). Culture and emotion. In J.W. Berry, P. Dasen, & T.S. Saraswathi (Eds.), *Handbook of cross-cultural psychology. Basic processes and human development* (Vol. 2, pp. 255–297). Boston: Allyn & Bacon.

Morling, B., & Kitayama, S. (August, 1999). *Cultural differences in influencing the environment and adjusting to the environment: Are there independent and collective styles of control?* Paper presented at the third conference of the Asian Association of Social Psychology, Taipe, Taiwan.

Nisbett, R. E., Peng, Kaiping, P., Choi, I., & Norenzayan, A. (2001). Culture and systems of thought: Holistic vs. analytic cognition. *Psychological Review, 108*, 291–310.

Rosaldo, M. (1984). Toward an anthropology of self and feeling. In R.A. Shweder & R.A. LeVine (Eds.), *Culture theory: Essays on mind, self, and emotion* (pp.137–157). Cambridge, MA: Cambridge University Press.

Scherer, K.R. (1997a). Patterns of emotion-antecedent appraisal across cultures. *Cognition and Emotion, 11*, 113–150.

Scherer, K.R. (1997b). The role of culture in emotion-antecedent appraisal. *Journal of Personality and Social Psychology, 73*, 902–922.

Skinner, B.F. (1971). *Beyond freedom and dignity*. New York: Knopf.

Smith, C.A., & Ellsworth, P.C. (1985). Patterns of cognitive appraisal in emotion. *Journal of Personality and Social Psychology, 48*, 813–838.

Spinoza, B. (1979). *Ethics*. (Dutch Trans. N. van Suchtelen). Amsterdam: Riemvest. (Original work published 1677.)

Tatara, M. (1998). Seishinbunsekiteki shinnrikyouhyouno tebiki [An introductory course on psychoanalysis]. Tokyo: SeshinSyobo.

Weisz, J.R., Rothbaum, F.M., & Blackburn, T.C. (1984). Standing out and standing in. The psychology of control in America and Japan. *American Psychologist, 39,* 955–969.

COGNITION AND EMOTION, 2002, *16* (1), 143–163

The role of honour concerns in emotional reactions to offences

Patricia M. Rodriguez Mosquera, Antony S.R. Manstead, and
Agneta H. Fischer

University of Amsterdam, The Netherlands

We investigated the role of honour concerns in mediating the effect of nationality
and gender on the reported intensity of anger and shame in reaction to insult
vignettes. Spain, an honour culture, and The Netherlands, where honour is of less
central significance, were selected for comparison. A total of 260 (125 Dutch, 135
Spanish) persons participated in the research. Participants completed a measure of
honour concerns and answered questions about emotional reactions of anger and
shame to vignettes depicting insults in which type of threat was manipulated. It
was found that Spanish participants responded especially intensely to insults that
threaten family honour, and that this effect of nationality on emotional reactions to
threats to family honour was mediated by individual differences in concern for
family honour.

Both the ethnographic record and social psychological research testify to the fact
that offences, such as humiliations and insults, have an especially strong impact
in honour cultures (Cohen & Nisbett, 1994; Cohen & Nisbett, 1997; Cohen,
Nisbett, Bowdle & Schwarz, 1996; Cohen, Vandello, & Rantilla, 1998; Miller,
1993; Murphy, 1983; Nisbett & Cohen, 1996; Peristiany, 1965; Pitt-Rivers,
1977; Stewart, 1994). Offences are often the object of intense emotional
experiences, especially of angry feelings and expressions, in honour cultures.
This effect of offences on emotion is related to the importance attached to
reputation in such cultures. In particular, the status of one's honour is strongly
based on the maintenance of a good reputation (see e.g., Peristiany, 1965; Pitt-
Rivers, 1977; Stewart, 1994). This implies a keen sensitivity to social approval

Correspondence should be addressed to Patricia M. Rodriguez Mosquera, Social Psychology
Program, Department of Psychology, University of Amsterdam, Roetersstraat 15, 1018 WB
Amsterdam, The Netherlands; e-mail: sp_rodriguez@macmail.psy.uva.nl

The review and editorial process for this paper was handled by W. Gerrod Parrott.

http://www.tandf.co.uk/journals/pp/02699931.html   DOI:10.1080/02699930143000167

and disapproval of one's behavior and personality in honour cultures. Situations in which social respect is withdrawn, as in the case of offences, therefore undermine one's reputation and threaten one's claim to honour, thereby provoking intense emotional reactions.

Empirical research on the determinants of emotional experiences in reaction to offences in honour cultures has, to date, mainly focused on the characteristics of offence situations that lead to emotion, and particularly to anger, in honour cultures. This research has documented that offences that: (a) take place in public; (b) question the reputation of one's female relatives in terms of sexual shame; or (c) threaten masculinity lead to intense anger in honour cultures (see e.g., Nisbett & Cohen, 1996; Peristiany, 1965; Stewart, 1994). These types of offence threaten core honour values, such as the importance of protecting one's reputation in public settings, thereby eliciting intense emotions in honour cultures. In other words, whether or not an offence has implications for the status of one's honour plays an important role in determining how members of honour cultures react emotionally.

Extrapolating from this line of argument, it seems reasonable to assume that the more one is concerned with maintaining honour, the more intense will be the emotional reactions to offences that jeopardise the status of one's honour. In other words, it can be argued that emotional reactions to honour-threatening offences should be mediated by *honour concerns*, that is, by the extent to which one is concerned with maintaining honour by conforming to prescriptions of the honour code. Although a psychological concern for maintaining honour is usually assumed to be the factor underlying emotional responses to offences in honour cultures, its role in emotion has mostly been inferred on the basis of the strength of an emotional response (such as anger). The stronger the response, the greater is the presumed concern for honour. Honour concerns have never been directly assessed.

The main objective of the present study was to address the role of honour concerns in emotional reactions to offences. We focused on a specific type of offence, namely verbal insults, and on two emotions that are closely related to the loss of honour, namely anger and shame. The research was carried out among young, middle class populations living in two countries which differ with respect to the significance attached to honour: Spain and The Netherlands. Previous cross-cultural studies on social values in these countries have established that honour and honour values (e.g., reputation, social interdependence, family honour) are more important in Spain than in The Netherlands (Fischer, Manstead, & Rodriguez Mosquera, 1999, study 1; Rodriguez Mosquera, 1999; Rodriguez Mosquera, Manstead, & Fischer, in press). This significance of honour and honour values in Spain is in line with ethnographic research on honour in that country (Gilmore, 1987; Gilmore & Gwynne, 1985; Murphy,

1983; Pitt-Rivers, 1965, 1977).[1] In contrast, individualistic values that empha-sise independence, autonomy, and the capacities and achievements of the self (e.g., ambition, capability) are more significant in the Netherlands than in Spain.[2]

There are two emotions that are especially associated with the loss of honour, according to the literature on honour: anger and shame. Anger has been studied in particular in relation to threats to male honour (Cohen & Nisbett, 1994, 1997; Cohen et al., 1996, 1998; Murphy, 1983; Nisbett & Cohen, 1996; Peristiany, 1965; Pitt-Rivers, 1977; Stewart, 1994). Honour cultures promote a view of manhood in which expressions of toughness, strength, and status in public behaviour are even more desirable than is the case in individualistic cultures (Gilmore, 1990). A refusal to submit to public humiliation is therefore a core characteristic of what it means to be a man in honour cultures. In the face of offences, this refusal is expressed in honour cultures by the experience and outward expression of male anger.

In contrast to men's emotional reactions to offences in honour cultures, women's emotional reactions have been less systematically studied. In the lit-erature on honour and offences women are usually portrayed as the instigators of angry reactions in men in offence situations, and as socialisation agents of such angry reactions in children (see e.g., Nisbett & Cohen, 1996). Previous research on honour and emotions has shown, nevertheless, that offences can also lead to female anger in honour cultures: When asked to recall autobiographical experiences of anger, both female and male Spanish participants reported that being offended by an intimate other was a common elicitor of anger (Rodriguez

---

[1] Two objections can be raised to using ethnographies in social psychological research. First, ethnographies are often carried out in populations quite different from the populations used by social psychologists. Second, ethnographies are often based on the discourse of informants whose ideol-ogies may not correspond to their psychologies. We agree that care should be taken when deriving predictions for social psychological research solely on the basis of the conclusions of ethnographic records, because the research goals, methodologies, and participant populations involved in the two types of research are often very different. However, in our view, neither objection can reasonably be levelled at the present research. First, our research predictions are based not only on the conclusions of ethnographic research, but also on our own studies of honour in Spanish and Dutch culture (e.g., Fischer et al., 1999, Study 1), and on research conducted by Cohen and Nisbett and their colla-borators (e.g., Cohen et al., 1996). Second, although early ethnographies on honour in the Medi-terranean area were mostly carried out in rural communities (e.g., Peristiany, 1965), there has been recently a shift in focus in anthropological studies on honour, with research being carried out also in urban areas (e.g., Murphy, 1983; Wikan, 1984). Moreover, cultural anthropological research on honour has used a variety of methodological approaches besides the use of local informants, such as participant observation and demographic analysis.

[2] Cultural differences between honour and individualistic cultures are seen as relative rather than absolute. Honour and individualistic value orientations are not regarded as opposite poles of a single dimension, but rather as two separate dimensions.

Mosquera, Manstead, & Fischer, 2000). There are grounds, therefore, for expecting that offences would also lead to angry feelings on the part of women in honour cultures.

Shame has been also associated with the loss of honour in the anthropological literature on honour. Shame has been described as an emotion that follows either disgraceful behaviour by the self or intimate others, or the withdrawal of social respect (Miller, 1993; Peristiany, 1965). Furthermore, "having a sense of shame" seems to be central in honour cultures, and in particular in Mediterranean honour cultures (see e.g., Gilmore, 1987; Peristiany, 1965; Pitt-Rivers, 1977). Shame in this context refers to an inner disposition or personal attribute of someone who has a sense of honour and is concerned with reputation issues. Feeling shame when social respect is withdrawn, as in the case of an offence, signals one's attachment to the honour code and is moreover consistent with a self-definition in terms of "having a sense of shame". In addition, such an emotional reaction should reinforce one's identity as a person who cares for his/her honour. Because reputation is emphasised for both sexes in honour cultures, experiencing shame in reaction to an offence should be elicited in both women and men in these cultures.

In sum, both anger and shame have been related to the withdrawal of social respect in the literature on honour. Anger in reaction to an offence implies a focus on others' negative behaviour, on a lack of respect shown by the offender. Shame in reaction to an offence implies an inward focus, that is, a focus on one's image being undermined in the eyes of others, which could lead to a lowering of self-esteem. We anticipate that both emotions are experienced more intensely in reaction to offences in honour cultures than in other cultures.

Intense anger and shame will not be elicited by *any* offence in honour cultures, but rather in response to those offences in which honour issues are at stake, such as one's family honour being jeopardised. In other words, the type of threat involved in an offence situation, the extent to which it is honour threatening, is assumed to be a moderator of the intensity of emotional reactions to offences in honour cultures. Moreover, the more significant honour concerns are for an individual, the more intense one's anger and/or shame should be in reaction to honour-threatening offences. The core concerns related to the maintenance of honour (i.e., honour concerns), can be derived from the honour code. The honour code involves a set of values and norms that define honourable and dishonorable behaviour, and thereby prescribes those things about which an individual with a sense of honour should be concerned. The honour code stresses the importance of family honour, social interdependence, masculine honour, and feminine honour (Gilmore, 1987, 1990; Gilmore & Gwynne, 1985; Jakubowska, 1989; Nisbett & Cohen, 1996; Peristiany, 1965; Pitt-Rivers, 1977; Stewart, 1994).

Family honour refers to values and norms concerning the protection of one's family's reputation. Being concerned with family honour implies caring for social evaluations of one's family, for the impact of one's behaviour on one's family honour, and for the defence of one's family's name. There is thus a strong interdependence between personal and family honour: The family's collective reputation is a reflection of the reputation of its individual members, while the status of the family's honour is shared by each family member. This strong interdependence between one's own and one's family's honour means that one is dependent on the actions of one's intimates, and how they are evaluated.

Social interdependence refers to a group of values and norms that focus on the strengthening of social bonds and the maintenance of interpersonal harmony, such as generosity, honesty or hospitality. Social interdependence therefore implies wanting to live up to others' expectations, to be honest, and to demonstrate reciprocity in one's relations with others as significant concerns in honour cultures. These concerns can also be understood as a desire to express one's integrity in social relations. Personal integrity (i.e., being loyal to one's own values and principles), has also been referred to in the literature as a relevant concern in relation to the maintenance of honour (see e.g., Peristiany, 1965).[3]

Being concerned with family honour and with one's integrity in social relations are conceived of in honour cultures as relevant to the maintenance of both women's and men's honour. However, there are also masculine and feminine honour codes that define gender-specific concerns. The masculine honour code entails being concerned with one's family's well-being, the maintenance of authority over one's family, and virility (e.g., being sexually active or being able to father many children). The feminine honour code, on the other hand, centers on sexual shame. Sexual shame entails the expression of restraint in sexual behaviour (e.g., maintaining virginity before marriage), modesty, and a sense of shame in women's social relations with men, and decorum in dress. Moreover, the behaviour and reputation of female relatives in terms of sexual shame is an important determinant of the status of family honour. This means that a lack of sexual shame on the part of female relatives is an important antecedent for the loss of family honour, and that caring for one's female relatives' sexual behaviour becomes a central concern with regard to the maintenance of family honour.

We assume that the core social values and the norms of the honour code are internalised to different degrees at the individual level, leading to individual differences in the extent to which an individual is attached to the honour code.

---

[3] There exist different views on the role of personal integrity in the maintenance of honour. Some ethnographers (e.g., Peristiany, 1965) have referred to it as part of the honour code, whereas other authors (Nisbett & Cohen, 1996; Stewart, 1994) have argued that personal integrity can be seen as a transcultural determinant of honour and prestige, implying that it is less characteristic of the honour code. We considered it important to include personal integrity in the present study in order to have a complete view of honour concerns.

Thus there will be individual differences in the extent to which one is concerned with family honour, maintaining integrity in social relations, masculine honour, and feminine honour. We propose that these honour concerns serve as mediators of the impact of honour-threatening offences on the intensity of anger and shame.

Finally, our assumption that the type of threat involved in an offence situation influences how people respond emotionally implies that type of threat could be a moderator of cultural differences in emotional reactions to offences. It seems reasonable to assume that types of threat other than those that are honour-related are relevant to the self in cultures in which honour is of less central significance, such as individualistic cultures. In particular, offences in which individualistic concerns are at stake, such as when one's independence or competence is questioned, should give rise to emotion in individualistic cultures.

THE PRESENT STUDY

Participants completed two sets of measures. The first was a measure of honour concerns, that is, family honour, integrity in social relations, feminine honour, and masculine honour. The second was a measure of the intensity of anger and shame in reaction to insult vignettes in which type of threat posed by the insult was manipulated.

Honour concerns were operationalised in the form of items describing either a behaviour or a reputation that violates the concern in question. This was intended to reflect the fact that the maintenance of honour is dependent both on one's actions and on one's maintenance of a reputation that conforms to the honour code (see, e.g., Peristiany, 1965). The items were phrased in such a way as to express a lack of concern for family honour, integrity in social relations, masculine honour, or feminine honour. Further, honour concerns should be a central aspect of one's identity in honour cultures. This means that self-esteem should be dependent on living up to honour concerns. Participants were therefore asked to rate the extent to which behaving or having a reputation as described in each item would damage their self-esteem, with a higher score expressing greater damage. This measure of honour concerns was constructed in order to: (1) investigate the effect of nationality and gender on honour concerns; and (2) be used as a mediating variable if nationality and gender proved to have effects on the reported intensity of anger and shame in reaction to honour-threatening offences.

The second set of measures involved six vignettes in which verbal insults were described. Because type of threat was assumed to be a factor moderating the impact of offences on emotion in honour and individualistic cultures, we varied the type of threat posed by the insults described in the vignettes. Three vignettes posed threats to honour concerns (i.e., threat to family honour; threat to masculine honour; and threat to feminine honour). The other three posed threats to individualistic concerns (i.e., threat to competence; threat to autonomy; and threat to assertiveness). Participants were presented with all six vignettes and asked to imagine as vividly as possible the situation described in each vignette happening to them and to report the extent to which it would elicit anger and shame.

Our predictions were as follows. First, we expected Spanish participants to be more concerned than Dutch participants with family honour and integrity in social relations, and therefore to score higher on the items associated with these honour concerns. Spanish males should also be more concerned than Spanish females or Dutch participants with masculine honour; likewise, Spanish females should be more concerned than Spanish males or Dutch participants with feminine honour.

Second, we expected type of threat in an offence situation to affect the intensity of the emotional reactions of Spanish and Dutch participants: Dutch participants should report more intense anger and shame than Spanish participants in reaction to the three vignettes in which threats to individualism were posed. By contrast, Spanish participants should report more intense anger and shame in reaction to the vignette in which family honour is threatened.

Third, Spanish males were expected to report more intense anger and shame in reaction to the vignette in which masculine honour was threatened, by comparison with Spanish females or Dutch participants. Spanish females, on the other hand, were expected to report more intense anger and shame in reaction to the vignette in which feminine honour was at stake, by comparison with Spanish males or Dutch participants.

Fourth, we expected individual differences in strength of honour concerns to mediate the predicted effects of nationality and gender on emotional reactions to the honour-threatening vignettes.

METHOD

Participants

A total of 125 Dutch (61 females, 64 males) and 135 Spanish (62 females, 73 males) university students participated in the study. The mean age of the Spanish participants was 22.3 years, and the mean age of the Dutch participants was 21.6 years, the mean age of the whole sample being 21.9 years. Spanish participants were students at the Autónoma University of Madrid, and Dutch participants were students at the University of Amsterdam. All Spanish and Dutch participants were born and had grown up in Spain or the Netherlands, respectively. Spanish and Dutch participants were only included if the nationalities of both parents were Spanish or Dutch, respectively.

Questionnaire and procedure

Participants completed a two-part questionnaire. One part included the measures of strength of concern for family honour, integrity in social relations, masculine honour, and feminine honour. Each honour concern was represented by an approximately equal number of items. The items are shown in Appendix A. Note that the word ''honour'' was not used in any of the items. Participants were asked to imagine as vividly as possible that they behaved or had the reputation described in each item, and to indicate the extent to which such a behaviour or reputation would damage their self-esteem by circling a point on a 7-point scale ranging from *not at all* (0) to *very much* (6). The items were presented in a random order.

Part 2 of the questionnaire consisted of the six insult vignettes and emotion measures in reaction to the vignettes. The content of the vignettes was varied so as to manipulate type of threat represented by the insult. Three vignettes posed threats to honour concerns: being depicted as a disgraceful member of one's family (threat to family honour); being depicted as unable to protect an intimate other in a threatening situation (threat to masculine honour); and being depicted as having various sexual partners (threat to sexual shame). The other three vignettes represented threats to individualism: being depicted as a failure in an academic context (threat to competence); being depicted as lacking autonomy and independence (threat to autonomy); and being depicted as someone who lacks assertiveness in social relations (threat to assertiveness). The vignettes were derived from real-life experiences as described in a previous interview study with Spanish and Dutch adults. In this interview study participants were asked to report autobiographical situations that had negatively affected their self-esteem. Content analysis of these descriptions showed that Dutch participants more often reported threats to self-esteem in which individualistic concerns were at stake, whereas Spanish participants more often reported self-esteem threats in which honour concerns were at stake. Situations that clearly reflected threats to individualism and threats to honour were selected for the present research. The vignettes described an act in which individualism or honour was made salient, followed by an insult made by someone else that was a criticism of the described act.[4] The insult was always initially phrased in the same way: ''If others were then to say to you . . .'' All vignettes are shown in Appendix B.

---

[4] Before the verbal insult was introduced some measures were taken to assess reactions to these self-esteem threatening situations. Thus we asked participants to report on a 7-point scale from *not at all* (0) to *very much* (6) the extent to which they would think about others' opinions, and the extent to which they would feel shame and anger in reaction to these situations. A MANOVA with nationality, gender, and type of self-esteem threatening situation (individualistic or honour) was performed on these measures. The main effect of gender was significant: Female participants scored higher on shame and anger than did male participants in reaction to the situations. The interaction between gender and type of situation was also significant: Female participants scored higher on a measure of concern with others' opinion and on shame than did male participants, but only in relation to the honour situations. However, the alphas of the measures of shame and anger within each set of self-esteem threatening situations were lower than .60, which led us to decide not to report these analyses. Cultural differences in emotional reactions to these self-esteem threatening situations were not found. As will be seen later, cultural differences did appear when insults were introduced into the vignettes.

Participants then answered five questions designed to assess the intensity of anger and shame in reaction to the insults. They were instructed to react specifically to the last part of the vignette (i.e., to the verbal insult). Three questions assessed the extent to which a vignette would elicit angry feelings, namely "To what extent would you feel enraged?" "To what extent would you feel insulted?" and "To what extent would this [i.e., the verbal insult] hurt your pride?"[5] Two questions assessed the extent to which a vignette would elicit feelings of shame: "To what extent would you feel shame?" and "To what extent would this [i.e., the verbal insult] damage your self-esteem?" These questions were answered on 7-point scales ranging from *not at all* (0) to *very much* (6).

Order of presentation of vignettes was counterbalanced across participants. Order of presentation of the measure of honour concerns and the vignettes was also counterbalanced across participants. Spanish respondents participated in this research on a voluntary basis. Dutch respondents were given either course credits or a small financial reward (Dfl5; approximately US$2.50) for participating in the study. All participants completed the questionnaire individually.

Questionnaires were prepared in Dutch and then translated into Spanish by a native speaker. The conceptual and linguistic equivalence of the Spanish and Dutch versions of the questionnaire was established by a process of back-translation performed by an independent linguistic expert fluent in both languages.

RESULTS

Effect of nationality and gender on honour concerns

We first assessed the internal consistency of the four group of items aimed at assessing honour concerns, that is, family honour, integrity in social relations, masculine honour, and feminine honour. These four measures will be referred to henceforth as *concern for family honour*, *concern for integrity*, *concern for masculine honour*, and *concern for feminine honour*. Cronbach's alphas were computed for each honour concern for the whole sample, as well as for the Spanish and Dutch sample separately. We therefore computed 12 Cronbach's alphas. All alphas were higher than .70, with several being higher than .80. Next,

---

[5] Previous research on honour and emotion suggests that a feeling of one's pride being hurt is also associated with offences in honour cultures (Rodriguez Mosquera et al., 2000). In this research, Spanish and Dutch participants were asked to report autobiographical experiences of pride (among other emotions). Some of the Spanish participants' pride stories focused on what we labelled hurt pride. These stories centred on offences committed by intimate others, and this type of emotional reaction involved a negative rather than a positive phenomenological experience (e.g., negative thoughts about the offender). Pride in this context can be understood as wounded honour or hurt dignity, and therefore as being closely related to feelings of being insulted in an offence situation.

scores on items within each honour concern measure were averaged, thereby obtaining an average measure of strength of each honour concern, and were entered into a MANOVA as multiple dependent variables. Nationality and gender served as independent factors.

The multivariate main effects of nationality, $F(4, 238) = 14.45, p < .001$, and of gender, $F(4, 238) = 10.62, p < .001$, were significant. The means and standard deviations for each honour concern measure as a function of nationality and gender, together with the corresponding univariate F-values are shown in Table 1. The univariate nationality main effect was significant only in the case of family honour: Spanish participants scored higher than Dutch participants. The univariate gender main effect was significant only in the case of feminine honour: Female participants scored higher than male participants. Contrary to expectations, the multivariate interaction between nationality and gender was not significant. Finally, comparing the relative importance of the four honour concerns, it is worth noting that respondents in both countries appear to be least concerned with feminine honour and most concerned with their integrity in social relations.

Anger and shame in reaction to the insult vignettes

In order not to lose information about the specific threats to honour or threats to individualism at stake in each vignette, the vignettes were analysed separately. We first computed composite scores for anger and shame reactions to each vignette. The anger score was computed by averaging responses to the questions "To what extent would you feel enraged?" "To what extent would you feel insulted?" and "To what extent would this [the verbal insult] hurt your pride?" The shame score was computed by averaging responses to the questions "To what extent would you feel shame?" and "To what extent would this [the verbal

TABLE 1
Effect of nationality and gender on honour concerns

| | Nationality | | Gender | | | |
| | Spanish | Dutch | Female | Male | | |
Concern for:	M (SD)	M (SD)	M (SD)	M (SD)	F^1	F^2
Family honour	5.35 (1.19)	4.51 (1.08)	4.99 (1.08)	4.92 (1.33)	31.66***	<1.00
Integrity	5.94 (0.75)	5.92 (0.70)	6.01 (0.69)	5.86 (0.75)	<1.00	1.58
Masculine honour	3.99 (0.95)	4.18 (1.00)	4.03 (0.97)	4.12 (0.99)	1.53	<1.00
Feminine honour	2.67 (1.27)	2.83 (0.95)	3.18 (1.06)	2.35 (1.04)	1.37	37.78***

Note: Spanish: $n = 135$; Dutch: $n = 125$. Female participants: $n = 123$. Male participants: $n = 137$. F^1, F^2 = Univariate effects corresponding to the multivariate main effect of nationality and the multivariate main effect of gender, respectively, with 1, 241 degrees of freedom.
***$p < .001$.

insult] damage your self-esteem?'' The internal consistency of these composite anger and shame scores was assessed by computing Cronbach's alphas for each of the vignettes, both for the sample as a whole and for the Spanish and Dutch sample separately. All of the resulting 36 alphas were higher than .70, with several being higher than .80.[6] These anger and shame scores were then entered into a MANOVA, with nationality and gender as factors.

The results relating to the threat to family honour, threat to masculine honour, and threat to sexual shame vignettes are shown in Table 2. The results relating to

TABLE 2

Threat to family honour, threat to masculine honour, and threat to sexual shame vignettes

| | Nationality | | | | Gender | | | | |
| | Spanish | | Dutch | | Female | | Male | | | |
Emotion	M	(SD)	M	(SD)	M	(SD)	M	(SD)	F^1	F^2
Threat to family honour										
Anger	4.59	(1.71)	4.49	(1.52)	5.05	(1.42)	4.08	(1.65)	<1.00	25.73***
Shame	4.14	(1.72)	3.53	(1.57)	4.35	(1.50)	3.40	(1.70)	10.09**	24.38***
Threat to masculine honour										
Anger	2.93	(1.86)	3.11	(1.73)	2.73	(1.79)	3.27	(1.76)	<1.00	5.88*
Shame	2.39	(1.63)	2.25	(1.37)	2.01	(1.18)	2.61	(1.71)	<1.00	10.23**
Threat to sexual shame										
Anger	3.39	(2.06)	3.46	(1.70)	4.51	(1.67)	2.45	(1.52)	<1.00	105.03***
Shame	3.14	(1.90)	3.26	(1.69)	4.09	(1.69)	2.41	(1.50)	<1.00	71.88***

Note: F^1 = Univariate effects corresponding to the multivariate main effect of nationality for each vignette. F^2 = Univariate effects corresponding to the multivariate main effect of gender for each vignette. Univariate effects for the threat to family honour and threat to masculine honour vignettes have 1, 256 degrees of freedom; univariate effects for the threat to sexual shame vignette have 1, 255 degrees of freedom.

*$p < .02$; **$p < .01$; ***$p < .001$.

---

[6] On the basis of our earlier (unpublished) interview study on self-esteem threats in Spain and The Netherlands, a further insult vignette was created. This vignette depicted an insult in which the self is portrayed as lacking integrity in social relations (i.e., as being dishonest). This situation was more often described as threatening to self-esteem by Spanish than by Dutch participants in the interview study. However, the reliability of the composite score of shame for this vignette was lower than .60 (regardless of whether the reliability was computed for the whole sample, or for the Spanish and Dutch samples separately). For this reason, the results for this vignette are not fully reported here. Surprisingly, however, Dutch participants reported more anger in reaction to this vignette than did Spanish participants. Further, female participants reported more anger and shame in reaction to this vignette than did male participants.

the threat to competence, threat to autonomy, and threat to assertiveness vignettes are shown in Table 3.

Threat to family honour vignette. The multivariate main effect of nationality was significant, $F(2, 255) = 6.88$, $p = .001$. The univariate effect was only significant for shame (see Table 2). As predicted, Spanish participants reported more shame in response to being portrayed as a disgraceful member of the family than did Dutch participants. The multivariate main effect of gender was also significant, $F(2, 255) = 15.12$, $p < .001$. The univariate effect was significant for both anger and shame (see Table 2). Female participants reported more anger and shame in response to this vignette than did male participants. The multivariate interaction was not significant.

Threat to masculine honour vignette. The multivariate main effect of gender was significant, $F(2, 255) = 5.11$, $p < .01$. The univariate effect was significant for both anger and shame (see Table 2). Male participants reported more anger and shame in reaction to being portrayed as unable to protect an intimate other in a threatening situation than did female participants. Neither the

TABLE 3
Threat to competence, threat to autonomy, and threat to assertiveness vignettes

| | *Nationality* | | *Gender* | | | |
| | *Spanish* | *Dutch* | *Female* | *Male* | | |
Emotion	*M* (SD)	*M* (SD)	*M* (SD)	*M* (SD)	F^1	F^2
Threat to competence						
Anger	4.59 (1.64)	4.83 (1.38)	5.12 (1.40)	4.33 (1.53)	1.36	17.71***
Shame	3.88 (1.84)	3.69 (1.46)	4.22 (1.58)	3.40 (1.66)	1.45	15.86***
Threat to autonomy						
Anger	3.63 (1.70)	4.53 (1.53)	4.61 (1.55	3.57 (1.64)	19.42***	27.25***
Shame	3.28 (1.60)	3.74 (1.53)	3.95 (1.56)	3.10 (1.50)	5.11**	19.31***
Threat to assertiveness						
Anger	3.89 (1.73)	3.90 (1.46)	4.10 (1.55)	3.71 (1.63)	<1.00	3.80
Shame	3.25 (1.61)	3.60 (1.45)	3.60 (1.46)	3.25 (1.60)	3.14*	3.24

Note: F^1 = Univariate effects corresponding to the multivariate main effect of nationality for each vignette. F^2 = Univariate effects corresponding to the multivariate main effect of gender for each vignette. Univariate effects for the threat to competence vignette have 1, 255 degrees of freedom, for the threat to autonomy vignette have 1, 256 degrees of freedom, and for the threat to assertiveness vignette have 1, 254 degrees of freedom.
*$p < .08$; **$p < .03$; ***$p < .001$.

multivariate main effect of nationality nor the multivariate interaction between nationality and gender was significant.

Threat to sexual shame vignette.   The multivariate main effect of gender was significant, $F(2, 254) = 52.48, p < .001$. The univariate effect was significant for both emotions (see Table 2). Female participants reported more anger and shame in response to being portrayed as being "easy to get off with" than did male participants. Neither the multivariate main effect of nationality nor the multivariate interaction between nationality and gender was significant.

Threat to competence vignette.   The multivariate main effect of gender was significant, $F(2, 254) = 10.48, p < .001$. The univariate effect was significant for both emotions (see Table 3). Female participants reported more anger and shame in reaction to this vignette than did male participants. Although the multivariate main effect of nationality was significant, $F(2, 254) = 3.48, p < .04$, none of the univariate effects was significant at the .05 level (see Table 3). However, both main effects were qualified by a significant multivariate interaction between nationality and gender, $F(2, 254) = 3.23, p < .05$. The univariate effect was significant for both anger, $F(1, 255) = 4.57, p < .04$, and shame, $F(1, 255) = 5.69, p < .02$. With regard to anger, an analysis of simple main effects revealed that Dutch male participants ($M = 4.65$, SD = 1.40) reported more anger when their competence was called into question than did their Spanish counterparts ($M = 4.05$, SD = 1.60), $F(1, 257) = 6.15, p < .02$. No significant differences were found between Spanish and Dutch female participants' reported intensity of anger. Unexpectedly, and in relation to shame, an analysis of simple main effects indicated that Spanish female participants ($M = 4.57$, SD = 1.64) reported more shame in reaction to this vignette than did their Dutch counterparts ($M = 3.85$, SD = 1.45), $F(1, 256) = 5.92, p < .02$.

Threat to autonomy vignette.   The multivariate main effect of nationality was significant, $F(2, 255) = 10.03, p < .001$. The univariate effect was significant for both anger and shame (see Table 3). Dutch participants reported more anger and shame in reaction to being portrayed as a person who is not autonomous than did Spanish participants. The multivariate main effect of gender was also significant, $F(2, 255) = 14.38, p < .001$. The univariate effect was significant for both anger and shame (see Table 3). As with the other vignettes, female participants reported more anger and shame in reaction to this vignette than did male participants. Both main effects were qualified by a significant multivariate interaction between nationality and gender, $F(2, 255) = 3.66, p < .03$. The univariate effect was only significant for anger, $F(1, 256) = 6.97, p < .01$. Analysis of simple main effects revealed that Dutch male participants ($M = 4.29$, SD = 1.53) reported more anger in reaction to this vignette than did Spanish male participants ($M = 2.95$, SD = 1.49), $F(1, 257) = 26.05, p < .001$. There was no significant difference between the anger scores of Spanish and Dutch female participants.

Threat to assertiveness vignette.   The multivariate main effect of nationality was marginally significant, $F(2, 253) = 2.95$, $p < .06$. The univariate effect was marginally significant for shame (see Table 3). Dutch participants reported more shame in reaction to being portrayed as not being assertive in social relations than did Spanish participants. Neither the multivariate main effect of gender nor the multivariate interaction between nationality and gender was significant.

In summary, Spanish respondents reacted more intensely when their family honour was threatened, but (contrary to our expectations) there was no difference between Spanish and Dutch respondents' reactions when masculine or feminine honour was threatened. As predicted, Dutch respondents reacted more strongly than did Spanish respondents to insults concerning their autonomy and assertiveness. Furthermore, Dutch male participants reacted more strongly than did their Spanish counterparts to insults concerning their competence and autonomy. On the whole, women reported more intense anger and shame in response to all threats, except the threat to masculine honour and the threat to assertiveness, suggesting that women are generally more emotionally reactive to social criticism than males are.

Honour concerns as potential mediators

In order to investigate the role of honour concerns in mediating the link between nationality, gender, and emotional reactions to the vignettes that depicted threats to honour, mediational analyses were performed following the procedure proposed by Baron and Kenny (1986). It has been already established that the independent variables (nationality and gender) had a significant impact on both the presumed mediator (honour concerns) and the outcome variable (emotional responses to the honour-threatening vignettes). Because nationality and gender differences were only found for concern for family honour and concern for feminine honour, respectively, further analyses are reported only in relation to these two honour concerns, and in relation to the corresponding threat to family honour and the threat to sexual shame vignettes.

The next step in mediational analysis involves showing that there is a relation between the mediator and the dependent variables. Concern for family honour correlated significantly with the reported intensity of shame ($r = .37$; $p < .001$) in reaction to the threat to family honour vignette. Further, concern for feminine honour correlated significantly with the reported intensity of anger ($r = .55$; $p < .001$), and shame ($r = .62$; $p < .001$) in reaction to the threat to sexual shame vignette.

Then a MANCOVA was performed using nationality as the factor, concern for family honour as the covariate, and the reported intensity of shame in reaction to the threat to family honour vignette as the dependent variable. The covariate accounted for a significant amount of variance in the reported intensity of shame, $F(1, 256) = 32.75$, $p < .001$. The main effect of nationality was no longer significant after controlling for the covariate, $F(1, 256) < 1.00$, n.s.

A further MANCOVA was performed using gender as the factor, concern for feminine honour as the covariate, and the reported intensity of anger and shame in reaction to the threat to sexual shame vignette as dependent variables. The covariate accounted for a significant amount of variance in the multivariate analysis, $F(2, 249) = 53.68$, $p < .001$. Univariate analyses showed that the covariate was significant for the reported intensity of both anger, $F(1, 250) = 62.92$, $p < .001$; and shame, $F(1, 250) = 107.41$, $p < .001$. However, the multivariate main effect of gender remained significant after controlling for the covariate, $F(2, 249) = 30.25$, $p < .001$. The effect of gender also remained significant in univariate terms for both anger, $F(1, 250) = 60.70$, $p < .001$; and shame, $F(1, 250) = 30.07$, $p < .001$.

In sum, these results show that concern for family honour mediated the influence of nationality on the reported intensity of shame in response to insults that threaten one's family honour. However, concern for feminine honour only partly mediated the impact of gender on the reported intensity of anger and shame in reaction to insults that threaten one's sexual shame.

DISCUSSION

The main objective of the present study was to examine the role played by different honour concerns in affecting the intensity of emotional reactions to offences. Our predictions with regard to the effect of nationality and gender on honour concerns were partly confirmed. As expected, Spanish participants rated injuries to family honour, such as being unable to defend one's family reputation or allowing others to insult one's family, as more damaging to their self-esteem than did Dutch participants. This reflects a greater concern for family honour on the part of Spanish participants. These results also imply that self-esteem is to a greater extent interpersonally determined in Spain than in The Netherlands, and that it is especially dependent on the reputation and actions of those with whom one shares honour (i.e., one's relatives).

However, and in contrast with what would be expected on the basis of cultural anthropological studies (e.g., Gilmore, 1987; Gilmore & Gwynne, 1985; Murphy, 1983; Pitt-Rivers, 1965, 1977), no cultural differences or interactions between nationality and gender were found for the other honour concerns. There was a significant impact of gender on honour concerns, albeit only in the case of feminine honour concerns. Lacking sexual shame was rated as more damaging for self-esteem by both Spanish and Dutch female participants than by their male counterparts. It is somewhat surprising to find that the impact of gender on these concerns was not moderated by nationality. Moreover, two supposedly core values in honour cultures, namely, the masculine and feminine honour codes, were both rated as being of relatively minor concern in relation to self-esteem. This may reflect the fact that more egalitarian attitudes towards men and women have become more commonplace in Spain in recent decades. The use of university students as participants makes it more likely that comparatively egalitarian attitudes were held by our Spanish respondents. The absence of significant cross-cultural differences in masculine and feminine honour concerns may also help to explain why transgressions of masculine and feminine honour codes did not evoke the expected differences in emotional reactions from Spanish and Dutch respondents. We will return below to this issue.

Turning now to the expected role of type of threat in moderating Spanish and Dutch emotional reactions to offences, here too our expectations were only partly confirmed. As predicted, Dutch participants reported more intense anger and/or shame in response to insults portraying them as lacking autonomy, and as not being assertive in social relations, by comparison with Spanish participants. Furthermore, a significant nationality by gender interaction was found for two of the vignettes that threatened individualistic concerns: Dutch males reported more intense anger than did their Spanish counterparts in response to insults that portrayed them as not being competent in an academic context, or as lacking in autonomy. These results support our prediction that members of honour cultures would not react with intense emotion to all types of offence, and our argument that the relevance for the self of the type of threat posed by an offence is central to the understanding of cultural differences in emotional reactions to offences. Both men and women in individualistic cultures appear to be sensitive to offences that question their assertiveness in social relations, as compared to men and women in honour cultures. Furthermore, men in individualistic cultures, when compared to men in honour cultures, seem to be especially sensitive to insults that question their competence and autonomy.

An unexpected finding was that Spanish female participants reported more intense shame than did their Dutch counterparts when they were portrayed by an insult as incompetent. The types of situations that Spanish female participants reported as threatening to their self-esteem in our earlier interview study may provide an explanation for this unexpected result. Spanish women who participated in the interview study were final year undergraduates who had already started working in or outside the university. These Spanish women referred quite often to situations in which their capacity to perform academic work successfully was called into question. Moreover, they believed that such expressions of doubt about their competence were often founded on their gender. This could explain why the Spanish female participants in the present study reacted more strongly to the threat to competence vignette.

Our predictions were confirmed in relation to the threat to family honour vignette: Spanish participants reported more intense shame in response to this vignette than did Dutch participants. In this vignette, the self is accused of bringing shame on his/her family, which could potentially damage family honour. These results are consistent with the fact that family honour was seen as a more important concern for one's self-esteem in Spain as compared to the Netherlands, and further demonstrate the significance of family honour in Spanish culture.[7]

In relation to threats to masculine honour, the predicted nationality by gender interaction was not found: Spanish and Dutch male participants reported equivalent levels of anger and shame in response to being described as someone who is incapable of protecting an intimate other. These results are consistent with what was found in relation to concern for masculine honour. Taken at face value these results suggest that protecting one's family and property, having authority over one's family, and virility are equally important concerns for men in both honour and individualistic cultures. However, this absence of cultural difference may be partly due to the fact that the participants were students and therefore less concerned with family-related issues than an older sample would be. Differences between honour and individualistic cultures with respect to masculine honour concerns and emotional reactions to insults that threaten male honour might be more apparent in an older group of men who have greater family responsibilities. It may also be that our paper-and-pencil measures could not capture cultural differences in this domain, and that behavioural measures would have revealed cultural differences in masculine honour, although the plausibility of this explanation is somewhat weakened by the fact that we did find nationality effects on reactions to other vignettes. These explanations could be explored in future research.

In the case of the threat to sexual shame vignette the results were consistent with those found in relation to concern for feminine honour. Emotional reactions to an insult that threatens one's sexual shame were influenced by gender, but not by nationality. Thus, female participants reported more intense anger and shame in reaction to being described as being "easy to get off with" than did their male counterparts. These results are in line with previous cross-cultural research on social values in these countries, in which it was found that the cultural importance attached to feminine honour values varied as a function of gender but not as a function of nationality (Rodriguez Mosquera, 1999).

---

[7] It could be argued that what we actually measured in the present research is a concern for familism rather than a concern for family honour. We believe, however, that familism and family honour are two different, albeit related, constructs that imply different types of psychological concerns. Familism has been defined as an orientation towards the welfare of one's immediate and extended family (Gaines et al., 1997). This value orientation is measured by items that express one's strong emotional ties to and identification with one's family members, such as "I cherish the times that I spend with my relatives", and "I cannot imagine what I would do without my family". Although a concern for family honour also implies emotional ties to and identification with one's family members, the primary focus of family honour is on the protection of the family's reputation. This is conceptually distinct from the fundamentally affective construct of familism.

Although feminine honour is an honour domain that appears to be more significant for women than for men in both Spain and The Netherlands, other aspects of our results suggest that these cultures do differ with respect to the family implications of not living up to feminine honour concerns. This conclusion is based on the results relating to concern for family honour. The measure of this domain of concern included the item: "One's sister or mother having the reputation of having diverse sexual relations."[8] Spanish participants rated injuries to their family honour, based partly on such lack of sexual shame on the part of female relatives, as more damaging to their self-esteem than Dutch participants did. This suggests that the differences between Spain and The Netherlands with regard to feminine honour focus on the *social implications* of violating this honour code: In Spain these implications extend beyond the individual, and negatively affect both the individual honour of relatives and the collective honour of the family.[9] This greater impact of female relatives' sexual shame on self-esteem and family honour in Spain is consistent with ethnographic research conducted in Mediterranean honour cultures (Gilmore, 1987; Gilmore & Gwynne, 1985; Murphy, 1983; Peristiany, 1965; Pitt-Rivers, 1977).

Our fourth and final hypothesis concerned the mediating role of honour concerns: We expected individual differences in strength of honour concerns to mediate the effects of nationality and gender on emotional reactions to the honour-threatening vignettes. There was good support for this prediction in relation to concern for family honour. Concern for family honour was positively related to the reported intensity of emotion: The more the self was concerned with family honour, the more intense was the shame in the face of insults threatening family honour. Furthermore, the effect of nationality on the reported intensity of emotional response to the vignette depicting a threat to family honour was no longer significant when controlling for individual differences in concern for family honour.

The prediction that concern for feminine honour would mediate the impact of gender on emotional reactions to the threat to sexual shame vignette was not confirmed. Concern for feminine honour was significantly and positively correlated with the reported intensity of emotional response to this vignette, showing that the more the self is psychologically concerned with feminine honour, the more intense are one's anger and shame in reaction to offences that

---

[8] This item was included in this honour concern domain on theoretical grounds, and concern for family honour had good levels of internal consistency. Moreover, the inclusion of this item in this honour concern domain was also supported by empirical results: In an exploratory principal components analysis this item loaded on the same factor as the other family honour items.

[9] A comparison between Spanish and Dutch participants' scores on the item "One's sister or mother having the reputation of having diverse sexual relations" further supported this conclusion: Spanish participants ($M = 4.79$, SD = 2.00) rated the lack of sexual shame of female relatives as more damaging for their self-esteem than did Dutch participants ($M = 3.89$, SD = 1.79), $t(257) = 3.78$, $p < .001$.

threaten sexual shame. However, the impact of gender on intensity of emotional reactions remained significant after controlling for individual differences in concern for feminine honour. Thus, concern for feminine honour only partly mediates the impact of gender on the reported intensity of anger and shame in reaction to the vignette in question. It nevertheless seems most unlikely that gender has a direct effect on intensity of emotional reactions to threats to sexual shame, without any psychological mediation. Future research should try to identify the nature of these psychological mediators.

In conclusion, we regard the present study as advancing our understanding of the relations among emotion, honour, and offences. First, we established that violations of family honour concerns have a greater impact on self-esteem in honour cultures than do violations of other honour concerns. Moreover, offences that threaten one's family honour seem to lead to more intense shame in honour cultures, as compared with offences in which other type of honour threats are involved. Second, it was shown that the type of threat posed by an offence is relevant to the understanding of cultural differences in emotional reactions to offences. Third, we found evidence that concern for family honour mediates the intensity of shame responses to situations in which family honour is threatened. Finally, there is suggestive evidence that the differences between honour and individualistic cultures in relation to feminine honour reside in the implications of lack of sexual shame for intimate others, rather than oneself.

Manuscript received 25 September 1999
Revised manuscript received 28 July 2000

REFERENCES

Baron, R.M., & Kenny, D.A. (1986). The moderator-mediator variable distinction in social psychological research: Conceptual, strategic, and statistical considerations. *Journal of Personality and Social Psychology, 51*, 1173–1182.

Cohen, D., & Nisbett, R.E. (1994). Self-protection and the culture of honour: Explaining southern violence. *Personality and Social Psychology Bulletin, 20*, 551–567.

Cohen, D., & Nisbett, R.E. (1997). Field experiments examining the culture of honor: The role of institutions in perpetuating norms about violence. *Personality and Social Psychology Bulletin, 23*, 1188–1199.

Cohen, D., Nisbett, R.E., Bowdle, B.F., & Schwarz, N. (1996). Insult, aggression and the southern culture of honor: An "experimental ethnography". *Journal of Personality and Social Psychology, 70*, 945–960.

Cohen, D., Vandello, J., & Rantilla, A.K. (1998). The sacred and the social: Cultures of honor and violence. In P. Gilbert & B. Andrews (Eds.), *Shame: Interpersonal behavior, psychopathology and culture* (pp. 261–282). Oxford, UK: Oxford University Press.

Fischer, A.H., Manstead, A.S.R., & Rodriguez Mosquera, P.M. (1999). The role of honor-related versus individualistic values in conceptualizing pride, shame and anger: Spanish and Dutch cultural prototypes. *Cognition and Emotion, 13*, 149–179.

Gaines, S.O., Marelich, W.D., Bledsoe, K.L., Steers, W.N., Henderson, M.C., Granrose, C.S., Barájas, L., Hicks, D., Lyde, M., Takahashi, Y., Yum, N., Ríos, D.I., García, B.F., Farris, K.R., &

Page M.S. (1997). Links between race/ethnicity and cultural values as mediated by racial/ethnic identity and moderated by gender. *Journal of Personality and Social Psychology*, 72, 1460–1476.

Gilmore, D.D. (1987). *Honor and shame and the unity of the Mediterranean.* Washington, DC: American Anthropological Association.

Gilmore, D. D. (1990). *Manhood in the making: Cultural concepts of masculinity.* New Haven, CT: Yale University Press.

Gilmore, D.D., & Gwynne, G. (1985) (Eds.). Sex and gender in Southern Europe. [Special Issue]. *Anthropology, 9.*

Jakubowska, L. (1989). A matter of honor. *The world and I*, April, 670–677.

Miller, W.I. (1993). *Humiliation and other essays on honour, social discomfort, and violence.* Ithaca, NY: Cornell University Press.

Murphy, M. (1983). Emotional confrontations between Sevillano fathers and sons. *American Ethnologist, 10*, 650–664.

Nisbett, R.E., & Cohen, D. (1996). *Culture of honour: The psychology of violence in the South.* Boulder, CO: Westview.

Peristiany, J.G. (Ed.) (1965). *Honour and shame: The values of Mediterranean society.* London: Weidenfeld & Nicolson.

Pitt-Rivers, J. (1965). Honor and social status. In J.G. Peristiany (Ed.), *Honour and shame: The values of Mediterranean society* (pp. 18–77). London: Weidenfeld & Nicolson.

Pitt-Rivers, J. (1977). *The fate of Shechem or the politics of sex: Essays in the anthropology of the Mediterranean.* Cambridge, UK: Cambridge University Press.

Rodriguez Mosquera, P.M. (1999). *Honor and emotion: The cultural shaping of pride, shame and anger.* Doctoral dissertation, University of Amsterdam.

Rodriguez Mosquera, P.M., Manstead, A.S.R., & Fischer, A.H. (2000). The role of honour-related values in the elicitation, experience and communication of pride, shame and anger: Spain and the Netherlands compared. *Personality and Social Psychology Bulletin, 26*, 833–844.

Rodriguez Mosquera, P.M., Manstead, A.S.R., & Fischer, A.H. (in press). Honor in Mediterranean and Northern Europe. *Journal of Cross-Cultural Psychology.*

Stewart, F.H. (1994). *Honor.* Chicago, IL: Chicago University Press.

Wikan, U. (1984). Shame and honour: A contestable pair. *Man, 19*, 635–652.

APPENDIX A

Items for each honour concern

Concern for family honour
"One's family having a bad reputation", "Self damaging one's family's reputation", "Being unable to defend one's family's reputation", "One's sister or mother having the reputation of having diverse sexual relations", and "Letting others insult your family".

Concern for integrity
"Betraying other people", "Not keeping up one's word", "Lying to others", "Not being loyal to one's values and principles", "Having the reputation of being dishonest with others", "Having the reputation of being someone who is not to be trusted", and "Being hypocritical".

Concern for masculine honour
"Not defending oneself when others insult you", "Not having authority over one's family", "Being unable to maintain one's family", "Not yet having had a sexual relationship", "Being incapable of

having children'', ''Being known as someone who does not have authority over family'', ''Being known as someone who cannot support a family'', ''Having the reputation of being someone without sexual experience'', and ''Everybody knowing that you are sterile''.

Concern for feminine honour
''Having sexual relations before marriage'', ''Changing partner often'', ''Sleeping with someone without starting a serious relationship with that person'', ''Wearing provocative clothes'', ''Being known as having different sexual contacts'', and ''Being known as someone with whom it is easy to sleep with''.

APPENDIX B

Insult vignettes

Threat to family honour vignette. ''You feel rejected by your own family. One of your uncles often makes negative comments about you, such as: ''You bring shame on the family.'' If others were then to say to you: ''Even your own family is ashamed of you,'' to what extent would you...?''

Threat to masculine honour vignette. ''You have a partner and you are with this person in a café. Another person you do not know begins to annoy your partner. Your partner reacts quickly and before you can do anything the other person leaves. If others were then to say to you: ''You are not even capable of protecting your own partner'', to what extent would you...?''

Threat to sexual shame vignette. ''You do not have a stable partner and you have a variety of sexual relations. If others were then to say to you: ''It is easy to get off with you'', to what extent would you...?''

Threat to competence vignette. ''At the beginning of the trimester you promise yourself to study hard and to prepare for all your courses well, but at the end of the trimester you have low grades. If others were then to say to you: ''You are worthless'', to what extent would you...?''

Threat to autonomy vignette. ''When you are with your parents they treat you as a little child who does not have an opinion or life of his or her own. They do things for you that you yourself can do because they think that you are not able to take any decisions. If others were then to say to you: ''You are not very independent'', to what extent would you...?''

Threat to assertiveness vignette. ''You share an apartment with someone. You have agreed to buy some things together, such as toilet paper, cleaning products, etc. The truth is that you are the one who almost always buys these things and your flatmate almost never does so. You believe that this person should buy more often, but you do not dare to say anything. If others were then to say to you: ''You are very weak, you are not even able to stand up for yourself'', to what extent would you...?''

The role of ethnicity, gender, emotional content, and contextual differences in physiological, expressive, and self-reported emotional responses to imagery

Scott R. Vrana and David Rollock

Purdue University, West Lafayette

Cardiovascular responses, skin conductance, corrugator ("frown"), and zygomaticus ("smile") electromyographic activity, and self-reported emotional responses were examined in response to scenarios that varied in emotional content and whether they involved interacting with a Black or White person. Black (33 women, 25 men) and White (28 women, 26 men) students imagined joy, neutral, fear, and anger situations. Emotional contents replicated patterns of physiological and self-reported emotion found in other studies, although gender differences in emotion found in other studies were evident only in White participants. Blacks exhibited more positive facial expressions, while Whites were more negatively expressive. Blacks, and particularly Black men, exhibited greater blood pressure reactivity to the emotional contexts. For both White and Black participants, imagined interactions with Blacks increased both positive and negative facial expression. Results suggest that, compared to Whites, Blacks are both more autonomically reactive to emotional interactions and may be responded to more emotionally. The results are discussed in terms of the need to study specific contextual factors rather than broad cross-cultural characterisations.

The study of emotion through the lens of cultural experience has been particularly useful in helping to clarify the range of environmental determinants, appraisal processes, self-management patterns, somatic experience, and communicative functions of emotion (Mesquita, Frijda, & Scherer, 1997; Shweder &

Correspondence should be addressed to Scott Vrana, Department of Psychology, Virginia Commonwealth University, 808 West Franklin St. Box 842018, Richmond, VA 23284-2018, USA; e-mail: srvrana@saturn.vcu.edu, or David Rollock, Department of Psychological Sciences, Purdue University, West Lafayette, IN 47907, USA; e-mail: rollock@psych.purdue.edu

This research was supported by National Institute of Child Health and Human Development grant HD30581 and by a Faculty Incentive Grant from the School of Liberal Arts, Purdue University. The data collection assistance of Miriam Delphin, Lisa Gordon, Natalie Milbrandt, Georgia Panayiotou, Andrea Waddell, and Charlotte Witvliet was invaluable in completing this study. Regina Todd Hicks provided the voice for the audiotaped imagery scenarios. The authors are grateful to Wendy Nilsen for comments on an earlier draft of this paper.

http://www.tandf.co.uk/journals/pp/02699931.html   DOI:10.1080/02699930143000185

Sullivan, 1993). However, there has been much less interest in intercultural examinations within individual societies. For example, although differences should be expected among diverse ethnic[1] groups within American society (Matsumoto, 1993), the implications of ethnic variation for emotional expression, experience, and physiology have only recently begun to be explored (Matsumoto, 1993; Tsai, Levenson, & Carstensen, 1992). Analysis of differences in emotion between cultural groups within a particular country offers a potentially useful complement to cross-cultural research that spans national boundaries, because national boundaries are only rough guides for identifying members of a particular culture, while ethnic groups are defined by the same meaning systems, interpersonal behaviour patterns, and social expectations that have been postulated to engender cross-cultural differences in emotion (Mesquita et al., 1997). Finding cultural differences within a society that shares a language, organisational structure, and media may help narrow the explanations for those differences, because these social structures help shape the way emotion is experienced and expressed (e.g., Russell, 1991).

Because emotion may be mediated by meaning systems, social learning, or social expectations, a contextual approach is useful in research on ethnic differences. Such an approach sees emotional responding in the laboratory as a function of multiple overlapping contexts. These include the broad sociocultural context that helps define intra-group commonalities in ethnic group experiences, beliefs, and values; extra-laboratory situational context that includes environmental factors and chronic stressors, such as racism and discrimination; intra-laboratory situational context, such as the experimental manipulations, perception of, and comfort in the experimental setting; and personal context, such as psychological and behavioural factors (L. P. Anderson, 1991; N. B. Anderson, 1989; N. B. Anderson & McNeilly, 1991). This study uses the contextual framework to examine group differences in emotion between African Americans and White Americans. Because culture influences gender differences and attitudes toward other groups, this study also investigates the effect of gender and the inter- and intra-ethnic social context on emotional response.

Emotional responding by African Americans

It has been speculated that African Americans are more emotionally expressive than White Americans, because African cultural heritage values emotional expression (Boykin, 1986; Dixon, 1976; White & Parham, 1990). However, as

---

[1] We follow the convention that race refers primarily to physical characteristics, whereas ethnicity has both physical and cultural components (see also footnote 2). Thus, the term "ethnicity" is used in referring to different groups participating as subjects in the experiment, whereas race is used to refer to the variable involving the manipulated variable of "Black" or "White" actors in the imagined scenarios (see Method section).

there are few data on this point, either within or across national boundaries, the nature of this hypothesised difference in expression is unclear. It is not known whether expressive differences manifest themselves generally or are restricted to specific emotions, or if they are evident in facial expressiveness, overt behaviour, or emotional report. Also, it is unclear whether there are similar sex differences in emotional expression among African Americans as in White cultures. Women report greater extremes of emotional experience than do men (Grossman & Wood, 1993), and express emotion facially more than do men (Dimberg & Lundquist, 1988; Schwartz, Brown, & Ahern, 1980) within European American culture. Such findings are generally interpreted in terms of social roles (e.g., Grossman & Wood, 1993). Because White and African Americans appear to learn different gender roles (Binion, 1990; Filardo, 1996), it is not expected that African American gender differences in emotion will parallel those of Whites.

Although the hypothesis that African Americans are more emotionally expressive remains speculative, there are clear ethnic differences in cardiovascular arousal. Compared to Whites, Blacks have higher resting levels of blood pressure, higher blood pressure reactivity, and higher mortality from hypertension (N. Anderson, 1989). Starting from a contextual approach, Anderson and McNeilly (1991) argue that the higher level of cardiovascular disease among African Americans is related in part to chronically stressful interactions associated with minority status (L. Anderson, 1991). However, most of the studies finding greater reactivity among Blacks have assessed only cognitive or physical challenges, such as mental arithmetic or cold stressor tasks (N. Anderson, 1989), rather than socioemotional stressors that would better test the social context approach.

As noted above, emotions have been suggested to be governed not only by general cultural norms and values, but also by social structural contexts such as expected interactions with outgroups and history of inter-group conflict (Gudykunst & Bond, 1997). The research that has assessed emotions in inter-group contexts among African Americans has done so primarily through studying overt racial discrimination (e.g., Sutherland, Harrell, & Isaacs, 1987). Although this is an important area of enquiry for the contextual approach, it leaves unexplored the larger and presumably more common experiences of emotionally evocative inter-racial interactions that do not involve gross racial antipathy or discrimination. These situations can still generate stress for an ethnic minority group member. Franklin (1992; 1998) uses the term "micro-aggressions" to describe experiences of African American men that are emotion arousing and frequent, but involve subtle affronts, such as being ignored in attempts to hail taxicabs in urban areas, rather than dramatic racism. The aggregation of such "daily hassles" is more highly related to the deleterious effects of stress than is the presence of a few overwhelming stressors (Lazarus, 1984; Monroe, 1983). Other lines of research suggest that ambiguous interactions with European Americans (Crocker & Major, 1989) or interactions that implicitly raise the spectre of stereotypes of African Americans (Steele & Aronson, 1995), generate suspicions of ethnic prejudice and initiate self-protective behaviour by African Americans. For these reasons, African Americans may remain particularly vigilant about the process and tone of interpersonal interactions with Whites (Whaley, 1998).

Emotions and inter-ethnic contact by White Americans

Mere activation of outgroup concepts automatically elicits negative affect or negative stereotypes, although when the social context is such that acknowledgement of the negative stereotypes is inappropriate, controlled report of affect may not reveal this negativity (Devine, 1989; Dovidio & Gaertner, 1993; Gaertner & Dovidio, 1986). Thus, Whites' emotions in inter-ethnic contexts depend on whether controlled self-reported affect or more automatic physiological response was being measured. For example, White college students self-report more positive emotional experience in imagined interactions with Blacks than with Whites, but evidence a more positive facial expression when imagining working with Whites than with Blacks (Vanman, Paul, Ito, & Miller, 1997) or when initially greeting a White person (compared to a Black person) in a neutral situation (Vrana & Rollock, 1998). Heart rate for White males increased by over 10 beats/minute when meeting and being touched by a Black male, compared to a nonsignificant decrease when encountering and being touched by a White male (Vrana & Rollock, 1998). Altogether, these data suggest a relatively negative facial expression and increased autonomic nervous system reactivity among European Americans when encountering an African American in an affectively neutral setting. This response pattern may be a function of aversive racism (Gaertner & Dovidio, 1986) or of the novelty of encountering a Black male in this setting (Fiske & Ruscher, 1993; Vrana & Rollock, 1998).

Fiske and Ruscher (1993) integrated the literature on African Americans' and White Americans' responses to inter-ethnic contact by arguing that in contexts requiring interdependence contact with outgroup members is disruptive and negatively arousing because of presumed goal blockage. Whether this disruption is caused by attributional ambiguity for African Americans, aversive racism for White Americans, or other processes, it leads to the prediction that inter-ethnic interactions will be more negative and arousing than intra-ethnic encounters. Because affectively toned encounters often involve strong motivation (i.e., ones in which goals are being pursued or thwarted), it is anticipated that inter-ethnic encounters may be particularly negative in these contexts.

The experimental approach

One reason these issues have not received much attention is that it can be difficult and unethical to evoke strong emotional responses in the lab, especially in a context potentially fraught with racial tension. Imagery has long been used to study physiological and subjective responses to situations that are hard to manipulate and study *in vivo*. Imagery has been used to examine response to fear, anger, and disgust (Vrana, 1993, 1995), phobias (Cook, Melamed, Cuthbert, McNeil, & Lang, 1988; Vrana, Constantine, & Westman, 1992), sexual material (Jones & Barlow, 1989), and racial discrimination (Sutherland et al., 1987). Physiological and self-reported responses during imagined situations parallel those found when experiencing the actual situation (see Cuthbert, Vrana, & Bradley, 1991 for a review). Furthermore, imagery is ideal for controlling precisely the context of emotional processing, for example, independently manipulating emotion and social context variables such as ethnicity and peer/authority status (Vrana & Rollock, 1996).

The current study examined self-reported emotion, cardiovascular, and sympathetic response, and facial expression (smiling and frowning) while listening to and then imagining fearful, joyful, and anger-evoking scenarios, the most studied emotions psychophysiologically (Cacioppo, Klein, Berntson, & Hatfield, 1993), and neutral control scenarios. Studying different "systems" of emotional response is important because these systems are partially independent, are differentially under automatic versus conscious control, and are reactive to different contextual variables (Lang, 1984). The scenarios were also varied as to whether they involved interacting with a White or Black actor. It was predicted *first* that the overall physiological and self-reported response to the emotion scenarios would replicate earlier studies of emotional imagery: There would be greater sympathetic response and self-reported arousal to arousing scenarios, greater negative facial expression, and self-reported emotion to negative scenarios, and greater positive expression and self-reported emotion to positive scenarios. Further, listening to and then imagining the emotional scenario involve different cognitive processes and can produce different response patterns (Lang, Kozak, Miller, Levin, & McLean, 1980). *Second*, African American participants were hypothesised to exhibit the emotion responses to a greater extent than White participants, although neither current theory nor existing data allows a prediction regarding whether this will be the case for all emotions, or all emotional response systems. *Third*, although the research literature generally finds that women report more intense emotional experience and express emotion facially more than men, these gender differences were expected to hold for White but not Black participants. *Finally*, imagined outgroup (inter-ethnic) interactions were expected to be more negative in self-report and facial expression, and to prompt more autonomic arousal than imagined ingroup (intra-ethnic) interactions.

METHOD

Participants

Participants were 58 African American[2] (33 women, 25 men) and 54 White (28 women, 26 men) undergraduate students at Purdue University. Students were recruited from the Introductory Psychology subject pool and by fliers posted around campus, and received course credit or money in exchange for participating. Table 1 contains information about age, year in school, home state, urbanization of home town, parental education, and imagery ability as measured by the Questionnaire Upon Mental Imagery (Sheehan, 1967). Group differences in age and imagery ability were analysed using a Sex × Ethnicity analysis of variance. Other variables were analysed using chi-square. Blacks reported better imagery ability than Whites, $F(1, 107) = 9.67, p < .005$. Blacks were more likely than Whites to report coming from an urban area, whereas Whites were more likely to report coming from a rural area, $\chi^2(2) = 20.54, p < .0001$.[3] No other group differences were found among these variables.

Experimental setting

This research took place on the West Lafayette campus of Purdue University. In the fall of 1993, the campus had a total enrolment of 35,161, including 83.3% White students and 3.6% African American students (Office of the Registrar, Purdue University, 1993).

---

[2] Participants in this study were classified according to ethnicity, rather than race. We accept the commonly repeated distinction that holds ''race'' to be an ill-defined biological categorisation based on presumed genotypic homogeneity. In contrast, ''ethnicity'', which refers to shared socially defined heritage based on factors that may include common culture and history, shared experiences and upbringing, self- and social identification, and sometimes biological characteristics (e.g., Gordon, 1983; Yinger, 1985). ''Race'' acquires psychological significance mainly as a stimulus for attitudes, identifications, and behaviour (Rollock & Terrell, 1996). Thus, consistent with all published empirical research cited in this paper, this study employs consensual identification of research participants by the individuals themselves and by the experimenters as African American/Black or European American/White.

[3] This confounding of ethnicity and urbanicity is, on the one hand, expected in this sample. Ethnicity includes common culture, history, shared experiences, and upbringing (see footnote 2), and, at least in the Northern and Midwestern United States, the African American ethnic experience is primarily urban. On the other hand, this presented a problem for interpretation of results, because the stress of chronic crowding can itself increase physiological reactivity in the laboratory (Fleming, Baum, Davidson, Rectanus, & McArdle, 1987). Urbanicity could not be included in the analyses, because one cell in the Urbanicity × Ethnicity × Gender matrix was empty (see Table 1). Therefore, to examine the effect of urbanicity, this variable was substituted for participant ethnicity, and all multivariate analyses reported in this paper were repeated. No effects of urbanicity were significant at the $p < .05$ level in any of the analyses. This was surprising given the strong effects of participant ethnicity and its significant overlap with urbanicity. Thus, it was concluded that the confound of ethnicity and urbanicity in this sample did not contribute appreciably to the current results.

TABLE 1
Demographic information

	Women		Men		
	Black	White	Black	White	Total
Sample size	33	28	25	26	112
Age	19.5	22.2	20.8	20.3	20.7
SD	(1.5)	(7.5)	(3.5)	(3.4)	(4.5)
Year in school					
Fresh/Soph	67	74	52	65	64
Junior/Senior	33	26	48	35	36
Home state					
Indiana	70	79	64	76	72
Other Midwest	21	11	24	12	17
Other states	9	10	12	12	11
Home town					
Urban	49	25	52	31	39
Suburban	49	36	48	42	44
Rural	3	39	0	27	17
Parental education					
No H.S. diploma	3	4	0	0	2
H.S. diploma	51	50	60	57	54
College diploma	15	21	24	15	19
Post-Bachelor's	30	25	16	27	25
Imagery ability	71.1	85.9	75.1	88.0	79.7
(SD)	(21.9)	(20.6)	(25.8)	(25.7)	(24.1)

Note: Age is presented in years. All other data are presented in percentages. Percentage columns may not add up to 100 due to rounding error. For "Home state", "Other Midwest" states were Illinois, Ohio, Michigan, Wisconsin, and Minnesota. Nine other states were represented in "Other states". Imagery ability is measured by the Questionnaire Upon Mental Imagery (Sheehan, 1967), on which lower scores (minimum score = 35) signify better imagery ability.

Apparatus. During the session the participant sat in a comfortable reclining chair in a dimly lit room adjacent to the equipment room. Timing of events and data collection were accomplished by an AT-compatible computer controlled by software designed for human psychophysiological experiments (Cook, Atkinson, & Lang, 1987). Imagery ratings were made using a joystick that manipulated a computer-controlled graphics display (Hodes, Cook, & Lang, 1985). All ratings were converted to a 0–20 scale.

Lead I electrocardiogram was obtained with 12.55 mm Med Associates Ag-AgCl electrodes filled with Med Associates electrode gel and placed on each inner forearm. The signal was filtered and amplified by a Coulbourn Hi-Gain

Bioamplifier and fed to a digital input on the computer, which detected R-waves and recorded the interval between R-waves in milliseconds. Skin conductance was measured by a Coulbourn Skin Conductance Coupler that applied constant 0.5 volts across two Med Associates 12.55 mm Ag-AgCl electrodes. These electrodes were filled with Unibase conductance medium (Fowles et al., 1981) and attached to the thenar and hypothenar eminences of the left hand after participants had rinsed their hands with tap water.

Electromyographic (EMG) activity at the zygomaticus ("smile") and corrugator ("frown") facial muscle regions was recorded from the left side of the face using electrode placements recommended by Fridlund and Cacioppo (1986). The skin was cleaned with Sea Breeze Facial Soap and rubbing alcohol, and Med Associates electrode gel and 4 mm Ag-AgCl electrodes were applied. Research assistants were trained in this technique to a criterion of reducing impedance below 10,000 ohms. Signals were filtered (below 90 Hz and above 250 Hz) with a Coulbourn Hi-Gain Bioamplifier. The signals were rectified and integrated using a Contour-Following Integrator set for a time constant of 80 ms. The skin conductance and facial EMG channels were sampled at 10 Hz with a 12-bit analogue-digital converter. Subjects were informed that the "sensors" measured "various bodily signals".

Blood pressure was measured on every heartbeat using an Ohmeda 2300 Non-Invasive Blood Pressure Monitor with a cuff attached to the middle finger of the nondominant hand. This equipment was added late to the study, so blood pressure was collected for only 22 participants. Two of these participants had missing data that precluded analysis, so blood pressure data analysis included six Black males, four Black females, seven White males, and three White females.

Materials. Data were analysed for eight imagery scenarios which were either taken from or written to be consistent in length and style with previous studies employing this imagery procedure with college students (Cuthbert et al., 1985; Lang et al., 1980; McNeil, Vrana, Melamed, Cuthbert, & Lang, 1993). Each script was designed as a realistic emotional situation for the subject population. Each script included at least one context-appropriate response proposition, which is a description of physiological and behavioural responding in the situation (e.g., "your heart pounds"; see Lang et al., 1980). Response propositions increase physiological responding during imagery (Lang et al., 1980). This research suggests that physiological response increases in a way that is consistent with responses in the actual situation, rather than resulting in a general activation consistent with increased responding due to demand characteristics. Each scenario was 100 ± 10 words long, and lasted 35–50 s when read at a normal rate. There were two scenarios in each of four emotional contents: neutral (e.g., sitting in a restaurant reading a newspaper), joy (e.g., approaching a smiling toddler), anger (e.g., people cutting in front of you in line when you are in a hurry), and fear (e.g., having someone break into your home while you are alone). All scenarios had been validated as producing self-reported emotions consistent with their emotional labels among Black and White students from the same population as this study (Vrana & Rollock, 1996). Each scenario included other actors (e.g., waiter in the restaurant, toddler, line-cutters, intruder) who were described as either "Black" or "White." For one of the scenarios in each emotion, the other actor or actors in the script were labelled as "White" and for the other scenario the actor(s) were labelled as "Black." The specific scenario in which the other actor(s) were labelled "Black" or "White" was balanced across subjects, so that "race" of the actor was not confounded with the specific scenario content. (All scenarios are available from the authors on request.)

The scenarios were played on tape over headphones to participants. To minimise effects of presumed ethnicity of the voice on the tape, pilot testing was used to select a reader who sounded ethnically ambiguous to both African American and White participants. Several people were asked to read aloud sample vignettes. Recordings of these readings were presented to African American and European American undergraduate raters who were blind to the ethnicity of the readers. These raters were asked to judge the extent to which each reader sounded like a "White" person, a "Black" person, or neither. Based on these ratings, scenarios were recorded on audiotape by an African American woman whose voice had been rated by both African American and European American respondents as being low on "sounding Black", low on "sounding White", and highly ethnically ambiguous.

Procedure

A female experimenter of the same ethnic background as the subject met the participant, explained the study, and attached the electrodes. After a brief experiment not reported here[4], the original experimenter returned and read the

---

[4] This experiment, reported fully in Vrana and Rollock (1998), involved a brief interaction with a research assistant who was the same sex and either the same or different racial background than the participant. Several analyses were undertaken with the current data to explore the possibility of carry-over effects from the earlier procedure. First, the baseline of all physiological responses for the initial practice imagery script (i.e., the measurement most closely following the brief interaction) were examined in an analysis of variance with participant Ethnicity and Gender, and the Race of the experimenter in the brief interaction as independent variables, and all data analyses reported in this paper were completed with race of experimenter as an additional between-subjects variable. The only significant finding for the baseline analyses was that baseline skin conductance was higher for participants who interacted with a same-race experimenter than for participants who interacted with a different-race experimenter, $F(1, 101) = 5.47$, $p < .05$. The only significant finding for race of experimenter for self-report was a multivariate main effect of race of experimenter $F(8, 83) = 2.48$, $p < .005$. Univariate follow-ups showed that, across all other within-subject and between-subject variables, subjects reported greater control following a same-race compared to a different-race

(Continued overleaf)

imagery instructions. These described the structure of the imagery trial and included the instruction to "Imagine you are actually in the scene and actively participating in it". After this instruction, brief audiotaped relaxation instructions were presented, followed by an affectively neutral practice trial. Each imagery trial consisted of a 30 s REST period that involved relaxing and waiting for the beginning of the scenario; a 50 s READ period that required listening to the scenario over headphones and imagining it while listening; a 30 s IMAGE period in which imagining continued after the scenario ended; a 30 s RECOVER period that involved relaxing; and an untimed rating period. During this time participants rated image vividness, the cross-culturally reliable emotional dimensions of valence, arousal, and control (Russell, 1991), and the specific emotions of fear, anger, and joy. Participants also rated how vividly they were able to imagine the other actor(s) in the image as Black or White. After making these ratings, the participant closed his/her eyes, relaxed, and waited for the next trial to begin.

Following the practice trial, the subject participated in the eight imagery trials described in the Materials section. These scenarios were presented in random order, with the constraints that one scenario in each of the four emotional categories appeared in the first four scenarios and one appeared in the second four scenarios, and no more than two negative (anger or fear) scenarios were presented in a row.

Data reduction and analysis.   Cardiac interbeat intervals were converted offline to heart rate in beats per minute. The mean skin conductance level was converted to μsiemens and facial EMG was converted to μvolts. Systolic,

---

[4] (Continued)

experimenter. The only significant finding involving race of experimenter for the physiological data analyses was a five-way multivariate interaction for the facial EMG data involving the variables Experimenter Race, participant Ethnicity, participant Gender, Actor Race, and emotional Content, $F(6, 552) = 2.18$, $p < .05$, the univariate follow-up of which was significant only for zygomaticus, $F(3, 277) = 3.50$, $p < .02$. Decomposition of this interaction suggested that Black male participants who had previously encountered a same-race research assistant smiled more during imagined joy scenarios with same-race actors. White males who had previously encountered a same-race research assistant showed a similar trend toward smiling more during imagined joy scenarios with same-race actors. Women showed no similar trend. This effect of African American males smiling less while imagining positive interactions with Blacks after a brief encounter with a White research assistant may be seen as evidence that emotional expressiveness in African Americans is muted in the presence of someone from the majority culture (Hecht, Ribeau, & Alberts, 1989). The perception of the laboratory environment, a microsocial context for subjects, may have significant effects on the physiological responses of African Americans (N. Anderson, 1989). Although this intriguing finding is consistent with the other social context effects reported in this paper, it should be interpreted with caution given the small number of subjects involved when decomposing this five-way interaction. Because each group of participants encountered an equal number of same-race and different-race research assistants prior to this study, this variable is unlikely to have biased the results reported here.

diastolic, and mean arterial blood pressure were calculated in mm/Hg. Data were averaged over the 30 s of the REST period, the last 30 s of the READ period, and the 30 s IMAGE period. Multivariate analyses of variance (ANOVA), evaluated using Wilk's lambda, were conducted separately on the facial EMG measures (corrugator and zygomaticus) and the autonomic nervous system measures (skin conductance and heart rate), with participant ethnicity (Black, White) and gender (male, female) as between-subjects variables and actor race (Black, White), emotional content (fear, anger, joy, neutral), and period (Read, Image) as within-subjects variables. Blood pressure was analysed in a separate univariate ANOVA because inclusion in the autonomic nervous system multivariate analysis would have drastically reduced the number of subjects in the analysis. The Rest period data were used as a covariate for all physiological analyses. Read and Image period data were subtracted from the Rest period for purposes of presentation. Physiological baseline (Rest period) data were handled in the same way except that Period was not a variable in the analyses and there was no covariate. A multivariate ANOVA with participant ethnicity and gender as between-subjects variables and actor race and emotional content as within-subjects variables was conducted to analyse the self-report data. Significant multivariate effects were followed up by univariate ANOVAs. Greenhouse–Geisser adjusted p-values and the associated ε are reported where appropriate to correct for violations of the sphericity assumption. When significant *post-hoc* comparisons are reported without statistical tests, t-tests were performed with alpha set at $p < .05$ corrected by the Bonferroni procedure.

RESULTS

Emotional self-reports

Emotional content.   Means, standard deviations, and F-tests for the main effect of emotional content are presented for all ratings in Table 2. The emotional content of the scenario significantly affected the emotion ratings, $F(24, 807) = 189.2, p < .0001$, in anticipated ways. Emotional dimension ratings were consistent with the a priori emotional contents. The specific emotion ratings also confirmed a priori emotional designations: fear scenarios were rated as prompting significantly more fear than all other contents, anger scenarios were rated as producing more anger, and joy scenarios were rated as producing more joy. Joy scenarios were found also to be the most vivid overall, replicating other imagery studies (e.g., Witvliet & Vrana, 1995). It also was significantly more difficult to imagine the race of the actor during the neutral scenarios compared to all other emotional contents.

Participant ethnicity.   There was a multivariate main effect for participant ethnicity, $F(8, 88) = 2.79, p < .01$. Univariate analyses found that Black participants reported feeling more in control in scenarios overall than did White

TABLE 2
Mean ratings (and standard deviations) by emotional content

Rating/Dimension	Emotional content				F
	Joy	Neutral	Fear	Anger	
Valence	17.09[a]	12.37[b]	3.20[c]	3.31[c]	654.4
	(3.95)	(2.83)	(3.71)	(3.42)	
Arousal	11.49[b]	4.98[c]	18.38[a]	17.56[a]	416.5
	(6.10)	(4.11)	(3.49)	(3.80)	
Control	11.90[b]	15.01[a]	3.95[d]	7.76[c]	216.5
	(5.99)	(4.45)	(4.71)	(5.28)	
Fear	3.47[b]	0.86[c]	16.26[a]	3.98[b]	477.3
	(5.19)	(2.46)	(4.39)	(5.09)	
Anger	3.79[c]	1.25[d]	14.29[b]	17.64[a]	616.1
	(5.70)	(3.23)	(5.68)	(3.68)	
Joy	16.38[a]	7.62[b]	0.72[c]	0.60[c]	612.0
	(3.97)	(5.83)	(2.41)	(1.90)	
Vividness	17.44[a]	16.26[b,c]	16.34[b,d]	17.07[a,c,d]	5.1
	(3.61)	(4.69)	(4.46)	(3.37)	
Race/Viv	17.56[a]	15.95[b]	16.93[a]	17.75[a]	10.6
	(3.72)	(4.65)	(4.04)	(3.59)	

Note: All ratings are on a 0–20 scale. Higher numbers indicate more positive valence, higher arousal, greater feelings of control, and greater vividness, fear, anger, and joy. Race/Viv involved a rating of how vividly one was able to imagine the race of the other actor in the scenario, with higher ratings indicating that this was more vividly imagined. All *F*-values are for the main effect of emotional category. All are significant ($p < .05$) and have 3 and 294 degrees of freedom, except Race/Viv, which has 3 and 285 degrees of freedom. Different superscripts on numbers within each row indicate that the means are significantly different at the .05 level using a *t*-test corrected by the Bonferroni procedure.

participants, $F(1, 95) = 9.80$, $p < .005$, and being able to imagine scenarios more vividly, $F(1, 95) = 5.61$, $p < .05$.

Actor race. We also found a multivariate main effect for actor race, $F(8, 88) = 2.56$, $p < .02$. Univariate analyses indicated that scenarios involving Black actors were rated as more positively valent, $F(1, 95) = 5.94$ $p < .05$, and more joyful, $F(1, 95) = 6.31$ $p < .02$, than scenarios involving White actors. However, this main effect was qualified by an Actor × Ethnicity multivariate effect $F(8, 88) = 2.01$, $p = .05$. Univariate analyses found the Actor × Ethnicity interaction significant for valence, $F(1, 95) = 9.42$, $p < .005$, and joy, $F(1, 95) = 7.82$, $p < .01$. *Post-hoc* exploration of these univariate effects found that imagined interactions with Black actors were rated as more positive by African American participants (valence $F(1, 47) = 8.73$, joy $F(1, 47) = 12.64$, both $ps < .005$) but not by White participants, both

TABLE 3
Means (and standard deviations) of valence ratings by emotional content of imagery, ethnicity, and gender of participants, and race of actor in the scenario

Emotion	Men			Women		
	Black Actors	White Actors	Mean	Black Actors	White Actors	Mean
Black participants						
Joy	18.2	15.9	17.0	16.5	17.1	16.8
	(2.8)	(3.8)	(3.5)	(6.3)	(4.0)	(5.2)
Neutral	12.3	12.0	12.2	13.7	12.0	12.8
	(3.4)	(3.0)	(3.2)	(3.6)	(3.3)	(3.5)
Fear	4.0	2.6	3.3	3.5	2.4	2.9
	(3.9)	(2.8)	(3.4)	(5.1)	(3.2)	(4.3)
Anger	3.4	2.3	2.9	2.9	2.2	2.6
	(3.5)	(3.5)	(3.5)	(3.9)	(4.0)	(3.9)
Mean	9.5	8.2		9.1	8.4	
	(7.1)	(6.7)		(5.2)	(7.4)	
White participants						
Joy	15.6	17.4	16.5	18.5	17.6	18.0
	(4.6)	(2.2)	(3.7)	(2.0)	(3.2)	(2.6)
Neutral	11.6	11.5	11.5	13.3	12.6	12.9
	(1.7)	(1.8)	(1.7)	(2.2)	(2.5)	(2.3)
Fear	3.6	3.6	3.6	2.7	3.1	2.9
	(3.9)	(3.2)	(3.5)	(3.4)	(3.6)	(3.5)
Anger	4.1	4.1	4.1	3.8	3.7	3.7
	(2.6)	(3.2)	(2.9)	(3.2)	(3.1)	(3.1)
Mean	8.7	9.2		9.6	9.3	
	(6.1)	(6.3)		(7.2)	(6.9)	

Note: Ratings are on a 0–20 scale. Higher numbers indicate more positive valence.

($F < 0.2$). Table 3 shows this effect for valence. Thus, emotional images were reported to be more negative in outgroup contexts for African Americans, as hypothesised, but not for Whites. Also, participants were able to imagine more vividly the actor's race in scenarios involving White actors ($M = 17.3$, $SD = 3.9$) than scenarios involving Black actors ($M = 16.8$, $SD = 4.3$), $F(1, 95) = 4.09$, $p < .05$.

A significant multivariate Actor race × Content interaction was also found, $F(24, 807) = 2.16$, $p < .005$. A significant univariate effect was found for fear ratings, $F(3, 285) = 4.80$, $p < .01$, $\varepsilon = .70$. Anger scenarios involving Black actors were rated as more fearful ($M = 5.1$, $SD = 5.5$) than anger scenarios involving White actors ($M = 3.1$, $SD = 4.6$), $F(1, 95) = 13.85$, $p < .0003$.

Gender.   One of the hypotheses was that gender differences in emotional report often found among White samples would not be found in Black samples. Although the overall multivariate statistic was not significant, an Actor × Ethnicity × Gender × Content interaction for valence was consistent with this hypothesis, $F(3, 297) = 3.20, p < .05, \varepsilon = .86$. The data are shown in Table 3. In order to disentangle this interaction, Black and White participants were analysed separately. Although both groups exhibited the expected strong main effects for emotional content, they differed in their pattern of scores in other respects. White men and women reacted differently to the different emotional scenarios, as evidenced by a significant interaction between Content and Gender, $F(3, 153) = 3.58, p < .05$. As previously found (Grossman & Wood, 1993), White women used a larger range on the rating scale than did White men, reporting more positive valence to joy and neutral scenarios and more negative valence to fear and anger scenarios. Black participants did not show this effect, $F = 0.3$, although they did report significantly more positive valence for scenarios involving Black actors, as described above. Thus, the gender differences in self-report of emotion often found in the literature were evident here in White, but not Black participants.

Physiological baseline

Baseline means and standard deviations for all physiological variables are presented in Table 4. For baseline EMG there was a main effect of participant ethnicity, $F(2, 97) = 7.09, p < .005$, and gender, $F(2, 97) = 5.69, p < .005$.

TABLE 4
Means (and standard deviations) of baseline data for physiological variables

	Women		Men	
	Black	*White*	*Black*	*White*
Corrugator EMG (μvolts)	1.85	3.44	1.67	2.11
	(1.10)	(2.11)	(0.78)	(1.12)
Zygomaticus EMG (μvolts)	1.97	1.17	1.15	0.95
	(2.51)	(0.80)	(0.79)	(1.23)
SCL (μSiemens)	1.52	2.80	2.18	3.59
	(1.43)	(3.88)	(2.10)	(2.99)
Heart rate (bpm)	72.55	68.88	62.56	61.44
	(9.38)	(8.97)	(8.08)	(9.36)
MABP (mm/Hg)	88.22	62.25	84.75	66.28
	(9.09)	(6.23)	(23.91)	(7.63)

Note: EMG, electromyographic activity; SCL, skin conductance level; MABP, mean arterial blood pressure. Standard deviations are presented in parentheses under their respective means.

Univariate analyses found that baseline corrugator EMG activity was greater for White than for Black participants, $F(1, 99) = 13.25$, $p < .0004$, and greater for women than for men, $F(1, 99) = 7.33$, $p < .01$. There was also a trend for ethnic differences in zygomaticus activity that was in the *opposite* direction to that found for corrugator: Black participants tended to have greater baseline zygomaticus than White participants, $F(1, 98) = 2.68$, $p < .11$. Thus, the ethnic differences in baseline activity appear expression-specific and not related to general facial muscle tension differences in Black and White participants.

Analysis of autonomic nervous system variables also revealed main effects of participant ethnicity, $F(2, 90) = 4.23$, $p < .02$, and gender, $F(2, 90) = 10.71$, $p < .0001$. White participants had greater baseline skin conductance level than did Black participants, $F(1, 99) = 5.96$, $p < .02$, a common finding given that people with darker skin have fewer active sweat glands than people with lighter skin (Boucsein, 1992). Women had greater baseline heart rate than did men, $F(1, 91) = 20.95$, $p < .0001$. Black participants had a higher baseline mean arterial blood pressure than did White participants, $F(1, 16) = 10.02$, $p < .01$, a common finding among adults (Anderson, 1989).

Facial expression

Emotional content.   As expected, facial expression differed depending on the emotional content of the imagery, $F(6, 582) = 24.6$, $p < .0001$. Corrugator (brow) region furrowing was greater during fear ($M = 1.24$ µvolts) and anger ($M = 1.07$ µvolts) scenarios than during neutral ($M = 0.62$ µvolts) scenarios, which in turn were larger than joy ($M = -0.02$ µvolts) scenarios, $F(3, 296) = 28.21$, $p < .0001$, $\varepsilon = .92$. The zygomaticus (smile) region increased more during joy scenarios ($M = 0.58$ µvolts) than during any other emotional scenario (means from -0.7 to $+0.03$ µvolts), $F(1, 293) = 30.43$, $p < .0001$, $\varepsilon = .42$. These data are presented in Figure 1, which shows within-subject standardised change scores for the effect of emotional content on all physiological variables. A multivariate interaction between Content and Period, $F(6, 586) = 9.94$, $p < .0001$, showed that the emotional content differences for both these regions were more pronounced during the Image compared to the Read period. This was the case for both the corrugator, $F(3, 297) = 7.70$, $p < .0003$, $\varepsilon = .79$, and the zygomaticus, $F(3, 294) = 14.43$, $p < .0001$, $\varepsilon = .40$.

Participant ethnicity and gender.   One of the hypotheses was that Black subjects would be more emotionally expressive than White subjects. In fact, Black and White subjects did differ in facial expressiveness to emotional imagery, as is shown by a significant multivariate two-way Content × Ethnicity interaction, $F(6, 582) = 2.41$, $p < .05$; and a three-way Content × Ethnicity × Period interaction, $F(6, 586) = 2.47$, $p < .05$. Follow-ups found that Blacks exhibited a trend toward greater zygomaticus (smiling) activity than did Whites

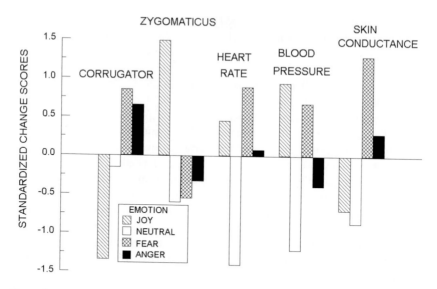

Figure 1. Standardised change scores for corrugator EMG, zygomaticus EMG, heart rate, mean arterial blood pressure, and skin conductance during the Read and Image period as a function of the emotional content of the image.

in the positive (joy) scenarios, Content $\times$ Ethnicity, $F(3, 293) = 2.89, p < .08$, $\varepsilon = .42$; Content $\times$ Ethnicity $\times$ Period, $F(3, 294) = 2.94, p < .08, \varepsilon = .40$. White participants exhibited a trend towards greater corrugator (brow furrowing) activity than did Blacks during negative (anger and fear) imagery, Content $\times$ Ethnicity $\times$ Period $F(3, 297) = 1.80, p < .16, \varepsilon = .79$. Thus, Blacks were more positively expressive than were Whites during positive images, and Whites were more negatively expressive than were Blacks during negative images.

Previous data have found that European American women are more facially expressive than men; however, these results were not expected to hold across ethnic groups. This was examined through decomposing the Content $\times$ Ethnicity $\times$ Gender $\times$ Period multivariate interaction, $F(6, 586) = 2.38, p < .05$. The univariate follow-up was significant for the corrugator region, $F(3, 297) = 3.21, p < .05, \varepsilon = .79$, and marginally significant for the zygomaticus region, $F(3, 294) = 1.74, p < .19, \varepsilon = .40$. The corrugator data are examined first. Because the emotion differences were greater during the Image than Read period, as described above, this interaction was examined separately for the Read and Image periods, and a Content $\times$ Ethnicity $\times$ Gender interaction was found only for the Image period, $F(3, 296) = 2.76, p < .05, \varepsilon = .85$. This interaction was followed up by examining the imagery data separately for men and women. As illustrated in Figure 2, both men and women exhibited a strong effect of emotional content. However, only for women was there a Content $\times$

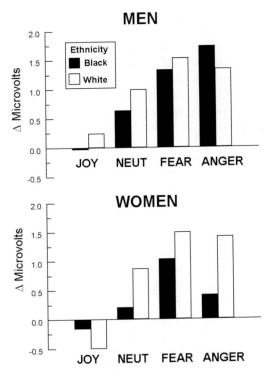

Figure 2. Corrugator EMG activity during joy, neutral, fear, and anger Image periods presented separately by participant gender and ethnicity.

Ethnicity interaction, $F(3, 161) = 5.32, p < .004, \varepsilon = .81$. White women exhibited a greater range of emotion-related corrugator region response than did Black women, with greater decrease in corrugator during joy scenarios and greater increase in corrugator during the neutral, fear, and anger scenarios. Follow-up examination of the trend in the zygomaticus region data showed that White *women* and Black *men* produced the greatest smiles during joy imagery. Thus, the gender differences in facial expressiveness found in many other studies were found here for White subjects, but not for African Americans, similar to the pattern found for the self-report data.

Actor race. Joy scenarios involving Black actors produced more smiling than did joy scenarios involving White actors, as is shown by a significant multivariate interaction between Actor and Content, $F(6, 582) = 2.34, p < .05$. Univariate follow-ups found that zygomaticus increase during joy scenarios was greater when the scenario involved a Black actor (0.79 μvolts) than when it involved a White actor (0.39 μvolts), $F(3, 293) = 4.36, p < .03, \varepsilon = .48$. A marginal univariate interaction suggested that the difference in smiling during joy scenarios with Black actors compared with White actors was greatest for Black men, Content × Actor × Ethnicity × Gender, $F(3, 293) = 2.34, p < .12$, $\varepsilon = .48$. That is, the greatest amount of smiling was found for *African American men* in *joy* scenarios involving *Black* actors.

In addition to the finding of increased positive expression in scenarios with Black actors, there was a suggestion of increased *negative* expression in scenarios with Black actors, as shown by a multivariate interaction between Actor and Period, $F(2, 97) = 2.97, p < .06$ and a univariate effect for corrugator, $F(1, 99) = 6.09, p < .02$. In scenarios involving Black actors, corrugator increased significantly from the Read ($M = 0.64$ µvolts) to Image ($M = 0.80$ µvolts) period, $F(1, 103) = 8.78, p < .005$. No difference was found for scenarios involving White actors (.71–.73 µvolts from Read to Image), $F < 0.3$.

Autonomic nervous system

Heart rate (HR) and skin conductance (SC). A multivariate Content × Period interaction, $F(6, 532) = 3.29, p < .005$, was found. Univariate analyses indicated a significant effect for HR, $F(3, 267) = 5.81, p < .001, \varepsilon = .97$. When Read and Image periods were analysed separately, no differences were found between emotional scenarios during the Read period, $F < 1$. However, in the Image period the change in HR was significantly greater during fear (0.56 beats/min), anger (0.43 beats/min), and joy (0.49 beats/min) imagery than during neutral (0.19 beats/min) imagery, $F(3, 266) = 3.02, p < .04, \varepsilon = .88$. Thus, the effects of emotional imagery on HR was greater during imagery than while participants were listening to the imagery script, just as was found for facial expression. Figure 1 shows that the pattern of SC means responded, like HR, to the affective arousal of the emotional scenario; however, these differences were not statistically significant, $F(3, 296) = 2.05, p < .15, \varepsilon = .45$.

We hypothesised that African American participants would be more autonomically reactive to emotional scenarios than would White participants, and that outgroup scenarios would be more arousing than ingroup scenarios. These hypotheses were not supported. Instead, a complicated and unexpected multivariate interaction was found between emotional content, gender, and the race of the actor in the imagined interaction, $F(6, 528) = 3.10, p < .006$. Univariate follow-ups found that this interaction was significant for both HR, $F(3, 266) = 3.47, p < .02, \varepsilon = .97$, and SC, $F(3, 296) = 3.34, p < .03, \varepsilon = .95$. To decompose this interaction for each measure, data for each scenario content were analysed separately. For HR, no significant gender or actor race differences were found for joy, fear, or anger imagery. During neutral imagery, men were more reactive to scenarios involving Black actors, while women did not respond differently to Black or White actors, Actor × Gender, $F(1, 98) = 6.75, p < .02$. Results were very similar for SC.

Mean arterial blood pressure.[5]   Figure 1 illustrates a marginally significant main effect of emotional content, $F(3, 47) = 2.42, p < .09, \varepsilon = .84$: blood pressure increase during fear scenarios (1.14 mm/Hg) was significantly different from the decrease found for neutral scenarios (-1.12 mm/Hg), with joy (0.75 mm/Hg) and anger (-0.05 mm/Hg) scenarios nonsignificantly between. Unexpectedly, however, this was modified by the ethnicity of the actor, Content × Actor × Period $F(3, 48) = 3.78, p < .03, \varepsilon = .90$. To follow up this interaction, data were analysed separately for Black and White actors, and a significant main effect for emotional content was found only for White actors, $F(3, 47) = 3.45, p < .04, \varepsilon = .78$.

Many studies have found that African Americans exhibit greater blood pressure reactivity than do White Americans (N. Anderson, 1989). This study replicated previous findings: Blood pressure increased among Black participants (mean $= +1.22$ mm/Hg) and decreased among White participants (mean $= -0.85$ mm/Hg), $F(1, 15) = 4.81, p < .05$. However, results were complicated by the following interactions: Ethnicity × Gender × Period, $F(1, 16) = 17.89$, $p < .0006$, Gender × Period, $F(1, 16) = 8.72, p < .01$, and Ethnicity × Period, $F(1, 16) = 14.84, p < .002$. Follow-up analyses found that, as can be seen in Figure 3, the increase for Black participants was found primarily among men,

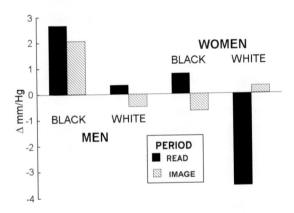

Figure 3. Mean arterial blood pressure shown separately by participant gender and ethnicity, and the Read and Image period of each trial.

---

[5] Results for analyses of systolic (SBP) and diastolic blood pressure (DBP) were substantially the same as that found for mean arterial blood pressure, including finding ethnicity differences in both baseline systolic and diastolic blood pressure. (Separate analyses of SBP and DBP are available from the authors.) One interesting finding was that the pattern of SBP and DBP change differentiated between fear and anger in a manner similar to that found in other studies of blood pressure changes in fear and anger (Ax, 1953; Roberts & Weerts, 1982).

and the decrease for White participants was found primarily among women during the Read period. The contextual approach hypothesised that reactivity among African Americans would be greatest during affective scenarios, and this was the case. The pattern of results showed that the greatest reactivity in any group was among African American males in emotionally arousing scenarios, Content × Gender × Period, $F(3, 48) = 3.65$, $p < .02$, $\varepsilon = .74$; Content × Ethnicity × Period $F(3, 48) = 2.75$, $p < .08$, $\varepsilon = .74$; Content × Ethnicity × Gender × Period, $F(3, 48) = 1.99$, $p < .15$, $\varepsilon = .74$.

Finally, it was hypothesised that outgroup interactions would be more arousing than ingroup interactions. This was the case only for African American males: the largest blood pressure response for any subject group in any condition was by *Black* males in *arousing* situations involving *White* actors, Content × Actor × Ethnicity × Gender × Period $F(3, 48) = 2.52$, $p < .08$, $\varepsilon = .90$. Unfortunately, the small sample size for blood pressure does not allow the power to assess the significance of specific differences in *post-hoc* follow-ups.

DISCUSSION

The first hypothesis was that the emotional scenarios would replicate the pattern of physiological and self-reported response found in other work. Results confirmed that the self-reported emotional response to the scenarios was as expected (see Table 2). That is, the scenarios were reported to fall along the dimensions of valence, arousal, and control, and to evoke the specific emotions of joy, fear, and anger. Physiological changes replicated previous findings as well (Lang et al., 1980; McNeil et al., 1993; Witvliet & Vrana, 1995). Figure 1 shows that greater heart rate, blood pressure, and skin conductance were found during imagery of arousing situations. Facial EMG data also mirrored previous findings (Dimberg, 1990; Fridlund & Izard, 1983; Witvliet & Vrana, 1995), with greater corrugator activity during negative (fear and anger) than neutral or positive (joy) scenarios, and greater zygomaticus activity during joy imagery than the other three emotional contents. Thus, the pattern of self-report, autonomic nervous system response, and facial expression found in this study replicated other emotional imagery studies, helping validate the scenarios and methods used here.

Ethnic and gender differences in response to emotional imagery

The patterns of emotional response described above were modified as a function of the ethnic background and sex of the participant. In contrast to Afrocentric theories positing generally deeper emotional experience and greater emotional expressiveness among African Americans (Boykin, 1986; Dixon, 1976; White & Parham, 1990), there were few differences between Whites and Blacks in self-reported emotional experience. Blacks and Whites did differ in facial expressiveness, although in a more complex way than was expected. Even though African Americans reported greater imagery vividness, which is typically associated with greater physiological responses (Miller et al., 1987), they did not exhibit generally greater emotional expression. Black participants had higher baseline zygomaticus (smile) activity, and exhibited greater zygomaticus differentiation between positive and negative scenarios than did White participants. On the other hand, White participants had higher baseline corrugator (frown) activity, and exhibited a trend toward greater corrugator differentiation between negative and positive emotions than did Black participants. Thus, African Americans showed more positive and less negative affective expression compared to their White counterparts. These expressive effects are different from those found when actually greeting an unfamiliar person (Vrana & Rollock, 1998). In that situation, Whites (especially women) exhibited a more positive expression than Blacks. The two ethnic groups may have different facial expression display rules (Ekman, 1973) that may take into account the affective valence and/or other aspects of the encounter.

These results, and those discussed below, pose theoretical problems for noncontextual cultural theories of emotional expressiveness. Emotional expressiveness appears to depend not only on one's own ethnic group values, but also on (at least) the situational context, gender roles, and the ethnic characteristics of others in the encounter. Therefore, the search for cultural determinants of emotion in interpersonal behaviour must proceed alongside more context-specific, multivariate explanations. In this case, the development of a calm appearance, particularly guarding against negative emotional expression in interracial settings, may be adaptive among African Americans (especially Black men) as a response to a racist society (Majors & Billson, 1992). Consistent with this hypothesis was the high degree of self-reported control by African Americans in these imagined emotional situations: "Losing one's cool can be a capital offense by Black standards, for it shows weakness in a world in which spiritual rigor is one of the few things we can call our own" (Page, 1996, p. 5). These tendencies might have been exacerbated in this study because, despite the presence of an African American researcher, the larger experimental context may have been perceived as fundamentally "White" (i.e., a predominantly White university, an experiment for a course taken primarily by Whites, and being asked questions about inter-ethnic contact), a context that restricts expression of affect among African American college students (Vrana & Rollock, 1996; see also footnote 4). This approach suggests that the hypothesis that African Americans are more emotionally expressive is too simplistic. A practical implication of these results is that discrepancies in expressive displays between Black and White Americans may underlie difficulties in social communication between these groups (Erickson, 1979; Vrana & Rollock, 1998).

Unlike expressivity, ethnic differences have been consistently found in autonomic nervous system activity and reactivity (Anderson & McNeilly, 1991). Most studies of reactivity have used nonsocial physical or cognitive stimuli such as cold pressor, exercise, or mental arithmetic as their stressor task[6] (N. Anderson, 1989), even though theories about the psychosocial influences on hypertension in Blacks highlight social-contextual factors (L. Anderson, 1991). This study measured cardiovascular reactivity to imagined stimuli with socio-emotional relevance. Results were similar to other studies, in that African Americans had higher resting blood pressure and exhibited greater increase to the stimuli (N. Anderson, 1989), although White participants exhibited greater heart rate reactivity. These results support the hypothesis that increased blood pressure in Blacks is mediated by peripheral vasoconstriction, rather than by increased heart rate or cardiac output (N. Anderson, 1989; Goldstein & Shapiro, 1995; Saab et al., 1992).

Looking more closely at the two cognitive tasks involved in this study suggests an interesting hypothesis about Black-White reactivity differences. Blacks (especially Black men) exhibited greater blood pressure reactivity while listening to the script (a stimulus intake task) compared to Whites (especially White women). Blacks then exhibited a decrease during imagery (a stimulus rejection/mental processing task) compared to their relatively high levels while taking in information. It may be that cardiovascular reactivity in Black adults is most likely to be expressed when attending to the environment (as opposed to internal cognitive activity), especially when this information is affectively toned. Alternatively, the greater reactivity may be specific to registration of auditory input, given the African American cultural emphasis on oral and aural modes of communication (Boykin, 1986). These possibilities are advanced very tentatively, as blood pressure was collected for only 20% of the total subject sample, and only for 13 males, the group of primary interest in this analysis. However, these intriguing and potentially important hypotheses about contributors to hypertension in African American males deserve further investigation.

Another hypothesis about ethnic differences was that gender differences in emotion found among White samples would not be evident in Black participants. Women are commonly found to report more intense emotional experiences and to facially express emotions more than do men. They further report to express more positive valence in positive situations and more negative valence in negative situations. These effects have been ascribed to gender role expectations and the enactment of these roles (Grossman & Wood, 1993). However, the "typical" gender patterns were found here only among the White participants. Black women may be less likely to subscribe to traditional European American female sex roles, particularly outside the family context (Binion, 1990), and all of the imagined scenarios used in this study occurred outside the family setting. Generalisations about sex differences and ethnic group differences in emotional expressiveness are typically made separately; however, rules

---

[6] Some recent studies have used a speech task (Saab et al., 1992; Turner, Sherwood, & Light, 1994) or interview (Ewart & Kolodner, 1993) as more socially relevant stressors.

about emotional expressiveness and display may be the result of social learning that is influenced in a complex, interactive way by gender, ethnicity, and other individual difference and situational factors. This suggests that theorists need to expand their view beyond a specific group difference (e.g., gender or ethnicity) to a broader social contextual perspective taking into account interactions between many variables.

One unexpected ethnic difference was that Blacks reported more vivid imagery, both in scenarios ratings and in a trait measure of imagery ability. This might be related to the reports of emotional control; that is, Blacks report more control in emotional situations and more control over their imagery (in the sense of being able to manipulate it as a vivid cognitive experience). Alternatively, it may be that imagery and affect are particularly important to the cognitive life of people with an African cultural background, as postulated by Afrocentric theorists. For example, Dixon (1976) suggested that "the Africanized personality is structurally oriented toward image construction and invention. In turn, Black metaphor ... is the use of imagery as the heart of reality" (p. 70).

Social context variables in emotion: Interacting with White or Black actors

This study manipulated whether the other actors in the imagined scenario were Black or White, and advanced the hypothesis that scenarios with out-group interaction would be more negative and arousing. There was some support for the hypothesis, but again results were more complex than was expected. African American participants perceived Black actors more positively than White actors, in that they rated scenarios with Black actors as higher in valence and joy. These rating differences were also apparent in facial expression: Joy scenarios involving Black actors evoked more zygomaticus (smiling) responses than did joy scenarios involving White actors, especially among African American men. However, in addition to this positive preference for Black actors primarily by African American participants, there was negative affect directed toward Black actors by *all* participants. All participants reported that anger scenarios with Black actors evoked more fear than anger scenarios with White actors. Moreover, corrugator (frowning) activity increased over time (from Read to Image) only during scenarios involving Black actors. Thus, compared to scenarios with White actors, scenarios with Black actors evoked more intense positive *and* negative responses. The greater intensity of emotional responding to Black actors is especially striking because scenarios with Black actors were reported by Black and White participants to be less easily imagined, which is usually associated with lesser affective response (Miller et al., 1987).

Social context also produced complex effects on cardiovascular and autonomic activity during imagery. For example, only men imagining White actors showed the "typical" heart rate effect, with greater acceleration during the arousing (joy, fear, anger) scenarios than the nonarousing neutral scenarios. Similarly, the "typical" blood pressure effect was found only when imagining White actors. This pattern of findings was unexpected. One tentative explanation is that White is the "default" ethnic category (Stroessner, 1996). This made scenarios involving White actors easier to imagine (all groups reported more vivid imagery of White actors), and perhaps such scenarios were processed with attention primarily focused on the emotional properties of the scenario. The higher heart rate response of men to Black actors in the neutral scenario is consistent with their response to a neutral encounter with an actual person (Vrana & Rollock, 1998). This could have to do with aversive racism among Whites (Gaertner & Dovidio, 1986), or it could be a function of disruption and novelty caused by lack of frequent encounters with Blacks in this campus context (Fiske & Ruscher, 1993). Women exhibited higher heart rate with Black than with White actors during the negative (fear and anger) scenarios. These results may be explained in that the sex of the actors in many of the scenarios was labelled as male or was left unlabelled, in which case "male" may be the default gender (Stroessner, 1996). Thus, the increased heart rate may be due to pervasive negative views of Black males, such as the generally negative portrayal of Black men in the media (DeLouth, Pirson, Hitchcock, & Rienzi, 1995), and the greater uncertainty of women in ambiguous or emotional interactions with men (Nilsen & Vrana, 1998). The pattern of self-report, facial expression, and autonomic results again defies a simple cross-cultural analysis of responsiveness to ingroup/outgroup interactions, and demands closer attention to the realities of gender and ethnic experiences within the specific cultural context.

This study showed that "race" (as defined here by the actors in the scenarios) is clearly a salient influence on emotional response across multiple channels. The greater cardiovascular reactivity on the part of Black participants underscores its particular significance to this ethnocultural group. Anderson (1991) described day-to-day hassles and unpleasant encounters as one type of acculturative stress potentially related to poor health outcome among African Americans. Although many daily hassles may be associated with overt racial discrimination, the current data suggest that ordinary, nondiscriminatory interpersonal encounters may add to daily stress. The self-reported and facial expressive reactions to Black actors suggests that social relations for African Americans may be more intensely charged, regardless of whether the encounter is positive or negative, or whether it is with another Black person or someone from the majority group. This suggests that African Americans may generally have more stressful social interactions than the majority group, and that they show greater cardiovascular reactivity to those interactions. This double risk may be an important variable in the disproportionate prevalence of cardiovascular and stress-related diseases seen in

African Americans. Such psychological and psychosomatic risks highlight the need for research to provide a view of functioning in varied emotional and social settings among diverse people.

Manuscript received 27 September 1999
Revised manuscript received 20 July 2000

REFERENCES

Anderson, L.P. (1991). Acculturative stress: A theory of relevance to Black Americans. *Clinical Psychology Review, 11*, 685–702.

Anderson, N.B. (1989). Racial differences in stress-induced cardiovascular reactivity and hypertension: Current status and substantive issues. *Psychological Bulletin, 105*, 89–105.

Anderson, N.B., & McNeilly, M. (1991). Age, gender, and ethnicity as variables in psychophysiological assessment: Sociodemographics in context. *Psychological Assessment: A Journal of Consulting and Clinical Psychology, 3*, 376–384.

Ax, A.F. (1953). The physiological differentiation between fear and anger in humans. *Psychosomatic Medicine, 15*, 433–442.

Binion, V.J. (1990). Psychological androgyny: A Black female perspective. *Sex Roles, 22*, 487–507.

Boucsein, W. (1992). *Electrodermal activity*. New York: Plenum.

Boykin, A.W. (1986). The triple quandary and the schooling of Afro-American children. In U. Neisser (Ed.), *The school achievement of minority children: New perspectives* (pp. 57–92). Hillsdale, NJ: Erlbaum.

Cacioppo, J.T., Klein, D.J., Berntson, G.G., & Hatfield, E. (1993). The psychophysiology of emotion. In M. Lewis & J.M. Haviland (Eds.), *Handbook of Emotions* (pp. 119–142). New York: Guilford Press.

Cook, E.W., III, Atkinson, L., & Lang, K.C. (1987). Stimulus control and data acquisition for IBM PC's and compatibles. *Psychophysiology, 24*, 726–727.

Cook, E.W., III, Melamed, B.G., Cuthbert, B.N., McNeil, D.W., & Lang, P.J. (1988). Emotional imagery and the differential diagnosis of anxiety. *Journal of Consulting and Clinical Psychology, 56*, 734–740.

Crocker, J., & Major, B. (1989). Social stigma and self-esteem: The self-protective properties of stigma. *Psychological Review, 96*, 608–630.

Cuthbert, B.N., Bradley, M.M., Spence, E.L., Vrana, S.R., Greenwald, M., Klein, W., & Lang, P.J. (1985). Emotional imagery: Effects of imagery ability and scene type on psychophysiological response. *Psychophysiology, 22*, 587.

Cuthbert, B.N., Vrana, S.R., & Bradley, M. (1991). Imagery: Function and physiology. In J.R. Jennings, P.K. Ackles, & M.G.H. Coles (Eds.), *Advances in Psychophysiology* (Vol. 4, pp. 1–42). London: Jessica Kingsley.

DeLouth, T.N.B., Pirson, B., Hitchcock, D., & Rienzi, B.M. (1995). Gender and ethnic role portrayals: Photographic images in three California newspapers. *Psychological Reports, 76*, 493–494.

Devine, P.G. (1989). Stereotypes and prejudice: Their automatic and controlled components. *Journal of Personality and Social Psychology, 56*, 5–18.

Dimberg, U. (1990). Facial electromyography and emotional reactions. *Psychophysiology, 27*, 481–494.

Dimberg, U., & Lundquist, O. (1988). Facial reactions to facial expressions: Sex differences. *Psychophysiology, 25*, 442–443.

Dixon, V.J. (1976). World views and research methodology. In L.M. King, V.J. Dixon, & W.W. Nobles (Eds.), *African philosophy: Assumptions and paradigms for research on Black persons* (pp. 51–100). Los Angeles: Fanon Center Press.

Dovidio, J.F., & Gaertner, S.L. (1993). Stereotypes and evaluative intergroup bias. In D.M. Mackie & D.L. Hamilton (Eds.), *Affect, cognition, and stereotyping: Interactive processes in group perception* (pp. 167–194). San Diego, CA: Academic Press.

Ekman, P. (1973). Cross-cultural studies of facial expression. In P. Ekman (Ed.), *Darwin and facial expression: A century of research in review* (pp. 169–222). New York: Academic Press.

Erickson, F. (1979). Talking down: Some cultural sources of miscommunication of interracial interviews. In A. Wolfgang (Ed.), *Nonverbal behavior: Applications and cultural implications* (pp. 99–126). New York: Academic Press.

Ewart, C.K., & Kolodner, K.B. (1993). Predicting ambulatory blood pressure during school: Effectiveness of social and nonsocial reactivity tasks in Black and White adolescents. *Psychophysiology, 30,* 30–38.

Filardo, E.K. (1996). Gender patterns in African American and White adolescents' social interactions in same-race, mixed-gender groups. *Journal of Personality and Social Psychology, 71,* 71–82.

Fiske, S.T., & Ruscher, J.B. (1993). Negative interdependence and prejudice: Whence the affect? In D.M. Mackie & D.L. Hamilton (Eds.), *Affect, cognition, and stereotyping: Interactive processes in group perception* (pp. 239–268). San Diego, CA: Academic Press.

Fleming, I., Baum, A., Davidson, L.M., Rectanus, E., & McArdle, S. (1987). Chronic stress as a factor in physiological reactivity to challenge. *Health Psychology, 6,* 221–237.

Fowles, D.C., Christie, M.J., Edelberg, R., Grings, W.W., Lykken, D.T., & Venables, P.H. (1981). Publication recommendations for electrodermal measurement. *Psychophysiology, 18,* 232–239.

Franklin, A.J. (1992). Therapy with African American men. *Families in Society, 73,* 350–355.

Franklin, A.J. (1998). Treating anger in African American men. In W.S. Pollack & R.F. Levant (Eds.), *New psychotherapy for men* (pp. 239–258). New York: Wiley.

Fridlund, A.J., & Cacioppo, J.T. (1986). Guidelines for human electromyographic research. *Psychophysiology, 23,* 567–589.

Fridlund, A.J., & Izard, C.E. (1983). Electromyographic studies of facial expressions of emotions. In J.T. Cacioppo & R.E. Petty (Eds.), *Social psychophysiology* (pp. 243–286). New York: Guilford Press.

Gaertner, S.L., & Dovidio, J.F. (1986). The aversive form of racism. In J.F. Dovidio & S.L. Gaertner (Eds.), *Prejudice, discrimination, and racism* (pp. 61–90). New York: Academic Press.

Goldstein, I.B., & Shapiro, D. (1995). The cardiovascular response to postural change as a function of race. *Biological Psychology, 39,* 173–186.

Gordon, E.W. (1983). Culture and ethnicity. In M.D. Levine, W.B. Carey, A.C. Crocker, & R.T. Gross (Eds.), *Developmental-behavioral pediatrics* (pp. 187–192). Philadelphia: W.B. Saunders.

Grossman, M., & Wood, W. (1993). Sex differences in intensity of emotional experience: A social role interpretation. *Journal of Personality and Social Psychology, 65,* 1010–1022.

Gudykunst, W.B., & Bond, M.H. (1997). Intergroup relations across cultures. In J.W. Berry, M.S. Segall, & Ç. Kagitçibasi (Eds.), *Handbook of cross-cultural psychology: Vol. 3. Social behavior and applications* (2nd ed., pp. 255–297). Boston, MA: Allyn & Bacon.

Hecht, M.L., Ribeau, S., & Alberts, J.K. (1989). An Afro-American perspective on interethnic communication. *Communication Monographs, 56,* 385–410.

Hodes, R.L., Cook, E.W., & Lang, P.J. (1985). Individual differences in autonomic response: Conditioned association or conditioned fear? *Psychophysiology, 22,* 545–560.

Jones, J.C., & Barlow, D.H. (1989). An investigation of Lang's bioinformational approach with sexually functional and dysfunctional men. *Journal of Psychopathology and Behavioral Assessment, 11,* 81–97.

Lang, P.J. (1984). Cognition in emotion: Concept and action. In C. Izard, J.K. Kagan, & R. Zajonc (Eds.), *Emotions, cognition, and behavior* (pp. 192–226). Cambridge, UK: Cambridge University Press.

Lang, P.J., Kozak, M.J., Miller, G.A., Levin, D.N., & McLean, A. (1980). Emotional imagery: Conceptual structure and pattern of somatovisceral response. *Psychophysiology, 17*, 179–192.

Lazarus, R.S. (1984). Puzzles in the study of daily hassles. *Journal of Behavioral Medicine, 7*, 375–389.

Majors, R., & Billson, J.M. (1992). *Cool pose: The dilemmas of Black manhood in America.* New York: Lexington.

Matsumoto, D. (1993). Ethnic differences in affect intensity, emotion judgments, display rule attitudes, and self-reported emotional expression in an American sample. *Motivation and Emotion, 17*, 107–123.

McNeil, D.W., Vrana, S.R., Melamed, B.G., Cuthbert, B.N., & Lang, P.J. (1993). Emotional imagery in simple and social phobia: fear versus anxiety. *Journal of Abnormal Psychology, 102*, 212–225.

Mesquita, B., Frijda, N.H., & Scherer, K.R. (1997). Culture and emotion. In J.W. Berry, P.R. Dasen, & T.S. Saraswathi (Eds.), *Handbook of cross-cultural psychology: Vol. 2. Basic processes and human development* (2nd ed., pp. 255–297). Boston: Allyn & Bacon.

Monroe, S.M. (1983). Major and minor life events as predictors of psychological distress: Further issues and findings. *Journal of Behavioral Medicine, 6*, 189–205.

Miller, G.A., Levin, D.N., Kozak, M.J., Cook, E.W., McLean, A., & Lang, P.J. (1987). Individual differences in imagery and the psychophysiology of emotion. *Cognition and Emotion, 1*, 367–390.

Nilsen, W.J., & Vrana, S.R. (1998). Some touching situations: The relationship between gender and contextual variables in physiological responses to human touch. *Annals of Behavioral Medicine, 20*, 270–276.

Page, C. (1996). *Showing my color: Impolite essays on race and identity.* New York: HarperCollins.

Roberts, R.J., & Weerts, T.C. (1982). Cardiovascular responding during anger and fear imagery. *Psychological Reports, 50*, 219–230.

Rollock, D., & Terrell, M.D. (1996). Multicultural issues in assessment: Toward an inclusive model. In J.L. DeLucia-Waack (Ed.), *Multicultural counseling competencies: Implications for training and practice* (pp. 113–153). Alexandria, VA: Association for Counselor Education and Supervision.

Russell, J.A. (1991). Culture and the categorization of emotions. *Psychological Bulletin, 110*, 426–450.

Saab, P.G., Llabre, M.M., Hurwitz, B.E., Frame, C.A., Reineke, L.J., Fins, A.I., McCalla, J., Cieply, L.K., & Schneiderman, N. (1992). Myocardial and peripheral vascular responses to behavioral challenges and their stability in Black and White Americans. *Psychophysiology, 29*, 384–397.

Schwartz, G.E., Brown, S.L., & Ahern, G.L. (1980). Facial muscle patterning and subjective experience during affective imagery: Sex differences. *Psychophysiology, 17*, 75–82.

Sheehan, P.W. (1967). A shortened form of Betts' questionnaire upon mental imagery. *Journal of Clinical Psychology, 23*, 386–389.

Shweder, R.A., & Sullivan, M.A. (1993). Cultural psychology: Who needs it? *Annual Review of Psychology, 44*, 497–523.

Steele, C.M. & Aronson, J. (1995). Stereotype threat and the intellectual test performance of African Americans. *Journal of Personality and Social Psychology, 69*, 797–811.

Stroessner, S.J. (1996). Social categorization by race or sex: Effects of perceived non-normalcy on response times. *Social Cognition, 14*, 247–276.

Sutherland, M.E., Harrell, J.P., & Isaacs, C. (1987). The stability of individual differences in imagery ability. *Journal of Mental Imagery, 11*, 97–104.

Tsai, J.L., Levenson, R.W., & Carstensen, L.L. (1992). Physiological and subjective responses to emotional films in Chinese Americans and European Americans. *Psychophysiology, 29*, S71.

Turner, J.R., Sherwood, A., & Light, K.C. (1994). Intertask consistency of hemodynamic responses to laboratory stressors in a biracial sample of men and women. *International Journal of Psychophysiology, 17*, 159–164.

Vanman, E., Paul, B.Y., Ito, T.A., & Miller, N. (1997). The modern face of prejudice and structural features that moderate the effect of cooperation on affect. *Journal of Personality and Social Psychology, 73*, 941–959.

Vrana, S.R. (1993). The psychophysiology of disgust: Differentiating negative emotional contexts with facial EMG. *Psychophysiology, 30*, 279–286.

Vrana, S.R. (1995). Emotional modulation of skin conductance and eyeblink responses to a startle probe. *Psychophysiology, 32*, 351–357.

Vrana, S.R., Constantine, J.A., & Westman, J.S. (1992). Startle reflex modification as an outcome measure in the treatment of phobia: Two case studies. *Behavioral Assessment, 14*, 279–291.

Vrana, S.R., & Rollock, D. (1996). The social context of emotion: Effects of ethnicity and authority/peer status on the emotional reports of African American college students. *Personality and Social Psychology Bulletin, 22*, 297–306.

Vrana, S.R., & Rollock, D. (1998). Physiological response to a minimal social encounter: Effects of gender, ethnicity, and social context. *Psychophysiology, 35*, 462-469.

Whaley, A.L. (1998). Cross-cultural perspective on paranoia: A focus on the Black American. *Psychiatric Quarterly, 69*, 325–343.

White, J.L. & Parham, T.A. (1990). *The psychology of Blacks: An African American perspective* (2nd ed.). Englewood Cliffs, NJ: Prentice Hall.

Witvliet, C.C., & Vrana, S.R. (1995). Psychophysiological responses as indices of affective dimensions. *Psychophysiology, 32*, 436–443.

Yinger, J.M. (1985). Ethnicity. *Annual Review of Sociology, 11*, 151–180.

Subject Index